A TEXT BOOK OF

COMPILER DESIGN

FOR

SEMESTER – VI

AF897608

THIRD YEAR (T.Y.) B. TECH COURSE IN COMPUTER ENGINEERING

Strictly According to New Revised Credit System Syllabus of Babasaheb Ambedkar Technological University (BATU), Lonere, (Dist. Raigad) Maharashtra,

(w.e.f. June 2019-20)

Dr. RAJESH S. PRASAD
Ph.D. (Computer Engineering)
Principal,
STES's Sinhgad Institute of Technology & Science
Narhe, PUNE.

Mrs. PRITI R. KUMBHAR-JORVEKAR
M. E. (Computer Engineering)
Assistant Professor, Comp. Engg. Deptt.
NBN Sinhgad School of Engineering
Ambegaon (Bk.), PUNE.

NIRALI PRAKASHAN
ADVANCEMENT OF KNOWLEDGE

N1122

COMPILER DESIGN (COMPUTER, BATU) **ISBN : 978-93-89686-62-3**

First Edition : **November 2019**

© : **Authors**

The text of this publication, or any part thereof, should not be reproduced or transmitted in any form or stored in any computer storage system or device for distribution including photocopy, recording, taping or information retrieval system or reproduced on any disc, tape, perforated media or other information storage device etc., without the written permission of Author with whom the rights are reserved. Breach of this condition is liable for legal action.

Every effort has been made to avoid errors or omissions in this publication. In spite of this, errors may have crept in. Any mistake, error or discrepancy so noted and shall be brought to our notice shall be taken care of in the next edition. It is notified that neither the publisher nor the author or seller shall be responsible for any damage or loss of action to any one, of any kind, in any manner, therefrom.

Published By :
NIRALI PRAKASHAN
Abhyudaya Pragati, 1312 Shivaji Nagar
Off J.M. Road, PUNE 411005
Tel : (020) 25512336/37/39
Email : niralipune@pragationline.com

➢ DISTRIBUTION CENTRES

PUNE

Nirali Prakashan (Local) : 119 Budhwar Peth, Jogeshwari Mandir Lane, Pune 411002, Maharashtra
Tel : (020) 2445 2044, Mobile : 9657703145, Email : niralilocal@pragationline.com

Nirali Prakashan (Outstation) : S. No. 28/27 Dhayari, Near Asian College, Dhayari, Pune 411041, Maharashtra
Tel : (020) 2469 0204, Fax : (020) 2469 0316, Mobile : 9657703143
Email : bookorder@pragationline.com

MUMBAI

Nirali Prakashan : 385 S.V.P. Road, Rasadhara Co-op. Hsg. Society Ltd., Girgaum, Mumbai 400004, Maharashtra
Tel : (022) 2385 6339 / 2386 9976, Fax : (022) 2386 9976, Mobile : 9320129587
Email : niralimumbai@pragationline.com

➢ DISTRIBUTION BRANCHES

JALGAON

Nirali Prakashan : 34 V. V. Golani Market, Navi Peth, Jalgaon 425001, Maharashtra
Tel : (0257) 222 0395, Mob : 94234 91860, Email : niralijalgaon@pragationline.com

KOLHAPUR

Nirali Prakashan : New Mahadvar Road, Kedar Plaza 1st Floor, Opp. IDBI Bank
Kolhapur 416012, Maharashtra. Mobile : 9850046155
Email : niralikolhapur@pragationline.com

NAGPUR

Nirali Prakashan : Above Maratha Mandir, Shop No 3, Second Floor,
Rani Jhanshi Square, Sitabuldi, Nagpur 440012, Maharashtra
Tel : (0712) 254 7129, Email : niralinagpur@pragationline.com

DELHI

Nirali Prakashan : 4593/15 Basement, Agarwal Lane, Ansari Road, Daryaganj
Near Times of India Building, New DelhiV 110002 Mobile : 8505972553
Email : niralidelhi@pragationline.com

BENGALURU

Nirali Prakashan : Maitri Ground Floor, Jaya Apartments, No. 99, 6th Cross, 6th Main,
Malleswaram, Bengaluru 560003, Karnataka
Mobile : 9449043034, Email : niralibangalore@pragationline.com

Note : Every possible effort has been made to avoid errors or omissions in this book. In spite this, errors may have crept in. Any type of error or mistake so noted, and shall be brought to our notice, shall be taken care of in the next edition. It is notified that neither the publisher, nor the author or book seller shall be responsible for any damage or loss of action to any one of any kind, in any manner, therefrom. The reader must cross check all the facts and contents with original Government notification or publications.

niralipune@pragationline.com | www.pragationline.com
Also find us on www.facebook.com/niralibooks

PREFACE

It gives us great pleasure to present the book **"Compiler Design"** for the students of **Semester VI Third Year (T.Y.) B. Tech. Course Computer Engineering of Dr. Babasaheb Ambedkar Technological University (BATU), Lonere, Dist. Raigad (Maharashtra).** This book is strictly as per the new revised syllabus 2019-20 Pattern, effective from the Academic Year July 2019-20.

In New Revised Syllabus, there will Class Assessment (CA) 20 Marks, Mid Sem. Exam. (MSE) 20 Marks and End Sem. Exam. (ESE) 60 Marks. End Sem. Exam. will be based on all Six units and each unit will carry 20 Marks.

The Theory Course will have 4 Credits.

The basic objective of this book is to bridge the gap between the vast contents of the reference books, written by the renowned International Authors and the concise requirements of Undergraduate Students. This book has been written in a comprehensive manner using Simple and Lucid language, keeping in mind students' requirements. The main emphasis has been given on exploring the basic concepts rather than merely the Information. Solved Examples and Exercises have been provided throughout the book and at the end of the Unit. Also we have given **Model Question Papers** for practice at the end of book.

Our special thanks to our family members, students and all those who directly or indirectly supported us in this project.

We also take this opportunity to express our sincere thanks to Shri. Dineshbhai Furia, Shri. Jignesh Furia, Mrs. Nirali Verma, Shri. M. P. Munde and entire team of Nirali Prakashan, namely Mrs. Deepali Lachake (Co-ordinator), and her colleagues who really have taken keen interest and untiring efforts in publishing this text.

The advice and suggestions of our esteemed readers to improve the text are most welcome and will be highly appreciated.

Pune **Authors**

SYLLABUS

Unit I : Introduction to Compiling — 6 Hrs

Definition, analysis of the source program, the phases of a compiler, the grouping of phases, Compiler Construction tools, A simple one-pass compiler,

Unit II : Lexical Analysis — 6 Hrs

The role of the Lexical analyzer, Input buffering, Specification of Tokens, A Language for Specifying Lexical Analyzers, Design of a Lexical Analyzer generator.

Unit III : Syntax Analysis — 6 Hrs

The role of the Parser, Context-free grammars, Writing a Grammar, Top-Down Parsing, Bottom-Up Parsing, Operator-precedence Parsing, LR Parsers, Using Ambiguous Grammars, Parser Generators.

Unit IV : Syntax-Directed Translation — 6 Hrs

Definitions, Construction of Syntax Trees, Bottom-Up Evaluation of S- Attributed definitions, Top-Down Translation, Bottom-Up Evaluation of Inherited attributes.

Unit V : Intermediate Code Generation — 6 Hrs

Intermediate Languages, Declarations, Assignment Statements, Boolean Expressions, Case Statements, Back patching, Procedure Calls.

Unit VI : Code Generation — 6 Hrs

Issues in the Design of a Code Generator, The target Machine, Run-Time Storage Management, Basic Blocks and Flow Graphs, Next-Use Information, Simple Code Generator, Register allocation and Assignment, The DAG Representation of Basic Blocks, Generating Code from DAGs, Dynamic Programming, Code-Generation Algorithm, Code-Generators.

CONTENTS

◈◈◈

UNIT I

INTRODUCTION TO COMPILING

1.1 COMPILER

- A compiler is a program that translates a high-level language program into a functionally equivalent low-level language program. Basically, it is a translator whose source language (the language to be translated) is a high-level language, and the target language (the language into which the source language is to be translated) is a low level language. In other words, a compiler is used to implement a high-level language on a computer.
- As an important part of this compilation process, a compiler reports the presence of any errors in the source program to its users.
- A language processing model using compilation is shown in Fig. 1.1.

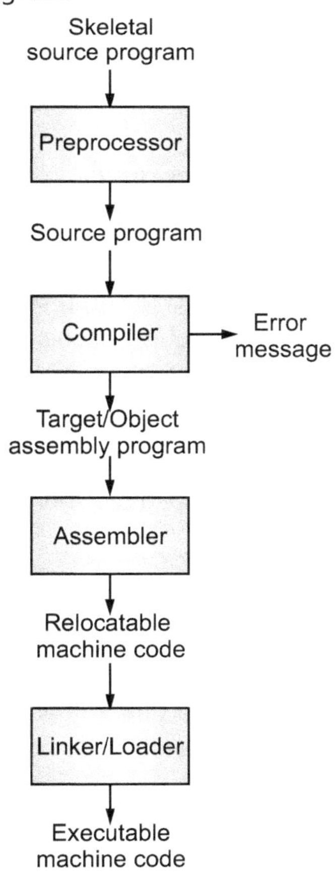

Fig. 1.1: Language processing model using compilation

The Steps Involved in Language Processing are as Follows :

1. The given source program may be divided into modules stored in separate files, if desired.
2. The preprocessor collects the source program.
3. The compiler translates the program written in high-level language to generate a target or object assembly code.
4. The assembler translates the assembly program to generate relocatable machine code.
5. The target machine determines the instructions to be used in the target program.
6. An executable machine code is generated by the compiler.

- The machine code generated by the compiler executes very efficiently, but it is not portable to other systems. One major drawback of this model is that the source program needs to be compiled for every modification.

1.2 ANALYSIS OF THE SOURCE PROGRAM

- Compilation refers to the process of translating a high-level language program into low-level language program by a compiler.
- There are two parts of compilation:
  1. Analysis of source program
  2. Synthesis of source program
- The analysis synthesis model of compilation is shown in Fig. 1.2.

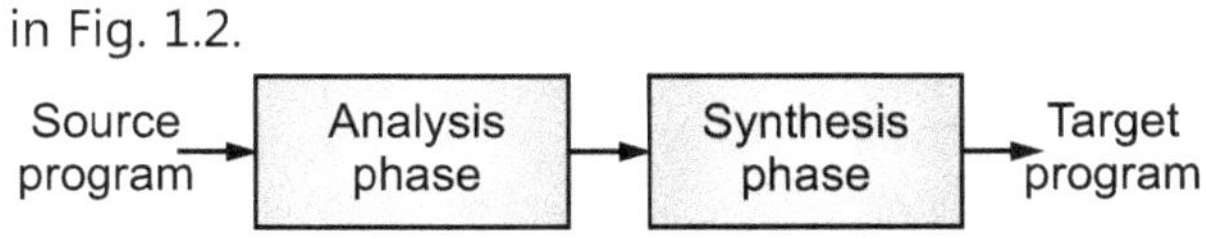

Fig. 1.2: Analysis synthesis model of compilation

- The analysis part breaks up the source program into constituent pieces and creates an intermediate representation of the source program.
- The synthesis part constructs the desired target program from the intermediate representation.

This two-step processing model is known as analysis synthesis model of compilation. The analysis step consists of three phases.

1. **Lexical Analysis:** It determines the lexical constituents in the source string by reading the stream of characters from left to right and grouping them into tokens. A token is a sequence of characters having a collective meaning.
2. **Syntax Analysis:** It determines the structure of the source string by grouping them into nested collections with collective meaning.
3. **Semantic Analysis:** It determines the meaning of source string and ensures that components of a program fit together meaningfully.

The synthesis step consists of two phases.

1. **Code Optimization:** It tries to improve the intermediate code to achieve a faster running machine code.
2. **Code Generation:** It generates the target code. Memory allocations are done for each of the variables used by the program. Intermediate instructions are then translated into a sequence of machine instructions.

1.3 PHASES OF COMPILER

A compiler operates in phases, each of which transforms the source program from one representation to another. A typical block diagram of a compiler is shown in Fig. 1.3.

1. Lexical Analysis:

- In a compiler, lexical analysis is known as linear analysis or scanning. In lexical analysis, the stream of characters making up the source program is read from left to right and grouped into tokens that are sequences of characters having collective meaning.

  For example, the assignment statement

  position = initial + rate * 60

  will be grouped into the following tokens.

  (i) identifier – { position, initial, rate}

  (ii) operator – { =, +, * }

  (iii) digits – { 60 }

2. Syntax Analysis:

- Syntax analysis is known as hierarchical analysis or parsing. It involves grouping the tokens of the source program into grammatical phrases that are used by the compiler to synthesize the output.

3. Semantic Analysis:

- The semantic analysis phase checks the source program for semantic errors and gathers type information for the subsequent code generation phase. It uses the hierarchical structure determined by the syntax analysis phase to identify the operators and operands of the expression and expression. An important part of the semantic analyzer is type checking.

4. Symbol Table Management:

- Symbol Table is a data structure containing a record for each identifier, with fields for the attributes of the identifier. The data structure allows us to find each identifier for the record quickly, and to store or retrieve data from that record quickly.
- An important function of compiler is to record the identifiers used in the source program and collect information about various attributes of each identifier.
- When an identifier in the source program is detected by the lexical analyzer (which partitions the input text, delivering a sequence of comments and basic symbols), the identifier is entered into the Symbol Table.
- The remaining phases of the compiler enter information about identifier into the Symbol Table and then use this information in various ways. In semantic analysis and intermediate code generation phase, we need to know what type of identifiers are there in the program. The code generation phase enters and uses the detailed information about the storage assigned to the identifiers.

5. Error Detection and Reporting:

- Errors can be encountered in any phase. Once an error is detected, a phase must know how to deal with it so that the compilation process can proceed smoothly. A compiler that stops at the first encountered error is not useful.
- Usually, the syntax and semantic analysis phases handle a large fraction of errors that can be detected by a compiler. Let us see how the different analysis phases handle errors.
  - ➢ **Syntax Analysis Phase:** This phase determines the errors where the token stream violates the structure rules of the language.
  - ➢ **Semantic Analysis Phase:** In this phase the compiler tries to detect those constructs which have the right syntactic structure, but have no meaning to the operation involved.
  - ➢ **Lexical Analysis Phase:** It can detect errors where the characters remaining in the input do not form any token of the language.

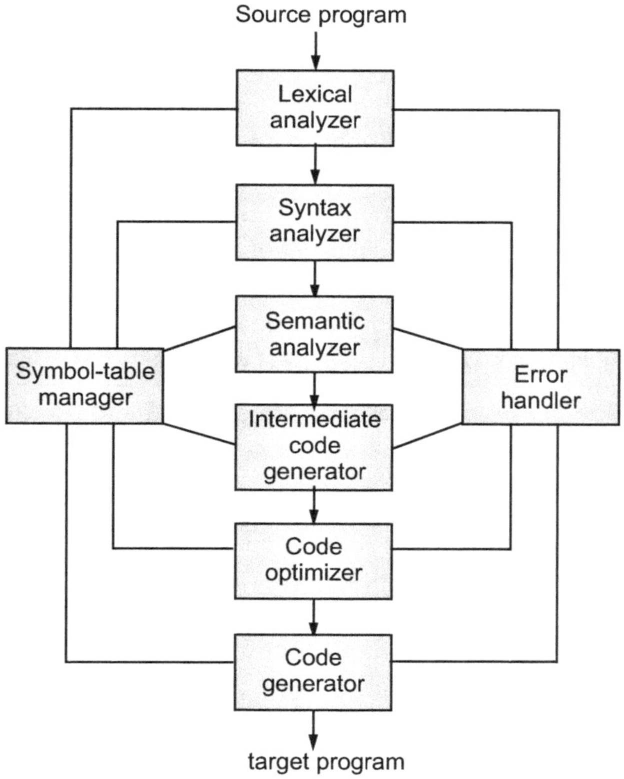

Fig. 1.3: Phases of compiler

6. **Intermediate Code Generation:**

- After syntax and semantic analysis, compilers generate intermediate representation of the source program. This intermediate representation should have two important properties:
  (i) It should be easy to produce.
  (ii) It should be easy to translate into the target program.

7. **Code Optimization:**

- The code optimization phase attempts to improve the intermediate code, so that the running time of the machine code can be improved.

8. **Code Generation:**

- The code generation phase of the compiler is the generation of the target code, consisting of relocatable machine code or assembly code. Memory locations are selected for each of the variables used by the program. Then intermediate instructions are translated into a sequence of machine instructions that perform the same task.

1.4 THE GROUPING OF PHASES

- The discussion of phases deals with the logical organization of a compiler. In an implementation, activities from several phases may be grouped together into a pass that reads an input file and writes an output file.
- For example, the front-end phases of lexical analysis, syntax analysis, semantic analysis, and intermediate code generation might be grouped together into one pass.
- Code optimization may be an not obligatory pass. Then there could be a back-end pass consisting of code generation for a particular target machine. Some compiler collections have been created around carefully designed intermediate representations that allow the front end for a particular language to interface with the back end for a certain target machine.
- With these collections, we can produce compilers for different source languages for one target machine by combining different front ends with the back end for that target machine.
- In the same way, we can produce compilers for different target machines, by combining a front end with back ends for different target machines

1.5 COMPILER CONSTRUCTION TOOLS

There are specialized tools that have been developed to assist in writing the various phases of a compiler. These are often referred to as compiler-compiler or compiler-generators. These tools can be used to implement a compiler. Generally these tools are oriented around a particular model of languages and they are most suitable for generating compilers for languages similar to that particular model of languages. Followings are the useful compiler construction tools:

1. **Parser Generator:** These tools produce syntax analyzers. These parser generators normally take input that is based on a context-free grammar. For example YACC is a LALR parser generator and is available as a command on the UNIX system.
2. **Scanner Generator:** These automatically generate lexical analyzers.
3. **Syntax-Directed Translation Engines:** These produce collections of routines that walk the parse tree, generating intermediate code.
4. **Automatic Code Generator:** This tool takes a collection of rules that define the translation of each operation of the intermediate language and changes them into the machine language for the target machine. The rules must include sufficient details that we can handle for different possible access methods for data. The basic technique is template matching. The intermediate code statements are replaced by

templates that represent sequences of machine instructions in such a way that the assumptions about storage of variables match from template to template.

5. **Data Flow Engines:** Much of the information needed to perform good code optimization involves "data-flow analysis". Here, the gathering of information about how values are transmitted from one part of the program to the each other part of the program is done. Different tasks of this kind can be performed by the same kind of routine. The user supplies details of the relationship between intermediate code statements and information being gathered.

1.6 PASSES OF COMPILER

- A pass means one complete scan of the source program or its equivalent representation. It includes reading an input file and writing an output file. It is difficult to compile source program in a single pass because of forward references.
- The statement goto jump cannot be compiled in one-pass, since the address of label 'jump' cannot be determined while compiling it. This problem can be solved by having two-pass compilers, so that storage may be allocated in first pass and code may be generated in the second pass. We can also use multi-pass compilers for reasons of storage limitation and optimization.
- The first-pass processes the source program and produces an easy-to-use form which is equivalent to the source program and contains additional information about the storage allocations. This equivalent program is processed by the second-pass. The front-end and the back-end each comprises one pass of compiler.
- There are several ways in which we can group the phases of the compilation process. Several phases of compilation are implemented as a single-pass consisting of reading an input file and writing an output file. It is desirable to have relatively few passes, since it takes time to read and write intermediate files.
- On the other hand, if we group several phases into one pass, we may be forced to keep the entire program in memory, because one phase may need information in a different order than the one in which the previous phase produces it. The internal form of the program may be considerably larger than either the source program or the target program, so this space could become a matter of concern.
- The memory requirements of a single-pass compiler are larger than multi-pass. The code generated is also less efficient. However, the advantage is that the time spent in constructing the intermediate code and scanning it in the subsequent passes, can be saved. Since these programs have short execution time, the relative inefficiency of the code is of minor importance.

1.6.1 Front-End and Back-End Models

- The phases of compilation are classified into front-end and back-end. This compiler organization is shown in Fig. 1.4.

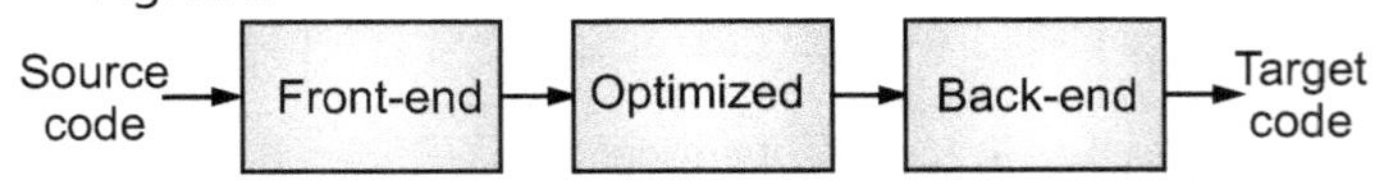

Fig. 1.4: Front-End and Back-End model of compilation

1. **Front-End:** The front-end consists of those phases, or parts of phases, that depend primarily on the source language and are largely independent of the target machine.

   These normally include:

   (i) Lexical analysis
   (ii) Syntax analysis
   (iii) Semantic analysis
   (iv) Creation of symbol table
   (v) Generation of intermediate code
   (vi) Certain amount of code optimization
   (vii) Error handling associated with these phases.

2. **Back-End:** The back-end includes those phases of compiler that depend on the target machine. These phases do not depend on the source language. They use only the intermediate language.

   Back-end normally includes:

   (i) Code optimization
   (ii) Code generation
   (iii) Necessary symbol table management
   (iv) Required error handling

The Advantages of using this Compiler Organization are:

- We can take the front-end of a compiler and attach a different back-end to produce a compiler for the same source language on a different machine.
- We can take a common back-end for different front-ends to compile several different languages on the same machine.

1.7 A SIMPLE ONE-PASS COMPILER

A Compiler pass refers to the traversal of a compiler through the entire program. Compiler pass are two types: Single Pass Compiler, and Two Pass Compiler or Multi Pass Compiler.

1. **Single Pass Compiler:** If we combine or group all the phases of compiler design in a single module known as single pass compiler. In Fig 1.5, there are all 6 phases are grouped in a single module, some important points of single pass compiler is as:

   A one pass/single pass compiler is that type of compiler that passes through the part of each compilation unit exactly once.

   Single pass compiler is faster and smaller than the multi pass compiler.

   As a disadvantage of single pass compiler is that it is less efficient in comparison with multipass compiler.

   Single pass compiler is one that processes the input exactly once, so going directly from lexical analysis to code generator, and then going back for the next read.

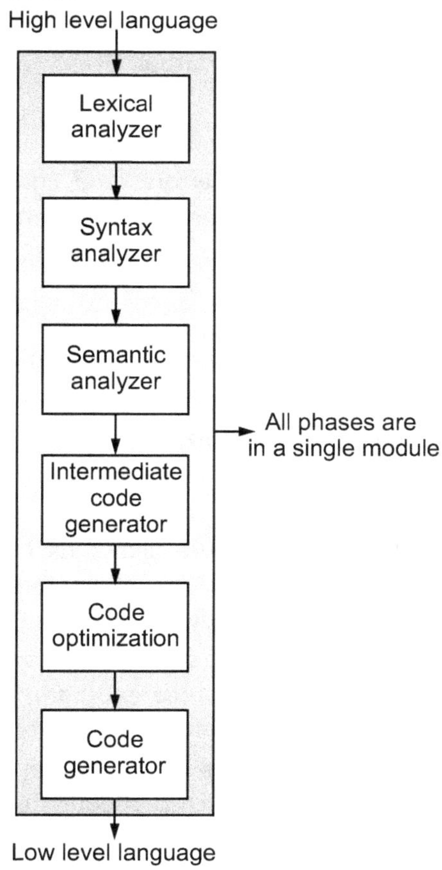

Fig. 1.5: One Pass Complier

SOLVED EXAMPLES

Example 1.1 : *Explain in detail various phases of compilation, describe output of the following statement after each phase of compiler a = b+ c*60*

Solution :

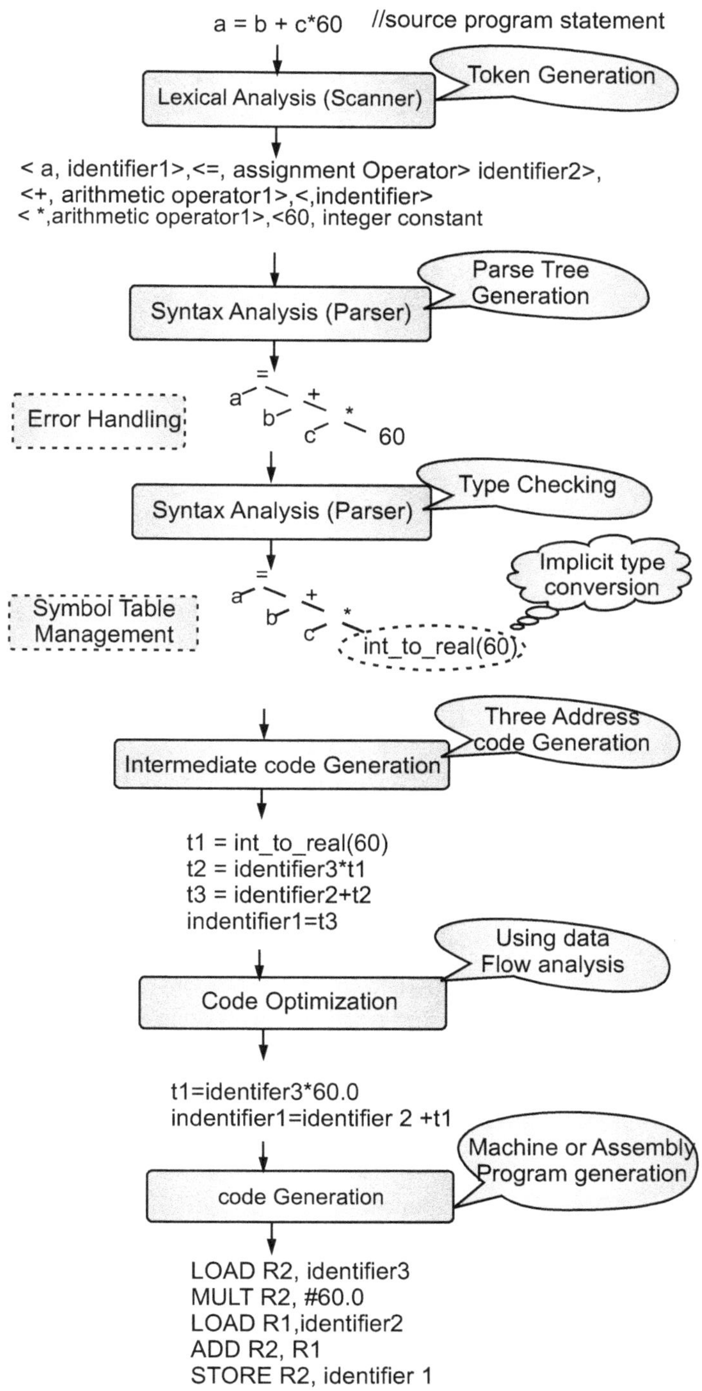

Fig. 1.6

Example 1.2 : *Explain in detail various phases of compilation, describe output of the following statement after each phase of compiler, c = a+b*5*

Solution :

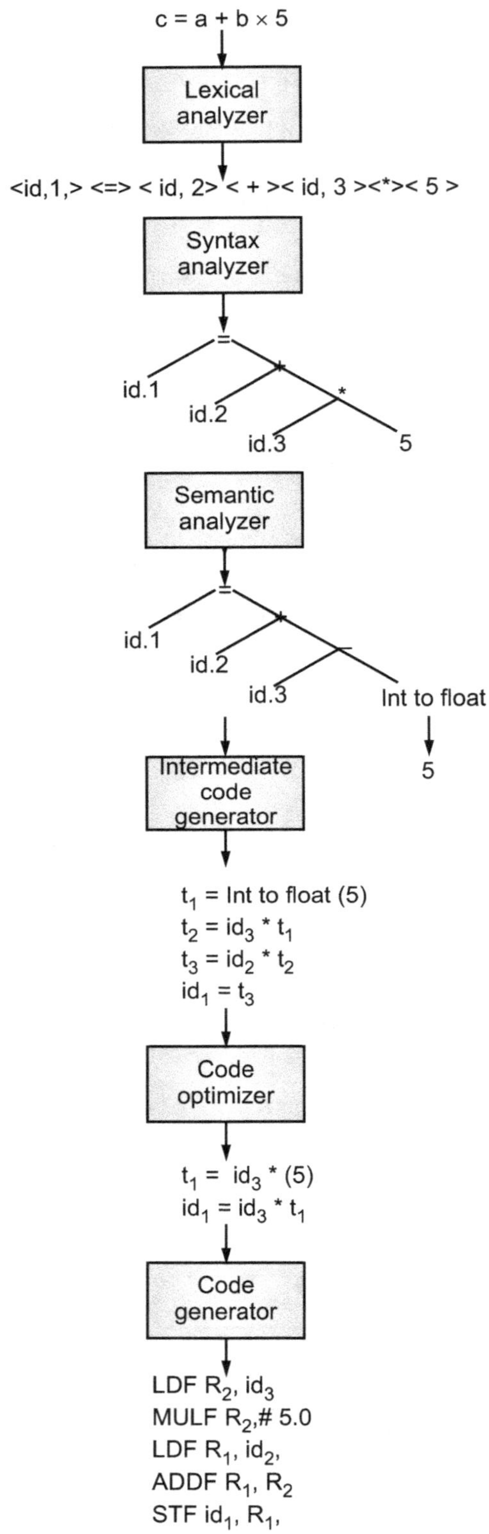

Fig. 1.7

SOLVED QUESTIONS AND ANSWERS

Questions 1 : Explain different phases of Compiler in detail.

Answer : A compiler operates in phases, each of which transforms the source program from one representation to another. A typical block diagram of a compiler is shown in Fig. 1.8.

1. **Lexical Analysis:**

- In a compiler, lexical analysis is known as linear analysis or scanning. In lexical analysis, the stream of characters making up the source program is read from left to right and grouped into tokens that are sequences of characters having collective meaning.

  For example, the assignment statement

  position = initial + rate * 60

  will be grouped into the following tokens.

  (i) identifier – { position, initial, rate}

  (ii) operator – { =, +, * }

  (iii) digits – { 60 }

2. **Syntax Analysis:**

- Syntax analysis is known as hierarchical analysis or parsing. It involves grouping the tokens of the source program into grammatical phrases that are used by the compiler to synthesize the output.

3. **Semantic Analysis:**

- The semantic analysis phase checks the source program for semantic errors and gathers type information for the subsequent code generation phase. It uses the hierarchical structure determined by the syntax analysis phase to identify the operators and operands of the expression and expression. An important part of the semantic analyzer is type checking.

4. **Symbol Table Management:**

- Symbol Table is a data structure containing a record for each identifier, with fields for the attributes of the identifier. The data structure allows us to find each identifier for the record quickly, and to store or retrieve data from that record quickly.
- An important function of compiler is to record the identifiers used in the source program and collect information about various attributes of each identifier.
- When an identifier in the source program is detected by the lexical analyzer (which partitions the input text, delivering a sequence of comments and basic symbols), the identifier is entered into the Symbol Table.

- The remaining phases of the compiler enter information about identifier into the Symbol Table and then use this information in various ways. In semantic analysis and intermediate code generation phase, we need to know what type of identifiers are there in the program. The code generation phase enters and uses the detailed information about the storage assigned to the identifiers.

5. **Error Detection and Reporting:**

- Errors can be encountered in any phase. Once an error is detected, a phase must know how to deal with it so that the compilation process can proceed smoothly. A compiler that stops at the first encountered error is not useful.

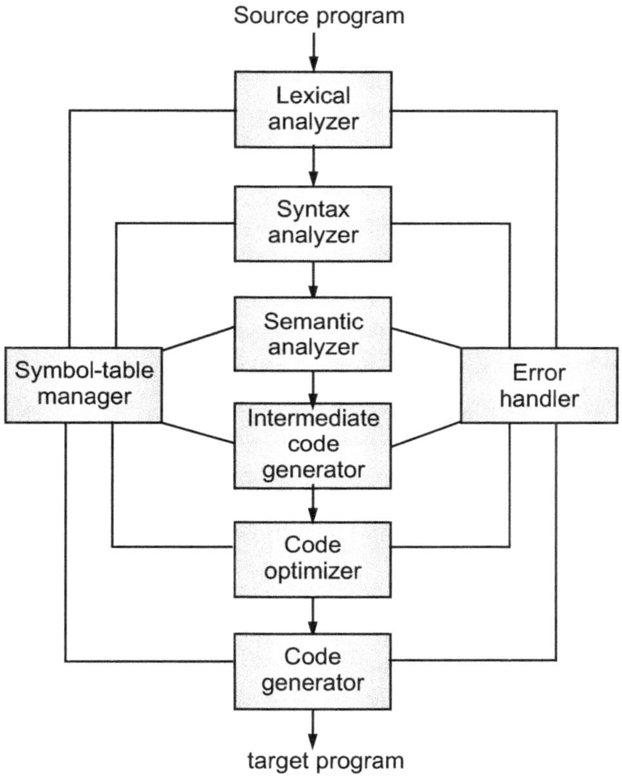

Fig. 1.8: Phases of compiler

- Usually, the syntax and semantic analysis phases handle a large fraction of errors that can be detected by a compiler. Let us see how the different analysis phases handle errors.
  - ➢ **Syntax Analysis Phase:** This phase determines the errors where the token stream violates the structure rules of the language.
  - ➢ **Semantic Analysis Phase:** In this phase the compiler tries to detect those constructs which have the right syntactic structure, but have no meaning to the operation involved.
  - ➢ **Lexical Analysis Phase:** It can detect errors where the characters remaining in the input do not form any token of the language.

6. **Intermediate Code Generation:**

- After syntax and semantic analysis, compilers generate intermediate representation of the source program. This intermediate representation should have two important properties:
  (i) It should be easy to produce.
  (ii) It should be easy to translate into the target program.

7. **Code Optimization:**

- The code optimization phase attempts to improve the intermediate code, so that the running time of the machine code can be improved.

8. **Code Generation:**

- The code generation phase of the compiler is the generation of the target code, consisting of relocatable machine code or assembly code. Memory locations are selected for each of the variables used by the program. Then intermediate instructions are translated into a sequence of machine instructions that perform the same task.

Question 2 : Differentiate between Compiler and Interpreter.

Answer :

Comparison	Compiler	Interpreter
Input	It takes an entire program at a time.	It takes a single line of code or instruction at a time.
Output	It generates intermediate object code.	It does not produce any intermediate object code.
Working mechanism	The compilation is done before execution.	Compilation and execution take place simultaneously.
Speed	Comparatively faster	Slower
Memory	Memory requirement is more due to the creation of object code.	It requires less memory as it does not create intermediate object code.
Errors	Display all errors after compilation, all at the same time.	Displays error of each line one by one.
Error detection	Difficult	Easier comparatively
Pertaining programming languages	C, C++, C#, Scala, typescript uses compiler.	PHP, Perl, Python, Ruby uses an interpreter.

Question 3 : Which are the various compiler construction tools

Answer : There are specialized tools that have been developed to assist in writing the various phases of a compiler. These are often referred to as compiler-compiler or compiler-generators. These tools can be used to implement a compiler. Generally these tools are oriented around a particular model of languages and they are most suitable for generating compilers for languages similar to that particular model of languages. Followings are the useful compiler construction tools:

1. **Parser Generator:** These tools produce syntax analyzers. These parser generators normally take input that is based on a context-free grammar. For example YACC is a LALR parser generator and is available as a command on the UNIX system.
2. **Scanner Generator:** These automatically generate lexical analyzers.
3. **Syntax-Directed Translation Engines:** These produce collections of routines that walk the parse tree, generating intermediate code.
4. **Automatic Code Generator:** This tool takes a collection of rules that define the translation of each operation of the intermediate language and changes them into the machine language for the target machine. The rules must include sufficient details that we can handle for different possible access methods for data. The basic technique is template matching. The intermediate code statements are replaced by templates that represent sequences of machine instructions in such a way that the assumptions about storage of variables match from template to template.
5. **Data Flow Engines:** Much of the information needed to perform good code optimization involves "data-flow analysis". Here, the gathering of information about how values are transmitted from one part of the program to the each other part of the program is done. Different tasks of this kind can be performed by the same kind of routine. The user supplies details of the relationship between intermediate code statements and information being gathered.

Question 4 : Write a note on Front-end and back-end model of compilation.

Answer : The phases of compilation are classified into front-end and back-end. This compiler organization is shown in Fig. 1.9.

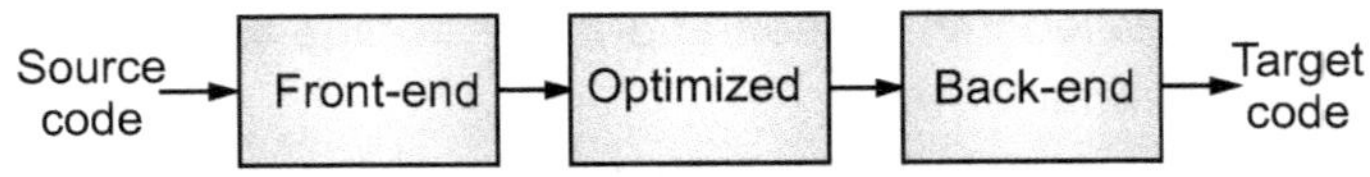

Fig. 1.9: Front-End and Back-End model of compilation

1. **Front-End:** The front-end consists of those phases, or parts of phases, that depend primarily on the source language and are largely independent of the target machine.

   These normally include:

   (i) Lexical analysis
   (ii) Syntax analysis
   (iii) Semantic analysis
   (iv) Creation of symbol table
   (v) Generation of intermediate code
   (vi) Certain amount of code optimization
   (vii) Error handling associated with these phases.

2. **Back-End:** The back-end includes those phases of compiler that depend on the target machine. These phases do not depend on the source language. They use only the intermediate language.

   Back-end normally includes:

   (i) Code optimization
   (ii) Code generation
   (iii) Necessary symbol table management
   (iv) Required error handling

The Advantages of using this Compiler Organization are:

- We can take the front-end of a compiler and attach a different back-end to produce a compiler for the same source language on a different machine.
- We can take a common back-end for different front-ends to compile several different languages on the same machine.

Question 5 : What is a Compiler?

Answer : Compiler is a systems program that translates a program written in source language into a program in target language.

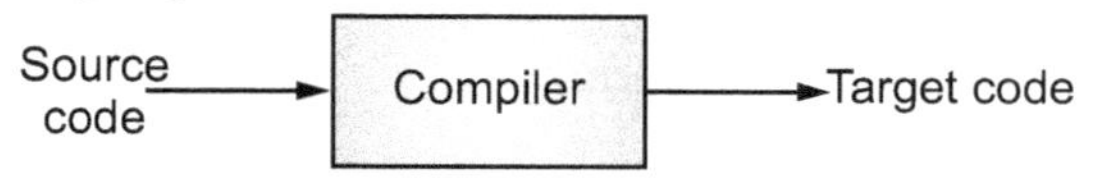

Fig. 1.10

Question 6 : What does the compiler simply do?

Answer: It translates the source code into machine language, which is run directly on a machine.

Question 7 : Describe the phases of the compiler.

Answer: The phases of a compiler can be described and implemented in many ways, but here is a representative picture of the process.

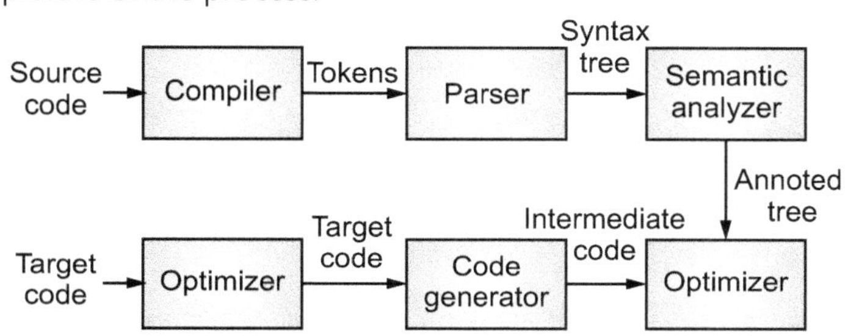

Fig. 1.11

Question 8 : What does the each phase do?

Answer: These phases transform the source code from a sequence of characters created by the program into an abstract representation of the program, and then into the desired target code. Each stage adds some new information to the representation.

Question 9 : What is the output of a compiler?

Answer: We generally think of the output of the compiler as the target code, rather than machine language. That is because a compiler may generate the code for a virtual machine, such as for Java or Squeak.

Question 10 : Do the compiler generate code in a language other than machine code?

Answer: It may also generate source code in another human programming language, such as C. Compiling to C is a common strategy for the implementers of new languages since C is relatively portable and low level; the reason being that the new language can be made quickly available in an efficient form on a wide variety of machines.

Question 11 : How the compilers came into existence?

Answer: The history of compilers parallels the history of programming. "In the beginning", when people were working with the first stored-program computers, programs really were codes. These codes were actual machine instructions that caused the computer to perform specific operations. Humans are language machines, and these first computer scientists soon created symbolic shorthand for machine instructions that made codes less tedious to write and easier to read. They wrote a program called an assembler to assemble the corresponding machine instructions from their symbolic codes.

Question 12 : What are the two parts to compilation?

Answer: A compiler performs two basic tasks:

- **Analysis :** Understand the components of the source program
- **Synthesis :** Generate the components of target program.

Question 13 : What does the analysis part of a compiler do?

Answer: Fig. 1.11 in the Answer to Question 7 shows the task breakdown of a compiler, with scanning and parsing doing the bulk of the program analysis, and the code generator and target code optimizer doing the bulk of the program synthesis.

Analysis uses knowledge of the source language to decompose the source program into its meaningful parts. An abstract syntax tree can serve as a first intermediate representation.

Question 14 : Give the types of analysis of the source program by the compiler.

Answer: Conceptually, there are three phases of analysis with the output of one phase taken as the input of the next. The phases are called lexical analysis or scanning, syntax analysis or parsing, and semantic analysis.

EXERCISE

1. Define passes and phases of Compiler. Explain different phases of Compiler in detail.
2. Differentiate between Compiler and Interpreter.
3. Explain in detail various phases of compilation, describe output of the following statement after each phase of compiler , a = b+c*5

4. Describe the analysis synthesis model of a compiler.
5. What do you mean by a pass ? How many passes a compiler should have
6. Draw a neat diagram showing various phases of compiler. Explain in brief each phase.
7. Write a note on :

   Front-end and back-end model of compilation.
8. Which are the various compiler construction tools.
9. Explain following points with respect to compiler :
   (i) Grouping of phases.
   (ii) No. of passes required.
   (iii) Intermediate languages.
   (iv) Tools needed.

◈◈◈

UNIT II

LEXICAL ANALYSIS

2.1 THE ROLE OF THE LEXICAL ANALYZER

- Lexical analysis is the first step in the compilation process. It is the process of converting a sequence of characters into a sequence of tokens. A program which performs the lexical analysis is known as a lexical analyzer.
- Lexical analyzer is the first phase of a compiler. The main task of a lexical analyzer is to read the input program and break it up into a sequence of tokens. These tokens are used by the syntax analyzer or parser, for syntax analysis.
- Fig. 2.1 is a block schematic of lexical analyzer and shows the interaction between the lexical analyzer and the parser.

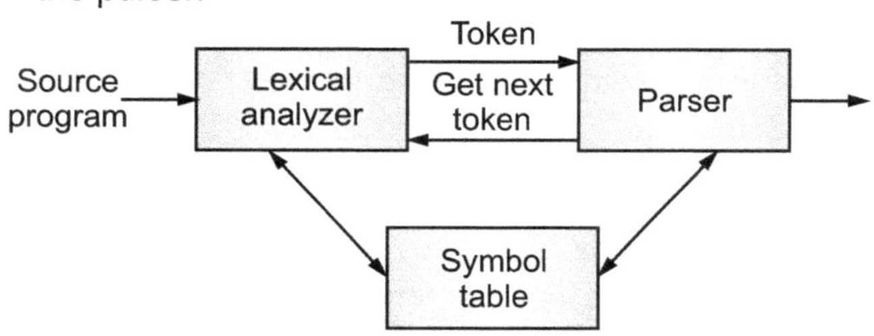

Fig. 2.1: Role of Lexical Analyzer

- Lexical analysis phase is divided into a cascade of two phases.
  1. Scanning
  2. Lexical analysis
- The lexical analyzer can also perform certain secondary tasks like removing the comments and white spaces from the source program. It may also make a copy of the source program with the error messages marked in it. Each error message may also be associated with the line number.

2.2 BASIC CONCEPTS

Let us understand some important terms associated with lexical analysis.

2.2.1 Lexeme

- Lexeme is the smallest logical unit of a program. It is defined as a sequence of characters in the source program that is matched by the pattern for a token.

  Consider the following Pascal statement.

  const pi = 3.1416

  Here, "const" is the lexeme for the token "const"

  "pi" is the lexeme for the token "identifier"

  "3.1416" is the lexeme for the token "num"

2.2.2 Alphabets and Token

- An alphabet or a character class is a finite set of symbols. Token is a sequence of characters that represents a unit of information in the source program. A string is a series of tokens put together based on the language rules. Whenever we come across a token which is not a part of the alphabets of the language, we encounter a lexical error. This is different from a syntax error.
- Classes of similar lexemes are identified by the same token.

2.2.3 Pattern

- A set of strings in the input for which the same token is produced as output, is described by a rule called a pattern.
- Pattern is a rule describing the set of lexemes that can represent a particular token in the source program.

Examples of token, pattern and lexeme are as given below.

Token	Lexeme	Description of Pattern
const	const	const
if	if	if
relation	<, <=, =, <>, >, >=	< or <= or = or <> or > or >=
id	pi, count, d2	letter followed by letters and digits
num	3.1416,0,6.02e23	any numeric constant
literal	"pascal"	Any characters between " and " except "

2.2.4 Lexical Errors

- Lexical analyzer has a very localized view of the program, hence few errors are easily detectable at the lexical level.

  Consider a C statement:

  fi(a == f (x))

when the string fi is encountered, a lexical analyzer cannot tell whether fi is a misspelling of the keyword if, or an undeclared function identifier. But since fi is a valid identifier, the lexical analyzer must return the token for an identifier and the error will be handled by some other phase of the compiler.

- But a situation may arise in which the lexical analyzer is unable to proceed because none of the patterns for the tokens matches a prefix of the remaining input. The simplest recovery strategy is the panic mode recovery.
- Other possible error recovery actions are:
  1. Deleting inappropriate character
  2. Inserting a missing character
  3. Replacing an incorrect character by a correct character
  4. Transposing two adjacent characters
- One way of finding errors in a program is to compute the minimum number of error transformations that are required to transform the erroneous program into the one that is syntactically correct.
- We say that the erroneous program has k errors if the shortest sequence of error transformations that will map it into some valid program has length k.

2.3 INPUT BUFFERING

- Before discussing the problem of recognizing lexemes in the input, let us examine some ways that the simple but important task of reading the source program can be speeded. This task is made difficult by the fact that we often have to look one or more characters beyond the next lexeme before we can be sure we have the right lexeme.
- The box on "Tricky Problems When Recognizing Tokens" gave an extreme example, but there are many situations where we need to look at least one additional character to the lead. For instance, we cannot be sure we have seen the end of an identifier until we see a character that is not a letter or digit, and therefore is not part of the lexeme for id. In C, single-character operators like - , =, or < could also be the beginning of a two-character operator like - > , ==, or <=. Thus, we introduce a two-buffer scheme that handles large look aheads safely.

2.3.1 Buffer Pairs

- Specialized buffering techniques have been developed to reduce the amount of overhead required to process a single input character because of the amount of time taken to process characters and the large number of characters that must be processed during the compilation of a large source program, An important scheme involves two buffers that are alternately reloaded.
- Each buffer is of the same size N , and N is usually the size of a disk block, for example 4096 bytes. Using one system read command we can read N characters into a buffer, rather than using one system call per character.
- If fewer than N characters remain in the input file, then a special character, represented by eof, marks the end of the source file and is different from any possible character of the source program.
- Two pointers to the input are maintained:
  1. Pointer lexeme Begin, marks the beginning of the current lexeme, whose extent we are attempting to determine.
  2. Pointer forward scans ahead until a pattern match is found
- Once the next lexeme is determined, forward is set to the character at its right end. Then, after the lexeme is recorded as an attribute value of a token returned to the parser, lexeme Begin is set to the character immediately after the lexeme just found.
- Advancing forward requires that we first test whether we have reached the end of one of the buffers, and if so, we must reload the other buffer from the input, and move forward to the beginning of the newly loaded buffer.
- As long as we never need to look so far ahead of the actual lexeme that the sum of the lexeme's length plus the distance we look ahead is greater than N , we shall never overwrite the lexeme in its buffer before determining it.

2.3.2 Sentinels

- If we use Buffer Pairs, we must check, each time we advance forward, that we have not moved off one of the buffer, if we do, then we must also reload the other buffer. Thus, for each character read, we make two tests: one for the end of the buffer, and one to determine what character is read.

- We can combine the buffer-end test with the test for the current character if we extend each buffer to hold a sentinel character at the end.
- The sentinel is a special character that cannot be part of the source program, and a natural choice is the character eof.

2.4 SPECIFICATION OF TOKENS

- Regular expressions are an important notation for specifying lexeme patterns. While they cannot express all possible patterns, they are very effective in specifying those types of patterns that we actually need for tokens.
- Here we shall study the formal notation for regular expressions, and we shall see how these expressions are used in a lexical-analyzer generator, how to build the lexical analyzer by converting regular expressions to automata that perform the recognition of the specified tokens.

2.4.1 Strings and Languages

- **Alphabet:** The term alphabet or character class denotes any finite set of symbols. Examples of symbols are letters and digits.
- **String:** A string over an alphabet is a finite sequence of symbols drawn from that alphabet. The term string refers to terms sentence and word in language theory.

  Length of the string s, denoted as |s| is the number of occurrences of symbols in s. The empty string, denoted as ε, is a special string of length zero.
- **Language:** The term language denotes any set of strings over some fixed alphabet. Languages like ϕ, the empty set { ε } are the languages under this definition.
- **Operations on Languages:** For lexical analysis, the important operations are given below.
  1. **Exponentiation Operator:** Exponentiation operator to language L can be defined as follows:

     L^0 is defined to be { ε },

     L^i is L concatenated with itself i-1 times.
  2. **Union:** Union of languages L and M written as $L \cup M$ is defined as follows:

     $L \cup M$ = { s | s is in L or s is in M }
  3. **Concatenation:** Concatenation of languages L and M written as LM is defined as follows:

     LM = { st | s is in L and t is in M }
  4. **Kleene Closure:** Kleene closure of L written as L+ is defined as follows:

     $$L^* = \bigcup_{i=0}^{\infty} L^i$$

     L^* denotes "zero or more" concatenations or occurrences of L.
  5. **Positive Closure:** Positive closure of L written as L^+ is defined as follows:

     $$L^+ = \bigcup_{i=0}^{\infty} L^i$$

     L^+ denotes "one or more" concatenations or occurrence of L.

Let L = { A, B, C, ..., Z, a, b, c, ..., z } and
D = { 0, 1, ..., 9 }

Let L and D be the two finite languages.

Following are the two examples of new languages created from L and D by applying the operators:

1. $L \cup D$ is the set of letters and digits.
2. LD is the set of strings consisting of a letter followed by a digit.
3. L^4 is the set of all four-letter strings.
4. L^* is the set of all strings of letters, including ε, the empty string.
5. D^+ is the set of all strings of one or more digits.
6. $L(L \cup D)^*$ is the set of all strings of letters and digits beginning with a letter.

2.4.2 Regular Expression

- A regular expression is built up out of simpler regular expressions using a set of defining rules. Each regular expression r denotes a language L(r).
- The rules that define the regular expressions over alphabet $\sum$ are as follows:
  1. ε is a regular expression that denotes { ε }, that is, the set containing the empty string.
  2. If a is a symbol in $\sum$, then a is a regular expression that denotes {a} i.e. the set containing the string a.
  3. Suppose r and s are regular expressions denoting the languages L(r) and L(s), then
     (i) (r)|(s) is a regular expression denoting $L(r) \cup L(s)$
     (ii) (r)(s) is a regular expression denoting L(r) L(s)
     (iii) $(r)^*$ is a regular expression denoting $(L(r))^*$
     (iv) (r) is a regular expression denoting $L(r)^2$

A language denoted by a regular expression is said to be a regular set.

2.4.3 Regular Definitions

If Σ is an alphabet of basic symbols, then a regular definition is a sequence of definitions of the form:

$d_1 \rightarrow r_1$

$d_2 \rightarrow r_2$

....

$d_n \rightarrow r_n$

where,

each d_i is a distinct name and each r_i is a regular expression over the symbols in

$\Sigma \cup \{d_1, d_2, ..., d_{i-1}\}$ i.e. the basic symbols and the previously defined names.

Examples of Regular Definitions:

1. Pascal identifier is a set of strings of letters and digits beginning with a letter. Regular expression for the identifier is:

   letter(letter|digit)*

   Regular definition for the regular expression is:

   letter → A|B|C|......|Z|a|b|.........|z

   digit → 0|1|2......|9

   id → letter(letter|digit) *

2. Regular expression for unsigned numbers in Pascal is:
   (([0-9]+) | ([0-9]+\.[0-9]+)) ([E][-+]?[0-9]+)?

   Regular definition for the regular expression is:

   digit → 0|1|........|9

   digits → digit digit*

   optional_fraction → .digits|ε

   optional_exponent → (E(+ |–|ε)digits)| ε

   num → digits optional_fraction optional_exponent

2.4.4 Non-Regular Sets

Some languages cannot be described by regular expression. Such languages are called as non-regular sets.

Examples of Non-Regular Sets are:

1. Regular expression cannot be used to describe the set of all strings of balanced parentheses. This set can be described by context-free grammar.
2. The set {wcw | w is a string of a's and b's} cannot be denoted by the regular expression nor can it be described by a context-free grammar.

2.4.5 Transition Diagram

Transition diagrams depict the actions that take place when a lexical analyzer is called by the parser to get the next token. Transition diagrams are used to keep track of the information about characters that are seen, as the forward pointer scans the input. For doing so, a transition diagram keeps moving from position to position in the diagram as the characters are read.

- Positions in transition diagram are drawn as circles and are called states.
- The states are connected by arrows called edges.
- Edges leaving the state s have label indicating the input character that can next appear after the transition diagram has reached the state s.
- The label other refers to any character that is not indicated by any of the other edges leaving s.
- One state is labeled as start state, it is the initial state of the transition diagram where the control resides at start.
- Certain state may have actions that are executed when the flow of control reaches that state.
- On entering a state, the next input character is read. If there is an edge from the current state with the label that matches the input character, it moves to the state that is reached from the current state with the current input character.

Examples of Transition Diagram:

1. Transition diagram for the pattern >= is given in Fig. 2.2. The transition diagram works as follows:
   (i) Its start state is 0.
   (ii) In state 0, we read the next input character. If the current input character is >, it moves to state 6.
   (iii) In state 6, if the current input is = then it reaches state 7. For any other input, it reaches state 8 with the edge labeled other.
   (iv) Double circle on state 7 indicates that it is an accepting state, i.e. it is the state in which the token >= is found.

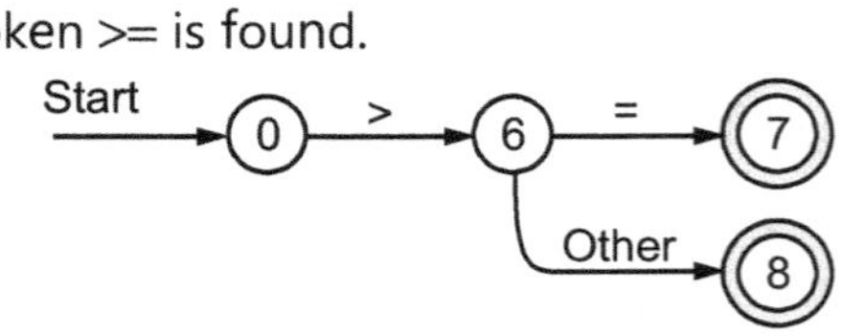

Fig. 2.2: Transition Diagram for >=

2. Transition diagram for Relational Operators is shown in Fig. 2.3.

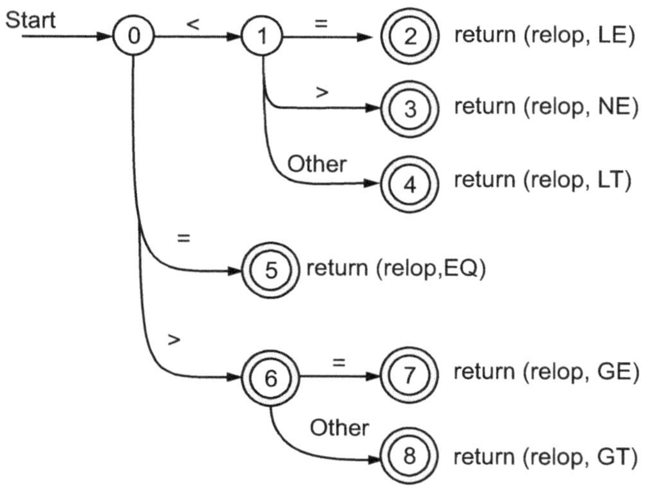

Fig. 2.3: Transition Diagram for Relational Operators

3. Transition diagram for Identifiers and Keywords is shown in Fig. 2.4.

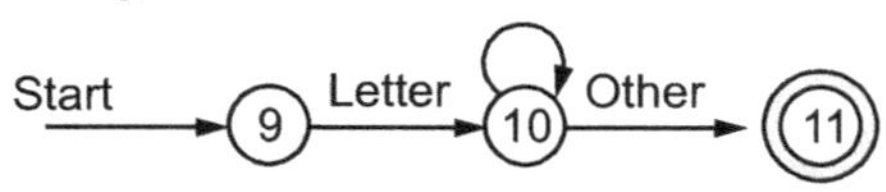

Fig. 2.4: Transition Diagram for Identifiers and Keywords

2.5 A LANGUAGE FOR SPECIFYING LEXICAL ANALYZERS

- Lex is the tool that has been widely used to specify lexical analyzers for a variety of languages. A lexer takes an arbitrary input stream and tokenizes it, i.e. divides it into lexical tokens. This tool is referred as the Lex Compiler, and its input specification is referred as Lex Language.
- While writing a lex specification, we create a set of patterns which lex matches against the input. Each time one of the patterns matches, the lex program invokes C code that we provide for doing something with the matched text. In this way a lex program divides the input into strings called as tokens.
- Lex itself doesn't produce an executable program. Instead, it translates the lex specification into a file containing a C routine called yylex( ). The program that you have written, then calls yylex ( ) to run the lexer.

  How to use Lex:

  ➢ Lexical analyzer is specified by creating lex.l in Lex language.

  ➢ lex.l is run through the Lex compiler to produce a C program lex.yy.c.

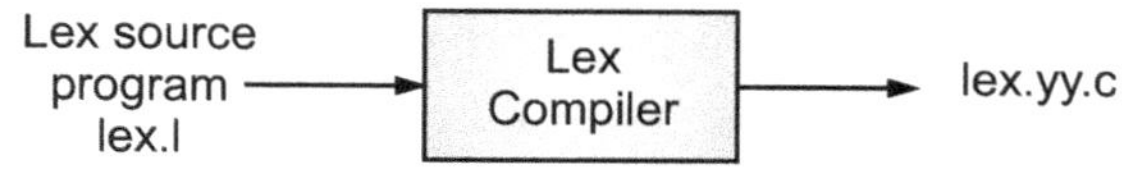

Fig. 2.5 : Lex Compiler

Program lex.yy.c Consists of:

- A tabular representation of a transition diagram constructed from the regular expressions of lex.l
- A standard routine that uses the table to recognise lexemes.
- The actions associated with regular expressions in lex.l are pieces of C code and are carried over directly to lex.yy.c.
- The lex.yy.c is run through the C compiler to produce an object program a.out.

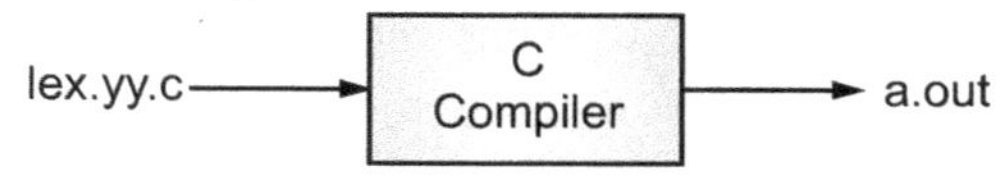

Fig. 2.6 : C Compiler

- a.out is the lexical analyzer that transforms an input stream into a sequence of tokens.

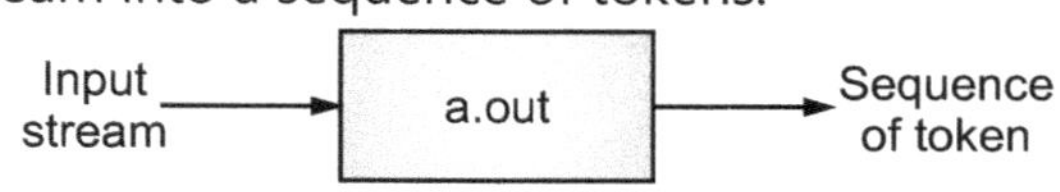

Fig. 2.7 : Output file

2.6 LEX SPECIFICATIONS AND FEATURES

A lex program consists of three parts.

1. Declarations

   %%

2. Translation rules

   %%

3. Auxiliary procedures

1. Declaration Section Includes the Declarations of:

   (i) Variables

   (ii) Manifest constants (these are identifiers that are declared to represent constants)

   (iii) Regular definitions (these are statements used as components of regular expressions appearing in translation rules.)

2. Translation Rules of a Lex Program are Statements of the Form:

   p_1 { $action_1$ }

   p_2 { $action_2$ }

   ......

   p_n { $action_n$ }

   where,

   p_i is a regular expression

$action_i$ is a program fragment describing what action the lexical analyzer should take when pattern p_i matches a lexeme.

In a Lex specification, actions are specified in C statements, however they can be in any implementation language.

3. **Auxiliary Procedures are Needed by the Actions :** Alternatively, these procedures can be compiled separately and loaded with the lexical analyzer.

2.7 REGULAR EXPRESSIONS

- A regular expression is a pattern description using a "meta" language, a language that is used to describe particular patterns of interest.
- The characters used in this metalanguage are a part of the standard ASCII character set used in UNIX and MS-DOS.
- The characters that form regular expressions are:

. Matches any single character except the newline character ("\n")

* Matches zero or more copies of the preceding expression.

[ ] A character class which matches any character within the brackets.

If the first character is a circumflex ("^"), it changes the meaning to match any character except the ones within the brackets.

A dash inside the square brackets indicates a character range. For e.g., "[0-9]" means the same thing as "[0123456789]".

A " – " or "]" as the first character after " [" is interpreted literally.

Other meta characters have no special meaning within square brackets, except that C escape sequences starting with "\" are recognised.

^ Matches the beginning of a line as the first character of a regular expression. Also used for negation within square brackets.

$ Matches the end of a line as the last character of a regular expression.

{ } Indicates how many times the previous pattern is allowed to match when containing one or two numbers.

For e.g.

A{1, 3}

Matches one to three occurrences of the letter A.

If they contain a name, they refer to a substitution by that name.

\ Used to escape meta characters, and also as a part of the usual C escape sequences.

For e.g., "\n" is a newline character, while "*" is a literal asterisk.

+ Matches one or more occurrences of the preceding regular expression.

For e.g.

[0–9]+

matches "1", "111", or "123456". But it can not match an empty string.

? Matches zero or one occurrence of the preceding regular expression.

For e.g.

-?[0-9]+

matches a signed number including an optional leading minus.

| Matches either the preceding regular expression or the following regular expression. For e.g.

is|am|are|were

matches any of the four words.

"..." Interprets everything within the quotation marks literally – meta characters other than C escape sequences lose their meaning.

/ Matches the preceding regular expression but only if it is followed by the following regular expression.

For e.g.

0/1

matches "0" in the string "01"

but it would not match anything in the strings "0" or "02".

( ) Groups a series of regular expressions together into a new regular expression.

For e.g.

(01)

represents the character sequence 01.

Parentheses are useful when building up complex patterns with *, +, and |.

Examples of Regular Expressions:

1. Regular expression for "digits": [0-9]
2. Regular expression for "integers"

[0-9]+ represents at least one digit & would not allow for no digit

[0-9]* represents zero or more digits

-?[0-9]+ an optional unary minus is added

3. Regular expression for "decimal numbers" [0-9]*\.[0-9]+
   This pattern matches "0.0", "4.15", or ".3145". But it would not match "0" or "2".
   Hence it can be modified as: ([0-9]+)|([0-9]*\.[0-9]+)
   -? (([0-9]+) | ([0-9]*\.[0-9]+))
4. Regular expression for "exponent" [eE][-+]?[0-9]+
5. Regular expression for "real numbers"
   -? (([0-9]+) | ([0-9]*\.[0-9]+)) ([eE][-+]?[0-9]+)

2.8 REFERENCE FOR LEX SPECIFICATIONS

1. Line Numbers and yylineno ( )

- Line number in the input file can be used to report the error at that line.
- Some versions of lex define yylineno ( ) to contain the line number and automatically update it. However, most do not support this.
- Keeping track of the line number is easy. Initialize your line number variable to 1, and increment it in any lex rule that matches a newline character, as shown below.

```
%{
int lineno = 1;
%}
%%
......
\n      { lineno++; }
```

- Lexers that handle nested include files have to store and restore line numbers associated with each file.

2. yyleng

- Whenever a scanner matches a token, the text of the token is stored in the null terminated string yytext, and its length is in yyleng. The length in yyleng is the same as the value that should be returned by strlen(yytext).

3. yyless ( )

- yyless ( ) can be called from the code associated with a rule to push back all but the first n characters of the token. This can be useful when the rule to determine the boundary between the tokens is inconvenient to express as a regular expression.

4. yylex ( )

- The scanner created by lex has the entry point yylex( ). We call yylex() to start or resume scanning.

5. yytext

- Whenever a lexer matches a token, the text of the token is stored in the null terminated string yytext. The contents of yytext are replaced each time a new token is matched. In AT&T lex, the standard size of yytext[ ] is 200 characters while in MKS lex, it is 100 characters.

6. yywrap

- When a lexer encounters the end of file, it calls the routine yywrap( ) to find out what to do next. If yywrap( ) returns 0, the scanner continues scanning. If it returns 1, the scanner returns a zero token to report the end of file.
- The standard version of yywrap( ) in the lex library always returns 1.

2.9 SAMPLE LEX PROGRAMS

1. Recognizing Words with Lex

Here we consider the following set of verbs to recognise

{is, am, are, were, was, be, being, been, do, does, did, will, would, should, can, could, has, have, had, go}

We consider the following set of nouns:

{pen, book, mirror, chalk, table, chair, computer}

Similarly for adverb, preposition, conjunction, adjective, pronoun, etc. A simple lex specification to recognise these verbs:

```
    %{
    %}
    %%
    [\t]+/* no action for white spaces*/
is| am|
are|
were|
was|
be|
being|
been|
do|
does|
did|
will|
would|
should|
can|
could|
has|
```

```
have|
had|
go      { printf(" %s : is a verb\n", yytext); }
he| she| I| we|
they    { printf(" %s : is a pronoun\n", yytext); }
very| simply| gently| quietly| calmly|
angrily|{ printf(" %s : is an adverb\n", yytext); }
to| from| behind| above| below| between|
below   { printf(" %s : is a preposition\n", yytext); }


if| then| and| but|
or  { printf(" %s : is a conjunction\n", yytext); }


their| my| your| his| her|
its { printf(" %s : is an adjective\n", yytext); }
pen| book| mirror| chalk| table| chair|
computer{ printf(" %s : is a noun\n", yytext); }
 [a-zA-Z]+{ printf(" %s : don't recognise, might be a
noun\n", yytext); }
.|\n{ECHO;}
%%
main( )
{
yylex( );
}
```

How to Execute

Consider that the program is placed in a file called word.l.

To create an executable program on UNIX system, we enter these commands:

% lex word.l

% cc lex.yy.c –o word –ll

Lex translates the lex specification into a C source file called lex.yy.c, which we compiled and linked with the lex library –ll.

Result of Execution of the Program :

Input to the program: did I have fun? did: is a verb

I: is a noun

have: is a verb

fun: don't recognise, might be a noun

?

^D

%

2. Lexical Analyzer for the Following Examples of Regular Expressions

Here we consider the regular expressions for integer, decimal number and real numbers

```
%{
%}
%% [\t]+
[0-9]+  printf("%s : is an integer number");}
([0-9]+)|( [0-9]*\.[0-9]+) printf("%s : is a decimal number");}
-?(([0-9]+)|([0-9]*\.[0-9]+))([eE][-+]?[0-9]+)
printf("%s : is a real number");}


%%
main( )
{
yylex( );
}
```

3. Lex Program for Counting Words, Lines and Characters

```
%{
unsigned charcount = 0, wordcount = 0, linecount = 0;
%}

word    [^ \t\n]+
eol \n

%%
{word}  {wordcount++; charcount+=yyleng;}
        /* yyleng is the lex variable which contains the
        length of the string the lexer has recognised.*/

{eol}   {charcount++, linecount++;}
   .    {charcount++;}


%%
main( )
{
yylex( );
printf("%dd %d %d\n", linecount,wordcount,charcount);
}
```

The same program can be written by using the command line arguments as follows:

```
main (int argc, char **argv)
{
    if(argv>1)
    {
        FILE * fp;
        fp = fopen(argv[1],"r");
        if(fp)
        {
            fprintf(stderr,"couldnot open%s\n",argv[1]);
            exit(1)
        }
        yyin=fp;
    }
    yylex( );
    printf(%u%u%u\n", charcount, wordcount, linecount);
    return 0;
}
```

4. Lexical Analyzer for Subset of C

```
%{
int line = 0;
%}

main        main
datatype    int|char|float|double|long
function    main|printf|scanf|clrscr
brackets    { | } | ( | )
operators   [*+—/=]
var         [a-z]
eol         \n
number      [0-9]+
symbols     ;|, | " | "
loop        while|do
conditional switch|if|else
%%
{eol}       {line++;}
{main}      {printf("main function found at line no %d\n",line);}
{datatype} {printf(" datatype %s found at line no %d\n", yytext,line);}
{function} {printf("function %s found at line no %d\n", yytext,line);}
{bracket}  {printf("bracket %s found at line no %d\n", yytext,line);}
{operator} {printf("operator %s found at line no %d\n", yytext,line);}
{var}      {printf("var %s found at line no %d\n", yytext,line);}
{number}   {printf("number %s found at line no %d\n", yytext,line);}
{symbol}   {printf("symbol %s found at line no %d\n", yytext,line);}
{loop}     {printf("loop %s found at line no %d\n", yytext,line);}
{conditional} {printf("conditional statement %s found at line no %d\n", yytext,line);}
%%
main (int argc, char **argv)
{
    if(argv>1)
    {
        FILE * fp;
        fp = fopen(argv[1],"r");
        if(fp)
        {
            fprintf(stderr,"could not open%s\n",argv[1]);
            exit(1)
        }
        yyin=fp;
    }
    yylex( );
    return 0;
}
```

2.10 DESIGN OF A LEXICAL ANALYZER GENERATOR

In this section we have to discuss two approaches, based on NFA's and DFA's; the final is basically the implementation of Lex.

2.10.1 The Structure of the Generated Analyzer

- Fig 2.8 shows the architecture of a lexical analyzer generated by Lex. The program that serves as the lexical analyzer includes a fixed program that simulates an automaton, at this point we leave open whether that automaton is deterministic or nondeterministic . The rest of the lexical analyzer consists of components that are created from the Lex program by Lex itself.

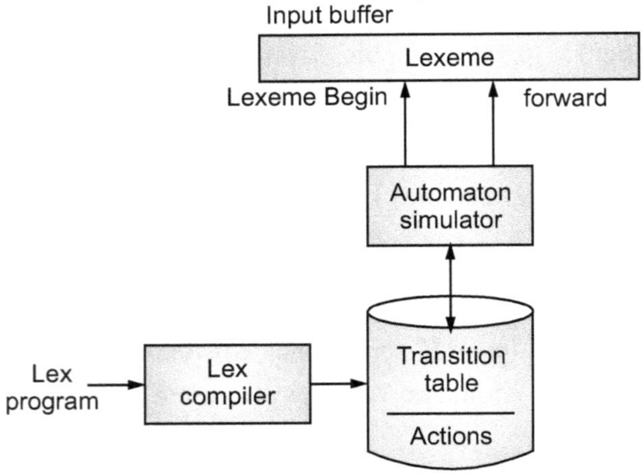

Fig. 2.8: Architecture of a lexical analyzer generated by Lex

- A Lex program is turned into a transition table and actions, which are used by a finite-automaton simulator
- These components are:
  1. A transition table for the automaton.
  2. The functions that are passed directly through Lex to the output
  3. The actions from the input program, which appear as fragments of code to be invoked at the appropriate time by the automaton simulator.

2.10.2 Pattern Matching Based on NFA's

- If the lexical analyzer simulates an NFA then it must read input beginning at the point on its input which we have referred to as lexeme Begin. As it moves the pointer called forward ahead in the input , it calculates the set of states it is in at each point, Eventually, the NFA simulation reaches a point on the input where there are no next states.
- At that face, there is no hope that any longer prefix of the input would ever get the NFA to an accepting state rather, the set of states will always be empty. therefore, we are ready to decide on the longest prefix that is a lexeme matching some pattern. We look backwards in the sequence of sets of states, until we find a set that includes one or more accepting states.
- If there are several accepting states in that set , pick the one associated with the earliest pattern Pi in the list from the Lex program. Move the forward pointer back to the end of the lexeme and perform the action Ai associated with pattern Pi.

2.10.3 DFA's for Lexical Analyzers

DFA's for Lexical Analyzers architecture, resembling the output of Lex is to convert the NFA for all the patterns into an equivalent DFA, using the subset construction Within each DFA state, if there are one or more accepting NFA states, It will determine the first pattern whose accepting state is represented and make that pattern the output of the DFA state.

SOLVED QUESTIONS AND ANSWERS

Question 1 : Explain the role of lexical analyzer

Answer : Lexical analysis is the first step in the compilation process. It is the process of converting a sequence of characters into a sequence of tokens. A program which performs the lexical analysis is known as a lexical analyzer.

- Lexical analyzer is the first phase of a compiler. The main task of a lexical analyzer is to read the input program and break it up into a sequence of tokens. These tokens are used by the syntax analyzer or parser, for syntax analysis.
- Fig. 2.9 is a block schematic of lexical analyzer and shows the interaction between the lexical analyzer and the parser.

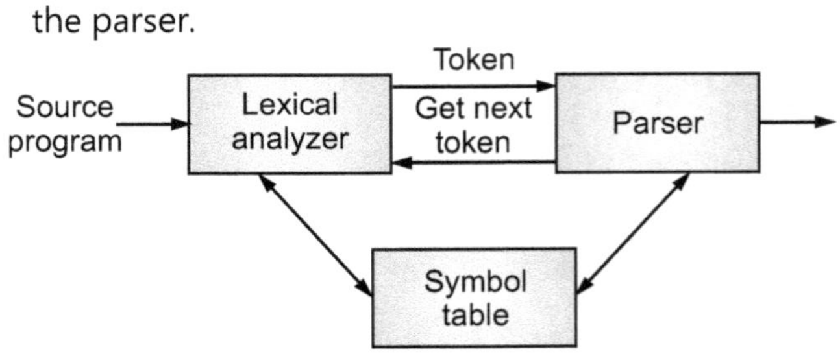

Fig. 2.9: Role of Lexical Analyzer

- Lexical analysis phase is divided into a cascade of two phases.
  1. Scanning
  2. Lexical analysis

- The lexical analyzer can also perform certain secondary tasks like removing the comments and white spaces from the source program. It may also make a copy of the source program with the error messages marked in it. Each error message may also be associated with the line number.

Question 2 : Define Lexeme

Answer : Lexeme

- Lexeme is the smallest logical unit of a program. It is defined as a sequence of characters in the source program that is matched by the pattern for a token.

  Consider the following Pascal statement.

  const pi = 3.1416

  Here, "const" is the lexeme for the token "const"

  "pi" is the lexeme for the token "identifier"

  "3.1416" is the lexeme for the token "num"

Question 3 : What is Regular Expression?

Answer : A regular expression is built up out of simpler regular expressions using a set of defining rules. Each regular expression r denotes a language L(r).

The rules that define the regular expressions over alphabet $\sum$ are as follows:

1. ε is a regular expression that denotes { ε }, that is, the set containing the empty string.
2. If a is a symbol in $\sum$, then a is a regular expression that denotes {a} i.e. the set containing the string a.
3. Suppose r and s are regular expressions denoting the languages L(r) and L(s), then
   (i) (r)|(s) is a regular expression denoting $L(r) \cup L(s)$
   (ii) (r)(s) is a regular expression denoting L(r) L(s)
   (iii) $(r)^*$ is a regular expression denoting $(L(r))^*$
   (iv) (r) is a regular expression denoting $L(r)^2$

A language denoted by a regular expression is said to be a regular set.

Question 4 : Explain the reference for lex specifications

Answer :

1. **Line Numbers and yylineno ( )**

- Line number in the input file can be used to report the error at that line.
- Some versions of lex define yylineno ( ) to contain the line number and automatically update it. However, most do not support this.
- Keeping track of the line number is easy. Initialize your line number variable to 1, and increment it in any lex rule that matches a newline character, as shown below.

```
%{
int lineno = 1;
%}
%%
......
\n      { lineno++; }
```

- Lexers that handle nested include files have to store and restore line numbers associated with each file.

2. **yyleng**

- Whenever a scanner matches a token, the text of the token is stored in the null terminated string yytext, and its length is in yyleng. The length in yyleng is the same as the value that should be returned by strlen(yytext).

3. **yyless ( )**

- yyless ( ) can be called from the code associated with a rule to push back all but the first n characters of the token. This can be useful when the rule to determine the boundary between the tokens is inconvenient to express as a regular expression.

4. **yylex ( )**

- The scanner created by lex has the entry point yylex( ). We call yylex() to start or resume scanning.

5. **yytext**

- Whenever a lexer matches a token, the text of the token is stored in the null terminated string yytext. The contents of yytext are replaced each time a new token is matched. In AT&T lex, the standard size of yytext[ ] is 200 characters while in MKS lex, it is 100 characters.

6. **yywrap**

- When a lexer encounters the end of file, it calls the routine yywrap( ) to find out what to do next. If yywrap( ) returns 0, the scanner continues scanning. If it returns 1, the scanner returns a zero token to report the end of file.
- The standard version of yywrap( ) in the lex library always returns 1.

Question 5 : Define Token.

Answer : Token

- An alphabet or a character class is a finite set of symbols. Token is a sequence of characters that represents a unit of information in the source program. A string is a series of tokens put together based on the language rules. Whenever we come across a token which is not a part of the alphabets of the language, we encounter a lexical error. This is different from a syntax error.

- Classes of similar lexemes are identified by the same token.

Question 6 : Define Pattern

Answer : Pattern

- A set of strings in the input for which the same token is produced as output, is described by a rule called a pattern.
- Pattern is a rule describing the set of lexemes that can represent a particular token in the source program.

Examples of token, pattern and lexeme are as given below.

Token	Lexeme	Description of Pattern
const	const	const
if	if	if
relation	<, <=, =, <>, >, >=	< or <= or = or <> or > or >=
id	pi, count, d2	letter followed by letters and digits
num	3.1416,0,6.02e23	any numeric constant
literal	"pascal"	Any characters between " and " except "

EXERCISE

1. Explain the Role of Lexical Analyzer, Explain interaction between Lexical Analyzer and Parser, Define Lexeme, Token and Pattern with suitable example.
2. Explain the role of Regular expression and DFA in Lexical Analyzer.
3. Define the term lexeme, token and pattern with example.
4. Specify lexical form (regular definition and DFA) of numerical constants, identifiers and keywords in the 'C' programming language.
5. How lexical analysis detect errors? Explain with suitable example.
6. Discuss the significance of lexemes with longest prefix and significance of ordering rules with suitable examples.
7. Explain LEX with suitable example.
8. Why white space characters are generally not allowed in identifier names. Justify.
9. Explain design of lexical analyzer generator.
10. Define regular exoression.

◈◈◈

UNIT III

SYNTAX ANALYSIS

3.1 INTRODUCTION

As we have already seen, syntax analysis (also known as parsing), is the process of analyzing a text made up of a sequence of tokens to determine whether the text conforms to the expected format or not. In this chapter, we understand the details of this analysis.

3.1.1 Role of Parsers

- The position of a syntax analyzer or parser in the compilation process is shown in Fig. 3.1.

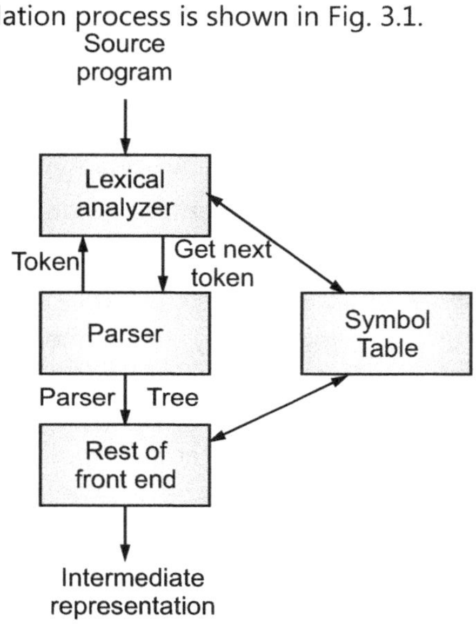

Fig. 3.1: Parser in Compiler Model

- In a compiler model, the parser obtains a string of tokens from the lexical analyzer, and verifies that the string can be generated by the grammar for the source language.
- If a syntax error occurs, the parser should be able to report it properly. It is also necessary that it should recover from commonly occurring errors so that the processing of the remaining input can proceed uninterrupted.
- The following section explains the nature of syntactic errors and general strategies for error recovery.

3.1.2 Error Detection and Recovery in Syntax Analysis

Syntax Error Handling

A program can contain errors at many different levels. For example, errors can be of the following types.

1. Lexical, such as misspelling an identifier, keyword, or operator.
2. Syntactic, such as an arithmetic expression with unbalanced parentheses.
3. Semantic, such as an operator applied to an incompatible operand.
4. Logical, such as an infinite recursive call.

In compilers, most of the error detection and recovery is focused around the syntax analysis phase. There are two reasons for this.

1. There are many errors which are syntactic in nature. These get detected when a stream of tokens coming from the lexical analyzer disobeys the grammar rules that define the programming language.
2. Modern parsing methods are very precise and can detect the presence of syntactic errors quite efficiently.

Goals of an Error Handler in a Compiler

An error handler is a routine in a program that respond to errors. It should have the following features.

1. It should report the presence of errors clearly and accurately and provide alternatives for dealing with them.
2. It should recover from each error quickly enough to be able to detect subsequent errors.
3. It should not significantly slow down the processing of correct programs.

Error Recovery Strategies :

A parser can employ the following strategies to recover from syntactic errors.

1. Panic Mode
2. Phrase Level
3. Error Productions
4. Global Corrections

1. Panic Mode Recovery: This is the simplest method to implement and can be used by most parsing methods.

This is a simple and most commonly used method.

When an error is detected, the parser discards the input symbols, one at a time, until it finds one of the designated sets of synchronizing tokens (synchronizing tokens are delimiters, such as semicolon or end, with a clear role in the source program.

Advantages :

- It is simple
- It does not to go into an infinite loop.
- It is adequate in situations where multiple errors are not there in the same statement.

Disadvantage:

- Panic mode correction often skips a considerable amount of input without checking it for additional errors.

2. Phrase Level Recovery: When an error is detected, the parser performs local corrections on the remaining input. For example, it replaces a prefix of the remaining input by some string which allows the parser to continue.

Some Typical Local Corrections:

- Replace a comma by a semicolon
- Delete an inappropriate semicolon
- Insert a missing semicolon

Disadvantage:

- Phrase level correction find it difficult to cope with situations in which the actual error has occurred before the point of detection.

3. Error Production: If we know the common errors that are likely to occur, we can supplement the grammar of the language with error producing constructs. When this grammar is used by the parser, error diagnostics can be generated to identify the erroneous construct found in the input.

4. Global Corrections: Ideally a compiler should make as few changes as possible, in processing of an incorrect input string.

Suppose we have an incorrect input string x and grammar G. There are algorithms which will find a parse tree for a related string y, such that the number of insertions, deletions and changes of tokens required to transform x into y, is as small as possible.

Disadvantage: Error production and global corrections are too costly to implement in terms of time and space.

3.2 CONTEXT-FREE GRAMMAR

In this section we understand the definition of context-free grammar and introduce terminology for talking about parsing.

1. Context-Free Grammar (CFG)

It is a four-tuple denoted by: G = (V, T, P, S)

where,

(i) V is a finite set of symbols called as non-terminals or variables.

(ii) T is a set of symbols called as terminals.

(iii) P is set of productions. Each production consists of a non-terminal on the left-hand side, and a string of terminals and non-terminals on the right-hand side.

(iv) S is a member of V, and is called as start symbol.

An Example of CFG:

The grammar with the following productions defines simple arithmetic expressions.

expr → expr op

expr expr → (expr)

expr → expr

expr → id

op → id |+ |- |* |/

In this grammar,

the terminal symbols are Id + - * / ( ) the non-terminal symbols are expr, op, the start symbol is expr.

2. Terminals

Terminals are the basic symbols from which the strings are formed. The word "token" is a synonym for "terminal".

3. Non-Terminals

Non-terminals are syntactic variables that denote sets of strings. In grammar, one non- terminal is distinguished as 'a'.

4. Productions

Productions of a grammar specify the manner in which the terminals and non-terminals can be combined to form strings. Each production consists of a non-terminal followed by an arrow, which is then followed by a string of non-terminals and terminals.

5. Notational Conventions

- **Conventions for Terminal Symbols:**
  - Lower case letters early in the alphabet such as a, b, c.
  - Operator symbols such as +, –, etc.
  - Punctuation symbols such as parentheses, comma, etc.
  - The digits 0, 1, 2, ...9.
  - Bold face strings such as id or if.
- **Conventions for Non-Terminals:**
  - Upper case letters early in the alphabet such as A, B, C.
  - The letter S, whenever it appears, is usually the start symbol.
  - Lower case italic names such as expr or stmt.
- Upper case letters late in the alphabet, such as X, Y, Z, represent grammar symbols that is, non-terminals or terminals.
- Lower case letters late in the alphabet, such as x, y, z represent string of terminals.

- Lower case greek letters, such as α, β, γ represent strings of grammar symbols.
- If $A \rightarrow \alpha_1$, $A \rightarrow \alpha_2$, $A \rightarrow \alpha_3$, ...$A \rightarrow \alpha_n$ are all productions with A on the left, we may write $A \rightarrow \alpha_1 | \alpha_2 | \alpha_3 | ...... \alpha_n$.

6. Derivation Tree or Parse Tree

Derivation tree or Parse tree is the graphical display of derivations as a tree. A tree is a derivation tree if it satisfies the following properties:

- All the leaf nodes of the tree are labeled by terminal symbols of the grammar.
- The root node of the tree is labeled by the start symbol of the grammar.
- The interior nodes are labeled by non-terminals.
- If an interior node has a label A, and it has n descendents with labels X_1, X_2,........., X_n from left to right, then the production rule $A \rightarrow X_1, X_2, ..., X_n$ must exist in the grammar.

7. Ambiguous Grammar

A grammar is said to be ambiguous when it produces more than one parse tree for a sentence. In other words, it produces more than one leftmost derivation or more than one rightmost derivation for the same sentence.

8. Left-Recursive Grammar

A grammar is left-recursive if it has a non-terminal A such that there is a derivation $A \Rightarrow + A\alpha$ for some string α.

Elimination of Left-Recursion

Top-down parsing methods cannot handle left-recursive grammar. Hence, a transformation that eliminates left-recursion is needed.

Rule for Eliminating Left-recursion

A left-recursive pair of productions $A \rightarrow A\alpha|\beta$ can be replaced by the non-left-recursive productions:

$A \rightarrow \beta A'$

$A' \rightarrow \alpha A'|\varepsilon$

First, group all the A-productions as:

$A \rightarrow A\alpha_1| A\alpha_2| A\alpha_3|...........| A\alpha_n|\beta_1|\beta_2|...........|\beta_m$

Then replace the A – productions by

$A \rightarrow \beta_1 A'|\beta_2 A'|..........|\beta_m A'$

$A' \rightarrow \alpha_1 A'|\alpha_2 A'|........|\alpha_n A'|\varepsilon$

The non-terminal A generates the same strings as before, but is no longer left-recursive.

This procedure eliminates all immediate left recursion from A and A' productions, but it cannot eliminate left recursion involving derivations of two or more steps.

Example:

Consider the grammar:

$E \rightarrow E+T |T$

$T \rightarrow T*F|F$

$F \rightarrow (E) |id$

For the production rule $E \rightarrow E+T |T$ string, α is +T and β is T.

Hence, by applying the rule for eliminating the left recursion, the productions are:

$E \rightarrow TE'$

$E' \rightarrow +TE'|\varepsilon$

Similarly, the left recursion can be removed for all other productions. The grammar after eliminating the left recursion is:

$E \rightarrow TE'$

$E' \rightarrow +TE'|\varepsilon$

$T \rightarrow FT'$

$T' \rightarrow *FT'|\varepsilon$

$F \rightarrow (E) |id$

Example:

Consider the grammar:

$S \rightarrow Aa | b$

$A \rightarrow Ac |Sd|\varepsilon$

Here, the non-terminal A is left-recursive because $S \Rightarrow Aa \Rightarrow Sda$, but it is not immediately left-recursive.

Hence we consider the following production rules:

$S \rightarrow Aa |b$

$A \rightarrow Ac|Aad|bd|\varepsilon$

After eliminating the left recursion, the resultant grammar is:

$S \rightarrow Aa |b$

$A \rightarrow bdA'|A'$

$A' \rightarrow cA'|adA'|\varepsilon$

Example:

Consider the following grammar:

$S \rightarrow aBDh$

$B \rightarrow Bb | c$

$D \rightarrow EF$

$E \rightarrow g | \varepsilon$

$F \rightarrow f | \varepsilon$

The grammar is left-recursive because it contains a pair of productions:

$B \rightarrow Bb | c$.

To eliminate the left-recursion, replace this production by the productions:

B → cB'

B' → bB'| ε

Hence the grammar is:

S → aBDh

B → cB'

B' → bB' | ε

D → EF

E → g | ε

F → f | ε

Example:

Consider the following grammar:

S → A

A → Ad | Ae | aB | aC

B → bBC | f

C → g

The grammar is left-recursive because it contains the production:

A → Ad | Ae | aB | aC

To eliminate the left-recursion, replace this by the set of productions:

A → aBA' | aCA'

A' → dA' | eA' |ε

Hence the set of productions is:

S → A

A → aBA' | aCA'

A' → dA' | eA' |ε

B → bBC | f

C → g

Example:

Consider the following grammar:

S → (L) | a

L → L, S | S

The grammar is left-recursive because it contains the productions:

L → L, S | S

To eliminate left recursion replace this by the set of productions:

L → SL'

L' → ,LL' |ε

Hence the set of productions is:

S → (L) | a

L → SL'

L' → ,LL' |ε

3.3 WRITING A GRAMMAR

- Grammars are capable of describing the largest part, but not all, of the syntax of programming languages. For example, the requirement that identifiers be declared before they are used, cannot be described by a context-free grammar. as a result, the sequences of tokens accepted by a parser form a superset of the programming language.
- Subsequent phases of the compiler must analyze the output of the parser to ensure compliance with rules that are not checked by the parser.
- One technique can remove ambiguity in the grammar, and other techniques - left-recursion elimination and left factoring - are useful for rewriting grammars so they become suitable for top-down parsing.

3.3.1 Lexical Versus Syntactic Analysis

Everything that can be described by a regular expression can also be described by a grammar. We may therefore reasonably ask: "Why use regular expressions to define the lexical syntax of a language?"

There are a number of reasons.

1. Separating the syntactic structure of a language into lexical and nonlexical parts provides a convenient way of modularizing the front end of a compiler into two manageable-sized components.
2. The lexical rules of a language are frequently quite simple, and to describe them we do not need a notation as powerful as grammars.
3. Regular expressions generally provide a more concise and easier-to-understand notation for tokens than grammars.
4. More efficient lexical analyzers can be constructed automatically from regular expressions than from arbitrary grammars.

There are no firm guidelines as to what to put into the lexical rules, as opposed to the syntactic rules. Regular expressions are most useful for describing the structure of constructs such as identifiers, constants, keywords, and white space. Grammars, on the other hand, are most useful for describing nested structures such as matching begin-end's, corresponding if-then-else's, and so on. These nested structures cannot be described by regular expressions.

3.3.2 Eliminating Ambiguity

- A grammar is said to be ambiguous if it can produce more than one parse tree for a particular sentence.
- This occurs when two different sequences of leftmost (or rightmost) derivations can produce the same sentence from the same start symbol.

Consider the following example:

ST AT	→	if EX PR then ST AT EST AT	Rule 1
	∈	at	Rule 2
EST AT	→	else ST AT	Rule 3
	∈	ε	Rule 4
EXPR	→	num	Rule 5

Suppose we wanted to parse the sentence: if num then if num then st else st

We could try to derive this (in the manner of a leftmost, top-down parse) as follows:

Table 3.1

Rules	Sentential Form
	ST AT
Rule 1	if EXPR then STAT ESTAT
Rule 5	if num then STAT ESTAT
Rule 1	if num then if EXPR STAT ESTAT ESTAT
Rule 5	if num then if num then STAT ESTAT ESTAT
Rule 2	if num then if num then st ESTAT ESTAT

1. Alternatively, we could apply rule 3 first, and then 2 and 4 to get:

Table 3.2

Rules	Sentential Form
Rule 3	if num then if num then st else STAT ESTAT
Rule 2	if num then if num then st else st ESTAT
Rule 4	if num then if num then st else st

3.3.3 Left-Recursive Grammar

A grammar is left-recursive if it has a non-terminal A such that there is a derivation $A \Rightarrow_+ A\alpha$ for some string α.

Elimination of Left-Recursion

Top-down parsing methods cannot handle left-recursive grammar. Hence, a transformation that eliminates left-recursion is needed.

Rule for Eliminating Left-Recursion

A left-recursive pair of productions $A \rightarrow A\alpha|\beta$ can be replaced by the non-left-recursive productions:

$A \rightarrow \beta A'$

$A' \rightarrow \alpha A'|\varepsilon$

First, group all the A-productions as:

$A \rightarrow A\alpha_1|\ A\alpha_2|\ A\alpha_3|..........|\ A\alpha_n|\beta_1|\beta_2|..........|\beta_m$

Then replace the A – productions by

$A \rightarrow \beta_1 A'|\beta_2 A'|.........|\beta_m A'$

$A' \rightarrow \alpha_1 A'|\alpha_2 A'|........|\alpha_n A'|\varepsilon$

The non-terminal A generates the same strings as before, but is no longer left-recursive.

This procedure eliminates all immediate left recursion from A and A' productions, but it cannot eliminate left recursion involving derivations of two or more steps.

Example:

Consider the grammar:

$E \rightarrow E+T\ |T$

$T \rightarrow T*F|F$

$F \rightarrow (\ E\ )\ |id$

For the production rule $E \rightarrow E+T\ |T$ string, α is +T and β is T.

Hence, by applying the rule for eliminating the left recursion, the productions are: $E \rightarrow TE'$

$E' \rightarrow +TE'|\varepsilon$

Similarly, the left recursion can be removed for all other productions. The grammar after eliminating the left recursion is:

$E \rightarrow TE'$

$E' \rightarrow +TE'|\varepsilon$

$T \rightarrow FT'$

$T' \rightarrow *FT'|\varepsilon$

$F \rightarrow (E)\ |id$

Example:

Consider the grammar:

$S \rightarrow Aa\ |\ b$

$A \rightarrow Ac\ |Sd|\varepsilon$

Here, the non-terminal A is left-recursive because $S \Rightarrow Aa \Rightarrow Sda$, but it is not immediately left-recursive.

Hence we consider the following production rules:

$S \rightarrow Aa\ |b$

$A \rightarrow Ac|Aad|bd|\varepsilon$

After eliminating the left recursion, the resultant grammar is: $S \rightarrow Aa\ |b$

$A \rightarrow bdA'|A'$

$A' \rightarrow cA'|adA'|\varepsilon$

Example:

Consider the following grammar:

$S \rightarrow aBDh$

$B \rightarrow Bb\ |\ c$

$D \rightarrow EF$

$E \rightarrow g\ |\ \varepsilon$

$F \rightarrow f\ |\ \varepsilon$

The grammar is left-recursive because it contains a pair of productions:

B → Bb | c.

To eliminate the left-recursion, replace this production by the productions:

B → cB'

B' → bB'| ε

Hence the grammar is:

S → aBDh

B → cB'

B'→ bB' | ε

D → EF

E → g | ε

F → f | ε

Example:

Consider the following grammar:

S → A

A → Ad | Ae | aB | aC

B → bBC | f

C → g

The grammar is left-recursive because it contains the production:

A → Ad | Ae | aB | aC

To eliminate the left-recursion, replace this by the set of productions:

A → aBA' | aCA'

A' → dA' | eA' |ε

Hence the set of productions is:

S → A

A → aBA' | aCA'

A' → dA' | eA' |ε

B → bBC | f

C → g

Example :

Consider the following grammar:

S → (L) | a

L → L, S | S

The grammar is left-recursive because it contains the productions:

L → L, S | S

To eliminate left recursion replace this by the set of productions:

L → SL'

L' → ,LL' |ε

Hence the set of productions is:

S → (L) | a

L → SL'

L' → ,LL' |ε

3.3.4 Left Factoring

In general, if A is a single non-terminal, and α, β and γ are strings of terminals or non-terminals, then a production rule of the form: A → $\alpha\beta$ | $\alpha\gamma$ can be left-factored into two rules of the form:

A → αB

B → β | γ

where β is some new non-terminal.

3.4 TOP-DOWN PARSING

In this section we will study the basic ideas behind top-down parsing and see how to construct an efficient non-backtracking form of a top down parser called as predictive parser.

Top down parsing can be attempted to find the leftmost derivation for an input string, as well as, to construct a parse tree for the input starting from the root, and creating the nodes of the parse tree in preorder.

In this section we are going to study the following forms of top-down parser.

1. Recursive-Descent Parser
2. Predictive Parser
3. Non-recursive Predictive Parsing

3.4.1 Recursive Descent Parser (RD)

Consider the grammar:

S → cAd

A → ab|a

and the input string w = cad.

To construct a parse tree for the input string, top down, we initially create a tree consisting of a single node labeled S. An input pointer points to c, the first symbol of w.

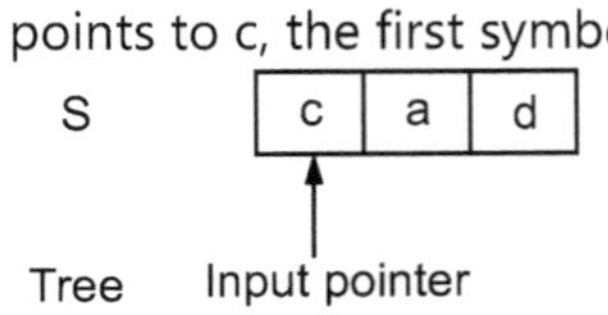

Fig. 3.2

Then using the first production rule for S to expand the tree, we obtain the following tree.

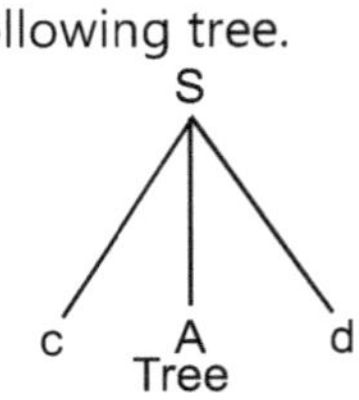

Fig. 3.3

The leftmost leaf c matches with the first symbol of w. Therefore, we advance the input pointer to a, the second symbol of w, and consider the next leaf of the tree labeled A.

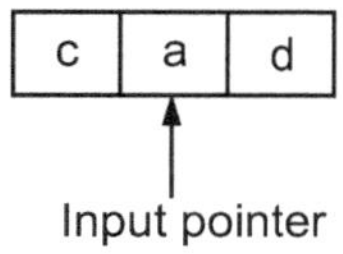

Fig. 3.4

Now A can be expanded using the first alternative for A to obtain the tree:

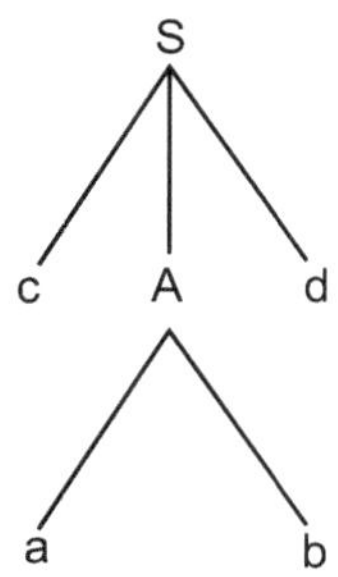

Fig. 3.5

We now have a match for the second input. Therefore, we advance the input pointer to d, the third input symbol, and compare this d against the next leaf, labeled b.

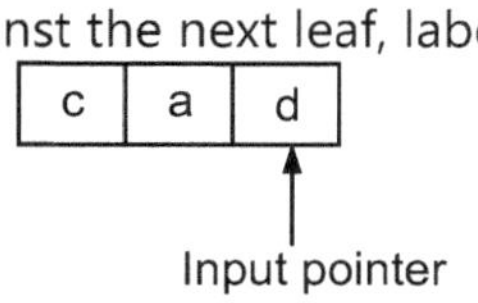

Fig. 3.6

Since b does not match d, we report failure and go back to A to see whether there is another alternative for A that we have not tried, but which might produce a match.

In going back to A, we must reset the input pointer to position 2, the position it had when we first came to A. This means that the procedure for A must store the input pointer in a local variable.

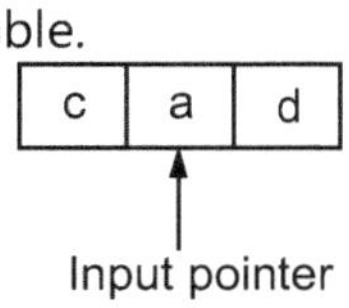

Fig. 3.7

We now try the second alternative for A and obtain the following tree.

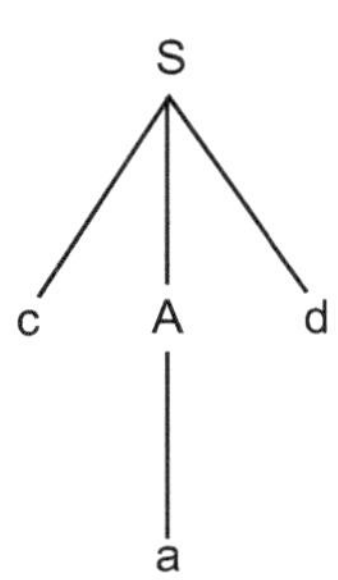

Tree

Fig. 3.8

The leaf a matches the second symbol of w and the leaf d matches the third symbol.

Since the parse tree for w is produced, we can stop and announce the successful completion of parsing.

A left-recursive grammar can cause a recursive descent parser to go into an infinite loop, even when it has backtracking.

3.4.2 Predictive Parsers

In many cases, if we write a grammar carefully, eliminate the left recursion from it, and then do left factoring of the resulting grammar, we can obtain a grammar which can be parsed by a recursive descent parser that requires no backtracking. This is called as predictive parser.

To construct a predictive parser when the current input symbol a, and the non-terminal A to be expanded are given, we must know which one of the alternatives of productions $A \rightarrow \alpha_1|\alpha_2|\alpha_3|......\alpha_n$ is the unique alternative that derives a string beginning with a.

For example, if the given productions are,

stmt → if expr then stmt else stmt

|while expr do stmt

|begin stmt_list end

then, the keywords if, while, and begin tell us which alternative is the only one that could possibly succeed if we are to find a statement.

Transition Diagrams for Predictive Parser

1. **How to Draw Transition Diagram For Predictive Parser.**

- There is one transition diagram for each non-terminal. The labels of edges are tokens (terminal) and non-terminals.
- A transition on a token means we should take that transition if that token is the next input symbol. A transition on a non-terminal A is a call of the procedure for A.
- To construct the transition diagram for a predictive parser from a grammar, follow the steps given below.
  1. First eliminate left recursion from the grammar, and then left factor the grammar.
  2. For each non-terminal do the following:
     (i) Create an initial and final (return) state.
     (ii) For each production $A \rightarrow X_1,X_2,.........X_n$ create a path from the initial to the final state, with edges labeled $X_1, X_2,.......X_n$

2. Behavior of the Predictive Parser Working with the Transition Diagram

It Begins in the Start State for the Start Symbol.

- If after some actions it is in state s, with an edge labeled by terminal a to state t, and if the next input symbol is a, then the parser moves the input cursor one position right, and goes to state t.
- On the other hand, if after some actions, it is in state s with an edge labeled by non- terminal A to state t, and if the next input symbol is a, the parser instead goes to the start state for A, without moving the input cursor.
- If it ever reaches the final state for A, it immediately goes to state t, in effect having "read" A from the input during the time it moved from state s to t.
- If there is an edge from s to t labeled ε, then from state s, the parser immediately goes to state t without advancing the input.
- A predictive parsing program attempts to match terminal symbol against the input, and makes potentially recursive procedure call whenever it has to follow an edge labeled by a non-terminal.

Example:

Consider the grammar for arithmetic expressions:

$E \rightarrow E+T \mid T$

$T \rightarrow T * F \mid F$

$F \rightarrow (E) \mid id$

After eliminating the immediate left recursion for E and T we obtain:

$E \rightarrow TE'$

$E' \rightarrow +TE' \mid \varepsilon$

$T \rightarrow FT'$

$T' \rightarrow *FT' \mid \varepsilon$

$F \rightarrow (E) \mid id$

Transition diagram for the grammar is shown in Fig. 3.9.

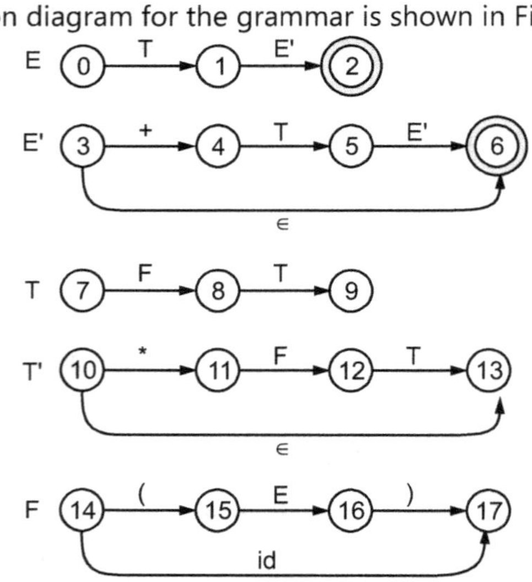

Fig. 3.9: Transition Diagrams for Grammar

The simplified transition diagrams for E', E, T' and T are shown in Fig. 3.10, Fig. 3.11, Fig. 3.12 and Fig. 3.13 respectively.

Substitute E' in the diagram for E.

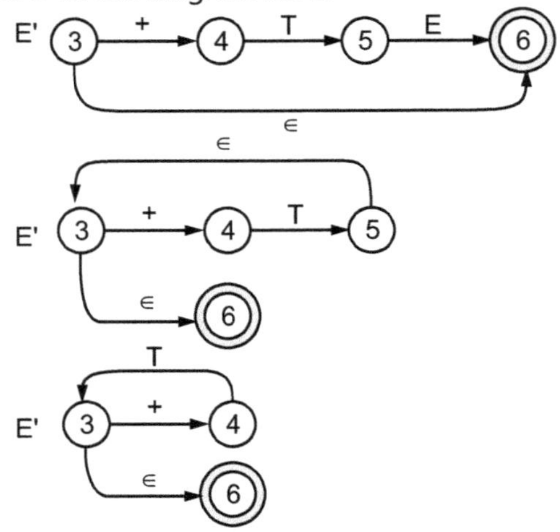

Fig. 3.10: Simplified Transition Diagram for E'

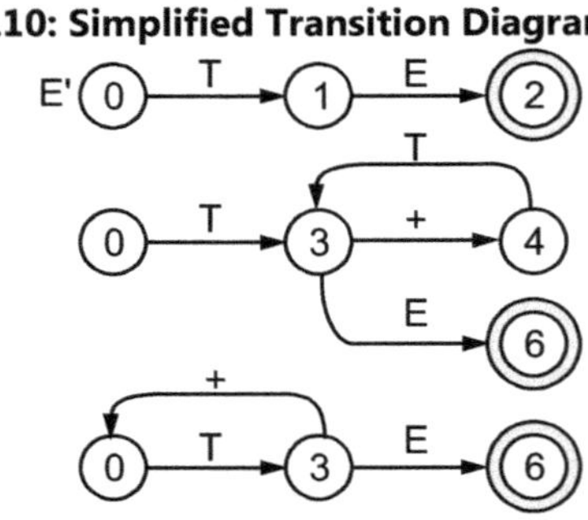

Fig. 3.11: Simplified Transition Diagram for E

Substitute T' in the diagram for T

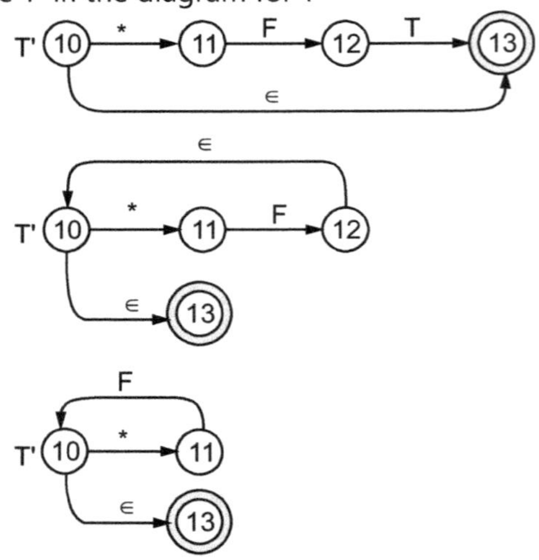

Fig. 3.12: Simplified Transition Diagram for T'

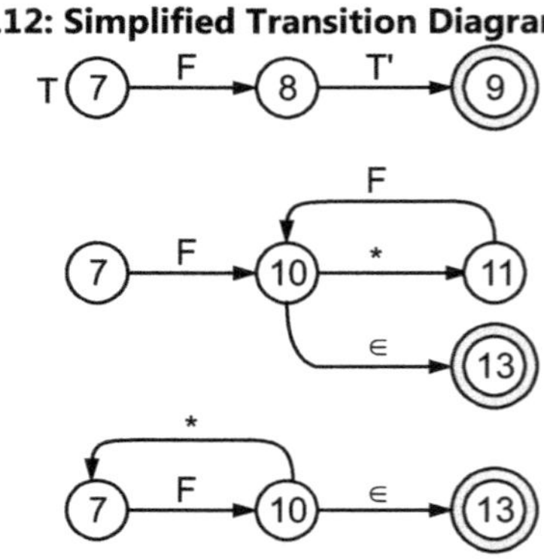

Fig. 3.13: Simplified Transition Diagram for T

The simplified transition diagram for the grammar is shown in Fig. 3.14.

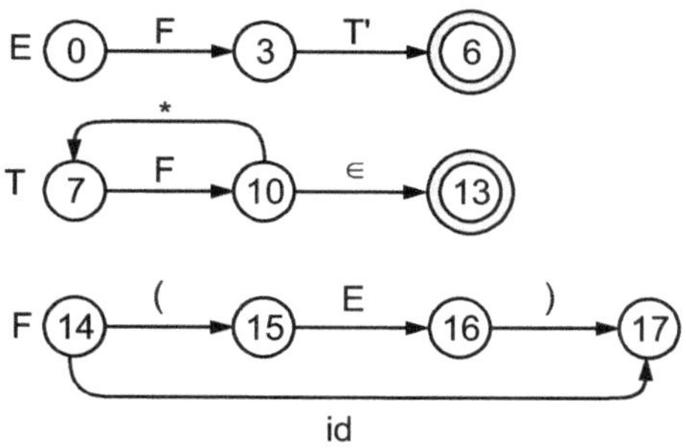

Fig. 3.14 : Simplified Transition Diagrams for Grammar

Now consider the input string: (id + id)

1. Predictive parser begins in start state 0.
2. It is in state 0 with an edge labeled by a non-terminal T and present input is (, hence it goes to the start state of T i.e. 7.
3. It is in state 7 with an edge labeled by a non-terminal F and present input is (, hence it reaches the start state of F i.e. 14.
4. It is in state 14 with two edges, one labeled with a terminal (, and the other labeled with terminal id, and the present input is (, hence it reaches the state 15 with the input (, and moves the input cursor one position right.
5. It is in state 15 with an edge labeled E, and the current input is id, hence it reaches the start state of E i.e., 0.
6. It is in state 0 with an edge labeled T, and the current input is id, hence it reaches the start state of T i.e. 7.
7. It is in state 7 with an edge labeled by a non-terminal F and present input is id, hence it reaches the start state of F i.e. 14.
8. It is in state 14 with two edges, one labeled with a terminal (, and the other labeled with terminal id, and the present input is id, hence it reaches the state 17 with the input id, and moves the input cursor one position right.
9. It is in state 17 which is the final or return state of F, hence it returns back and reaches state 10 via state 7.
10. It is in state 10 with two edges one labeled by a terminal * and the other labeled by a terminal ε and the current input is +, hence it reaches the state 13 with ε.
11. It is in state 13 which is the final or return state of T, hence it returns back and reaches the state 3 from state 0.
12. It is in state 3 with two edges, one labeled by a terminal + and the other labeled by a terminal ε and the current input is +, hence it reaches the state 0 with +.
13. It is in state 0 with an edge labeled T, and the current input is id, hence it reaches the start state of T i.e. 7.
14. It is in state 7 with an edge labeled by a non-terminal F and present input is id, hence it reaches the start state of F i.e., 14.
15. It is in state 14 with two edges, one labeled with a terminal (, and the other labeled with terminal id, and the present input is id, hence it reaches the state 17 with the input id, and moves the input cursor one position right.
16. It is in state 17, which is the final or return state of F, hence it returns back and reaches state 10 from state 7.
17. It is in state 10 with two edges one labeled by a terminal * and the other labeled by a terminal ε and the current input is), hence it reaches the state 13 with ε.
18. It is in state 13, which is the final or return state of T, hence it returns back and reaches the state 3 from state 0.
19. It is in state 3 with two edges one labeled by a terminal + and the other labeled by a terminal ε and the current input is), hence it reaches the state 6 with ε.
20. It is in state 6, which is the final state of E, and the current input is), hence it reaches the state 16 from state 15 with the non-terminal E.
21. It is in state 16 with an edge labeled by), and the current input is), hence it reaches the state 17 with the input).
22. It is in state 17 which is the final state or return state, and the complete input is processed. Hence the successful completion.

3.4.3 Non-Recursive Predictive Parser

The non-recursive predictive parser can be built by maintaining a stack explicitly rather than implicitly, via recursive calls. A model of the non-recursive predictive parser is shown in Fig. 3.15.

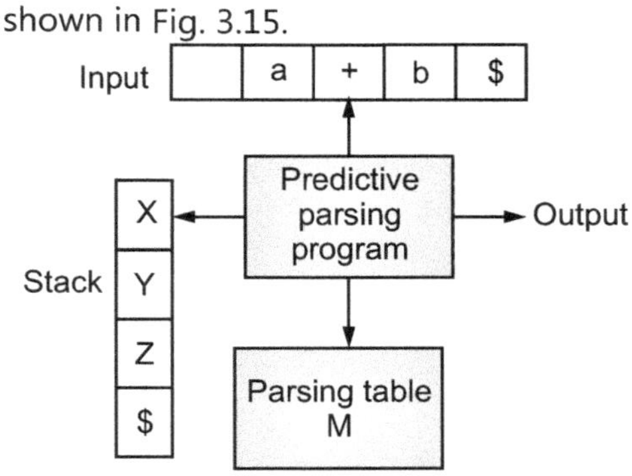

Fig. 3.15 : Model of Non-recursive Predictive Parser

- A Table driven non-recursive predictive parser has:
  1. Input Buffer
  2. Stack
  3. Parsing Table
  4. Output Stream

1. Input Buffer contains the string to be parsed, followed by $, which is a symbol used as a right-end marker to indicate the end of the input string.
2. Stack contains a sequence of grammar symbols with $ at the bottom, indicating the bottom of the stack. Initially, the stack contains the start symbol of grammar on top of $.
3. Parsing table is a two dimensional array M[A, a], where 'A' is a non-terminal, and 'a' is a terminal or the symbol $.

- The parser is controlled by a predictive parsing program that behaves as follows.
- The program considers X as the symbol on top of the stack, and 'a' as the current input symbol. These two symbols determine the action of the parser.
- There are three possibilities:

1. If X = a = $, the parser halts and announces the successful completion of parsing.
2. If X = a ≠ $, the parser pops X off the stack and advances the input pointer to the next input symbol.
3. If X is a non-terminal, the program consults entry M[X, a] of the parsing table M. This entry will be either an X-production of the grammar or an error entry. If, for example, M[X, a] = {X → UVW}, then the parser replaces X on top of stack by WVU (with U on top). If M[X, a] = error, the parser calls an error recovery routine.

Example:

Consider the grammar for arithmetic expressions:

E → E + T |T

T → T * F |F

F → (E) |id

After eliminating the immediate left recursion for E and T we obtain:

E → TE'

E' → +TE'|ε

T → FT'

T' → *FT'|ε

F → (E)|id

Predictive Parsing Table for this grammar is:

Table 3.3

Non-terminal	Input Symbol					
	Id	+	*	(	)	$
E	E →TE'			E → TE'		
E'		E'→+TE'			E'→ε	E'→ε
T	T → FT'			T → FT'		
T'		T' → ε	T' → *FT'		T'→ε	T'→ε
F	F → id			F → (E)		

Moves made by the parser for the input id + id*id are as follows:

Table 3.4

$E	id+id*id$	
$E'T	id+id*id$	E →TE'
$E'T'F	id+id*id$	T → FT'
$E'T'id	id+id*id$	F → id
$E'T'	+id*id$	
$E'	+id*id$	T'→ ε
$E'T+	+id*id$	E' → +TE'
$E'T	id*id$	
$E'T'F	id*id$	T → FT'
$E'T'id	id*id$	F → id
$E'T'	*id$	
$E'T'F'	*id$	T' → *FT'
$E'T'F	id$	
$E'T'id	id$	F → id
$E'T'	$	
$E'	$	T' → ε
$	$	E' → ε

Construction of Predictive Parsing Table

1. FIRST Function:

If α is any string of grammar symbols, let FIRST(α) be the set of terminals that begin the strings derived from α. If α $\overset{*}{\Rightarrow}$ ε, then ε is also in FIRST(α).

To compute FIRST(X) for all grammar symbols X, apply the following rules until no more terminals or ε can be added to any FIRST set.

1. If X is terminal, then FIRST(X) is {X}.
2. If X → ε is a production, then add ε to FIRST(X)

3. If X is non-terminal and $X \rightarrow Y_1, Y_2, ...Y_k$ is a production, then place a in FIRST(X) if for some i, a is in FIRST(Y_i), and ε is in all of FIRST(Y_1),.........FIRST(Y_{i-1}); that is $Y_1, ...Y_{i-1} \stackrel{*}{\Rightarrow} \varepsilon$.

If ε is in FIRST(Y_j) for all j=1, 2,.........k, then add ε to FIRST(X).

The rules can be simplified as follows:

FIRST(α)=Set of those terminals with which the strings derivable from α start. If α = XYZ, then FIRST(α) is computed as follows:

1. FIRST(α) = FIRST(XYZ) = {X} if X is terminal.
2. FIRST(α) = FIRST(XYZ) = FIRST(X) if X does not derive to an empty string; that is if FIRST(X) does not contain ε.
3. FIRST(α) = FIRST(XYZ) = FIRST(X)-{ε} ∪ FIRST(YZ) FIRST(YZ) is computed in an identical manner. FIRST(YZ) = {Y} if Y is terminal, otherwise,

   FIRST(YZ) = FIRST(Y) if Y does not contain ε, otherwise

   FIRST(YZ) = FIRST(Y) - {ε} ∪ FIRST(Z)

2. FOLLOW Function:

FOLLOW(A) for a non-terminal A, is defined to be a set of terminals a that can appear immediately to right of A in some sentential form. In other words, it is a set of terminals a such that there exists a derivation of the form $S \stackrel{*}{\Rightarrow} \alpha A a \beta$ for some α and β.

To compute FOLLOW(A) for all non-terminals A, apply the following rules until nothing can be added to any FOLLOW set:

1. Place $ in FOLLOW(S), where S is the start symbol and $ is the input right-end marker.
2. If there is a production $A \rightarrow \alpha B \beta$, then everything in FIRST(β) except ε is placed in FOLLOW(B).
3. If there is a production $A \rightarrow \alpha B$, or a production $A \rightarrow \alpha B \beta$ where FIRST(β) contains ε (i.e. $\beta \stackrel{*}{\Rightarrow} \varepsilon$), then everything in FOLLOW(A) is in FOLLOW(B).

Example:

Consider the grammar given below:

E → TE'

E' → +TE'|ε

T → FT'

T' → *FT'|ε

F → (E)|id Compute FIRST(E)

According to rule 3,

E → TE'

T → FT'

F → (E)|id

Hence,

FIRST(E) = { (, id }

Similarly, FIRST(T) = FIRST(F) ={ (, id }

Compute FIRST(E')

According to rule 3,

E' → +TE'

Add + to FIRST(E')

According to rule 2,

E' → ε

Add ε to FIRST(E')

FIRST(E')={ +, ε }

Compute FIRST(T')

According to rule 3,

T' → *FT'

Add * to FIRST(T')

According to rule 2,

T' → ε

Add ε to FIRST(T')

FIRST(T') ={ *, ε }

Compute FOLLOW(E)

According to rule 1, E is the start symbol hence place $ in FOLLOW(E)

According to rule 3,

F → (E)

Place FIRST() in FOLLOW(E) Hence FOLLOW(E) = { $,) }

Compute FOLLOW(E')

According to rule 3,

E → TE'

Hence put every thing in FOLLOW(E) in FOLLOW(E') FOLLOW(E')={ $,) }

Compute FOLLOW(T)

According to rule 2,

E → TE'

FIRST(E') ={ +, ε}

Hence put + in FOLLOW(T)

FIRST(E') contains ε, hence put everything in FOLLOW(E) in FOLLOW(T) Hence FOLLOW(T) = { +,), $ }

Compute FOLLOW(T')

According to rule 3,

T → FT'

Put everything in FOLLOW(T) in FOLLOW(T') FOLLOW(T') = { +,), $ }

Compute FOLLOW(F)

According to rule 2,

T → FT'

FIRST(T')={ *, ε}

Add * in FOLLOW(F)

FIRST(T') contains ε, hence, add everything in FOLLOW(T) to FOLLOW(F)

Hence,

FOLLOW(F) = {*, +,), $}

3. **Algorithm for Construction of Predictive Parsing Table:**

(i) For each production A → α of the grammar, do steps 2, and 3.

(ii) For each terminal 'a' in FIRST(α), add A → α to M[A, a].

(iii) If ε is in FIRST(α), add A → α to M[A, b] for each terminal 'b' in FOLLOW(A). If ε is in FIRST(α) and $ is in FOLLOW(A), add A → α to M[A, $].

(iv) Make each undefined entry of M be error.

Example:

Consider the grammar given below:

E → TE'

E' → +TE'|ε

T → FT'

T' → *FT'|ε

F → (E)|id

1. For the production rule

E → TE'

FIRST(TE')=FIRST(T)={ (, id}

Add E → TE' to M[E, ( ] and M[E, id]

2. For the production E' → +TE'

FIRST(+TE') = {+}

Add E' → +TE' to M[E' , +]

3. For the production rule E' → ε

FOLLOW(E') = {), $}

Add E' → ε to M[E',)] and M[E' , $]

4. For the production rule

T → FT'

FIRST(FT') = FIRST(F) = { (,id}

Add T → FT' to M[T, ( ] and M[T, id]

5. For the production rule T' → *FT'

FIRST(*FT') = {*}

Add T' → *FT' to M[T' , *]

6. For the production rule T' → ε

FOLLOW(T') = { +,), $}

Add T' → ε to M[T',+], M[T',)] and M[T' ,$]

7. For the production rule F → (E)

FIRST((E)) = { (}

Add F → (E) to M[F, ( ]

8. For the production rule F → id

FIRST(id) = {id}

Add F → id to M[F, id]

Hence the predictive parsing table is:

Table 3.5

Non-terminal	Input Symbol					
	id	+	*	(	)	$
E	E → TE'			E→ TE'		
E'		E' → +TE'			E' → ε	E' → ε
T	T → FT'			T → FT'		
T'		T' → ε	T'→ *FT'		T' → ε	T' → ε
F	F → id			F → (E)		

3.5 BOTTOM-UP PARSING

Bottom-up parsing can be done by using various types of parsers. Some of these are explained below.

3.5.1 Shift Reduce Parser

Shift-Reduce parsing attempts to construct a parse tree for an input string beginning at the leaves and working up towards the root. We can think of this process as "reducing" a string w to the start symbol of a grammar.

At each reducing step, a particular sub-string matching the right side of a production rule is replaced by the symbol on the left side of that production, and if the sub-string is chosen correctly at each step, the rightmost derivation is traced out in reverse.

Example:

Consider the grammar:

S → aABe

A → Abc|b

B → d

The sentence abbcde can be reduced to S by the following steps:

abbcde

Use the production rule A → b

aAbcde

Use the production rule A → Abc

aAde

Use the production rule B → d

aABe

Use the production rule S → aABe

S

Thus, by sequence of four reductions, we are able to reduce abbcde to S. These reductions trace out the following right-most derivation in reverse:

S ⇒ aABe ⇒ aAde ⇒ aAbcde ⇒ abbcde

Handle

- Handle of a string is a substring that matches the right side of a production, and whose reduction to the non-terminal on the left side of the production represents one step along the reverse of a rightmost derivation.
- But in many cases the leftmost substring β that matches the right side of some production $A \to \beta$ is not a handle, because a reduction by the production $A \to \beta$ yields a string that cannot be reduced to start symbol.
- Hence, handle of a right sentential form γ is a production $A \to \beta$ and a position of γ, where the string β may be found and replaced by A to produce the right sentential form in a rightmost derivation of γ.

Example:

Consider the grammar:

S → aABe

A → Abc|b

B → d

For the right sentential form: abbcde

A → b is the handle at position 2.

For the right sentential form: aAbcde

A → Abc is the handle at position 2.

For the right sentential form: aAde

B → d is the handle at position 3.

For the right sentential form: aABe

S → aABe is the handle at position 3.

Example:

Consider the grammar:

E → E + E

E → E * E

E → (E)

E → id

For the string id+id*id the rightmost derivation is:

E ⇒ E+E

⇒ E + E * E

⇒ E +E * id

⇒ E + id * id

⇒ id + id * id

Hence, while reducing the string id + id * id, we can use leftmost derivation as follows

id + id * id (handle for the right sentential form is E → id at position 1)

E + id *id (handle for the right sentential form is E → id at position 2)

E + E * id (handle for the right sentential form is E → id at position 3)

E + E * E (handle for the right sentential form is E → E * E at position 2)

E + E (handle for the right sentential form is

E → E + E at position 1)

Because the grammar is ambiguous there is another rightmost derivation for the same string:

E ⇒ E *E

⇒ E * id

⇒ E +E * id

⇒ E + id * id

⇒ id + id * id

Handle Pruning

- A rightmost derivation can be obtained by handle pruning. Handle pruning means, we start with a string of terminals w that we wish to parse. If w is a sentence of the grammar at hand, then $w = \gamma_n$, where γ_n is the right sentential form of some rightmost derivation which is not yet

  known:

  $S = \gamma_0 \Rightarrow \gamma_1 \Rightarrow \gamma_2 \Rightarrow \ldots\ldots\ldots\ \gamma_{n-1} \Rightarrow \gamma_n = w$
- To reconstruct this derivation in the reverse order, we locate the handle β_n in γ_n and replace β_n by the left-side of some production $A_n \to \beta_n$ to obtain the $(n-1)^{st}$ right sentential form γ_{n-1}. Then repeat the same process. If by continuing this process we produce a right sentential form consisting only of the start symbol S, then we stop and announce the successful completion of parsing.

Stack Implementation of Shift-Reduce Parsing

Shift-reduce parser can be implemented by using:

1. Stack to hold grammar symbols.
2. Input Buffer to hold the input string to be parsed.

We use $

To mark the bottom of the stack

To mark the right end of the input string.

Initially the stack is empty, and the string w is on the input, which can be shown as follows:

STACK

$

INPUT

W $

Working of the parser can be described as follows:

- The parser operates by shifting zero or more input symbols onto the stack until a handle β is on the top of the stack.
- Then it reduces β to the left-side of the appropriate production.
- It repeats this cycle until it has detected an error; or until the stack contains the start symbol and the input is empty, which can be shown as:

```
STACK
$S

INPUT
$
```

- After entering this configuration, the parser stops and announces the successful completion of parsing.

Actions of Shift-Reduce Parser

- The primary operations of the shift-reduce parser are shift and reduce, but actually a shift-reduce parser can perform four actions:
  1. Shift
  2. Reduce
  3. Accept
  4. Error

1. In a shift action, the next input symbol is shifted onto the top of the stack.
2. In a reduce action, the parser knows that the right end of the handle is at the top of the stack. It must then locate the left end of the handle within the stack and decide, with what non-terminal to reduce the handle.
3. In an accept action, the parser announces successful completion of parsing.
4. In an error action, the parser discovers that a syntax error has occurred and calls error recovery routine.

Example:

Consider the grammar:

E → E + E

E → E * E

E → (E)

E → id

and the input string is id + id * id.

The actions of shift-reduce parser are given below.

Table 3.6

Stack	Input	Actions
$	id + id * id $	shift
$id	+ id * id $	reduce by E→ id
$E	+ id * id $	shift
$E +	id * id $	shift
$E + id	* id $	reduce by E → id
$E + E	* id $	shift
$E + E *	id $	shift
$E + E * id	$	reduce by E → id
$E + E * E	$	reduce by E → E * E
$E + E	$	reduce by E → E + E
$E	$	accept

3.5.2 Operator Precedence Parsing

Operator Grammar: The grammar with the property that no production right side is ε or has two adjacent non-terminals, is called operator grammar.

Example of Operator Grammar:

E → E + E | E – E | E ∗ E | E / E | E ↑ E |(E) |–E| id

Precedence Relations:

In operator precedence parsing, three disjoint precedence relations,

<· , ≐ , and ·> are defined between certain pairs of terminals.

These precedence relations guide the selection of handles and have the following meaning.

Table 3.7

Relation	Meaning
a <· b	a yields precedence to b
a ≐ b	a has the same precedence as b.
a ·> b	a takes precedence over b.

Parsing using Operator Precedence Relations:

Precedence relations are used to delimit the handle of a right sentential form in the following way.

<· - marking left end

≐ - appearing in the interior of the handle.

·> - marking the right end.

Right sides of productions cannot have adjacent non-terminals. Hence, the right sentential form will not have two adjacent non-terminals.

Thus, the right sentential form can be written as:

$\beta_0 \alpha_1 \beta_1 \alpha_2 \ldots\ldots \alpha_n \beta_n$.

where each β_i is either $\in$ or a single non-terminal, and each a_i is a single terminal.

Let us assume that between a and a exactly one of the relations <· , $\doteq$, and ·> holds true. Let us use $ to mark each end of the string and define $ <· b and b ·> $ for all terminals b.

Now consider that the non-terminals are removed from the string and correct relation <·, $\doteq$, and ·> between each pair of terminals, and between the endmost terminals and $'s marking the ends of the string.

Example :

Right sentential form is:

id + id * id

The precedence relations are:

Table 3.8

	id	+	*	$
id		·>	·>	·>
+	<·	·>	<·	·>
*	<·	·>	·>	·>
$	<·	<·	<·	

Then the string with the precedence relations inserted is:

$ <· id ·> + <· id ·> * <· id ·> $

The handle can be found by the following process.

1. Scan the string from the left end until the first ·> is encountered for the above string.

   $ <· id ·> + <· id ·> * <· id ·> $

   ↑

   First ·> is found

2. Then scan backwards (to left) over any $\doteq$'s until a < · is encountered

   In the above string, scan backwards to $.

   $ <· id ·> + <· id ·> * <· id ·> $

   ↑

3. The handle sometime contains things to the left of the first ·> and to the right of the <· encountered in step 2, including any intervening or surrounding non-terminals. In the above string.

   $ <· id ·> + <· id ·> * <· id ·> $

   ↑ ↑

   The handle is id.

Example:

Consider the string with precedence relations inserted.

$ <· id ·> + <· id ·> * <· id ·> $

The first handle is first id, which is reduced to E. Then the right sentential form is E + id * id. The string with precedence relations for this right sentential form can be written as:

$ <· + <· id ·> * <· id ·> $

Then the handle can be found by following the three steps given below.

1. $ <· + <· id ·> * <· id ·> $

   ↑

   First ·> is encountered

2. $ <· + <· id ·> * <· id ·> $

   ↑

   First <· in left direction is found

3. Hence the handle is id.

Then id is reduced to E. Similarly the third id is reduced to E, and we get the right sentential form.

E + E * E

The string with precedence relations inserted is:

$ <· + <· * ·> $

By following the three steps we get the handle * i.e. E * E, which is reduced to E. The right sentential form is

E + E

The string with precedence relations inserted is:

$ <· + ·> $

Hence the handle is + i.e. E + E which is reduced to E.

3.5.3 LR Parser

LR(k) parsing is an efficient bottom-up syntax analysis technique that can be used to parse a large class of context-free grammars.

1. The "L" is for left-to-right scanning of the input.
2. The "R" is for constructing rightmost derivation in reverse.
3. "k" is for the number of input symbols of lookahead that are used in making parsing decisions. When k is omitted, k is assumed to be 1.

LR Parsing Algorithm

A model of the LR parser is shown in Fig. 3.16.

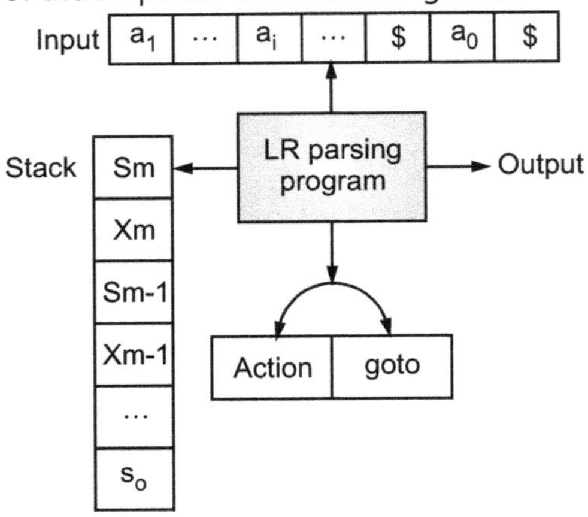

Fig. 3.16: Model of LR Parser

LR parser consists of:

1. Input
2. Output
3. Stack
4. Driver Program
5. Parsing Table with two parts
   (i) action
   (ii) goto

Driver Program

- It is the same for all parsers, only the parsing table changes from parser to parser. The parsing program reads characters from an input buffer one at a time. The program uses stack to store a string of the form:

  $s_0X_1s_1X_2.........X_ms_m$

  where s_m is on top.
- Each X_i is a grammar symbol and each s_i is a symbol called a state.
- Each state symbol summarizes the information contained in the stack below it.
- A combination of state symbol on the top of the stack and the current input symbol is used to index the parsing table and determine the shift reduce parsing decision.

Parsing Table

- A parsing table consists of two parts, a parsing action function action, and a goto function goto.
- LR parsing table can be constructed by using three methods:
  1. Simple LR (SLR)
  2. Canonical LR
  3. LookAhead LR (LALR)

Configuration of LR Parser

- It is a pair whose first component is the stack contents, and second component is the unexpended input.

  $(s_0X_1\,s_1X_2\,s_2X_3.........\,X_ms_m,\ a_i\,a_{i+1}...........a_n\$)$.

  This configuration represents the right sentential form $X_1, X_2,.........X_ma_ia_{i+1}...........a_n$
- The program driving the LR parser behaves as follows.
  1. It determines s_m, the state on the top of the stack, and a_i, the current input symbol.
  2. It then consults action $[s_m, a_i]$, the parsing action table entry for state s_m and input a_i, which can have one of the following four values:
     (i) shift s, where s is a state
     (ii) reduce by a grammar production $a \rightarrow \beta$
     (iii) accept d. error
- The configurations resulting after each of the four types of move are as follows:
  1. If action$[s_m, a_i]$=shift s, the parser executes a shift move, entering the configuration

     $(s_0X_1\,s_1X_2\,s_2X_3.........\,X_ms_m\,a_i\,s,\ a_{i+1}...........a_n\$)$

     Here, the parser has shifted both the current input symbol a_i, and the next state s which is given in action$[s_m,a_i]$, onto the stack; a_{i+1} becomes the current input symbol.
  2. If action$[s_m,a_i]$ = reduce $A \rightarrow \beta$, then the parser executes a reduce move, entering the configuration

     $(s_0X_1\,s_1X_2\,s_2X_3.........\,X_{m-r}\,s_{m-r}\,A\ s,\ a_i\,a_{i+1}...........a_n\$)$

     where s = goto$[s_{m-r}, A]$ and r is the length of β, the right side of the production.
  3. If action$[s_m, a_i]$=accept, parsing is completed.
  4. If action$[s_m, a_i]$=error, the parser has discovered an error and calls an error recovery routine.

     The function goto takes a state and grammar symbol as arguments and produces a state.

Example:

Consider the grammar:

$E \rightarrow E + T$

$E \rightarrow T$

$T \rightarrow T$ *

F $T \rightarrow F$

$F \rightarrow (E)$

$F \rightarrow id$

The parsing table for the expression grammar is given below.

Table 3.9

State	action						goto		
	Id	+	*	(	)	$	E	T	F
0	s5			s4			1	2	3
1		s6				acc			
2		r2	s7		r2	r2			
3		r4	r4		r4	r4			
4	s5			s4			8	2	3
5		r6	r6		r6	r6			
6	s5			s4				9	3
7	s5			s4					10
8		s6			s11				
9		r1	s7		r1	r1			
10		r3	r3		r3	r3			
11		r5	r5		r5	r5			

If the input string is id * id + id, the sequence of stack and input contents is as follows:

Table 3.10

Stack	Input	Action
(1) 0	id * id + id $	Shift
(2) 0 id 5	* id + id $	Reduce by F → id
(3) 0 F 3	* id + id $	Reduce by T → F
(4) 0 T 2	* id + id $	Shift
(5) 0 T 2 * 7	id + id $	Shift
(6) 0 T 2 * 7 id 5	+ id $	Reduce by F→ id
(7) 0 T 2 * 7 F 10	+ id $	Reduce by T → T * F
(8) 0 T 2	+ id $	Reduce by E → T
(9) 0 E 1	+ id $	Shift
(10) 0 E 1 + 6	+ id $	Shift
(11) 0 E 1 + 6 id 5	$	Reduce by F → id
(12) 0 E 1 + 6 F 3	$	Reduce by T → F
(13) 0 E 1 + 6 T 9	$	Reduce by E → E + T
(14) 0 E 1	$	Accept

LR Grammar

A grammar for which we can construct a parsing table, is said to be an LR Grammar.

LR(k) Grammar

A grammar that can be parsed by an LR parser that examines up to k input symbols on each move, is called an LR(k) grammar.

Difference Between LL(k) Grammar and LR(k) Grammar

- In LR(k) parsing there is an overhead of recognizing all of what is derived from the right hand side of a production for LL(k) grammar this requirement is quiet simple.
- For LL(k) grammar, it is sufficient be able to recognise the use of a production by seeing only the first k symbols of what its right side derives.
- LR(k) grammar can describe more languages than LL(k) grammar.

3.6 USING AMBIGUOUS GRAMMAR

- Let consider writing parsers for ambiguous grammar. If we note that ambiguous grammar has less number of non terminals. Hence parsing table will be small in size. But when we construct LR parser tables for ambiguous grammar, multiple entries like "shift and reduce" in same cell of parsing table may come, we call it as shift/reduce conflict. Then it is hard to take decision whether to shift or reduce.
- So we may think of first unambiguous the grammar and then generate the parsing table. But instead of removing ambiguity from grammar we may handle conflicts by giving preference to reduce or shift using associative and precedence rule.

Example : if current state in derivation reduce action is coming for '+' terminal but next reading symbol is '*' so give preference to shift '*' instead of reduce for '+'.

3.7 PARSER GENERATORS

YACC stands for " yet another compiler-compiler" and was created by S.C. Johnson. YACC is available as a command on the Unix system, and has been used to help implement hundreds of compilers.

Input/Output Translator with YACC

First a file say translate.y is transformed into a C program called y.tab.c using the LALR method. The program y.tab.c is a representation of an LALR parser written in C, along with other C routines that the user may have prepared.

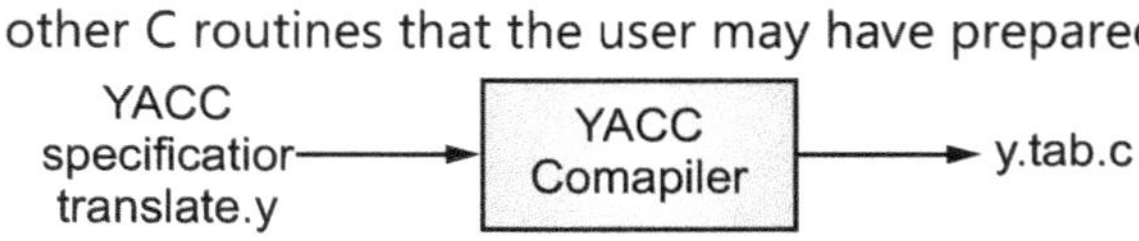

Fig. 3.17 : YACC Compiler

By compiling y.tab.c along with the ly library that contains the LR parsing program using the command,

cc y.tab.c – ly

We obtain the desired object program a.out that performs the translation specified by the original YACC program.

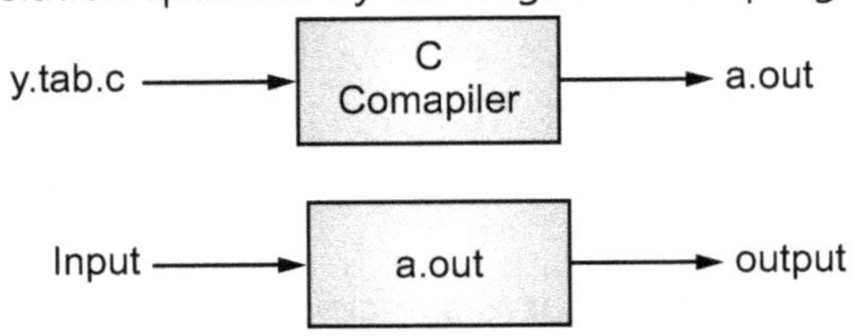

Fig. 3.18 : YACC compilation process

YACC program has three parts:

1. declarations

   %%

2. translation rules

   %%

3. supporting C-routines

1. Declaration Part (Also Called as Definition Section)

There are two optional sections in the declarations part of a YACC program. In the first section we put ordinary C declarations, delimited by % { and %}. Here we can place declarations of any temporaries used by the translation rules or procedures of the second and third sections.

The second section includes declarations of tokens used in the grammar.

2. Translation Rules Part (Also Called as Rules Section)

The rules section simply consists of a list of grammar rules. Each rule consists of a grammar production and the associated semantic action.

3. Supporting C Routines Part

This part consists of supporting C routines. A lexical analyzer by the name yylex() must be provided. Other procedures such as error recovery routines may be provided as necessary.

YACC Specification for Simple Desk Calculator

Consider the grammar for constructing the desk calculator:

$E \rightarrow E+T|T$

$T \rightarrow T * F|F$

$F \rightarrow (E)|id$

```
%{
#include <ctype.h>
%}
%token DIGIT
%%
S   : E'\n'  {printf("%d\n", $1);}
    ;
E   : E+T   {$$ = $1 + $3; }
    : T
    ;
T   : T * F  {$$=$1 * $3;}
    : F
    ;
F   : '(' E ')' {$$ = $2;}
    : DIGIT
    ;
%%
yylex( )
{
        int c;
        if (isdigit(c))
        {
            yylval = c-'0' ;
            return DIGIT;
        }
        return c;
}
```

SOLVED EXAMPLES

Example 3.1: *Show whether grammar1 and grammar2 are LL(1). Also show the parsing table for both grammars.*

Grammar1: $E \rightarrow TE'$

$E' \rightarrow *TE'|\varepsilon$

$T \rightarrow FT'$

$T' \rightarrow \wedge T|\varepsilon$

$F \rightarrow (E) | id$

Grammar2: $X \rightarrow YZ$

$Y \rightarrow m|n|\varepsilon$

$Z \rightarrow m$

Solution: A grammar whose parsing table has no multiply-defined entries is said to be LL(1). The first "L" in LL(1) stands for scanning the input from left to right, the second "L" stands for producing the leftmost derivation, and the "1" for using one input symbol of lookahead at each step to make parsing action decisions.

Parsing table for grammar1:

Table 3.11

Non-Terminal	Input Symbol					
	id	+	*	(	)	$
E	E → TE'			E → TE'		
E'			E' → *TE'		E' → ε	E' → ε
T	T → FT'			T → FT'		
T'		T' → +FT'	T' → ε		T' → ε	T' → ε
F	F → id			F → (E)		

This grammar is LL(1) grammar because the parsing table does not have any multiply- defined entries.

Parsing table for grammar2:

Table 3.12

Non-Terminal	Input Symbol			
	m	**n**	**ε**	**$**
X	X → YZ	X → YZ		
Y	Y → ε Y → M	Y → n		
Z	Z → m			

This grammar is not LL(1) because the table entry [Y, m] is multiply defined.

Example 3.2: *Construct the LR parsing table for the grammar*

S → iSeS | iS |a

Solution: The grammar after augmentation is: S' → S

S → iSes

S → iS

S → a

The LR(0) items are:

I_0 = Closure(S' → •S)

S' → •S

S → •iSeS

S → •iS

S → •a

I_1 = goto(I_0, S)

S' → S•

I_2 = goto(I_0, i)

S → i•SeS

S → i•S

S → •iSeS

S → •iS

S → •a

I_3 = goto(I_0, a)

S → •a

I_4 = goto(I_2, S)

S → iS•eS

S → iS•

goto(I_2,i) = I_2

I_5 = goto(I_4,e)

S → iSe•S

S → •iSeS

S → •iS

S → •a

I_6 = goto(I_5,S)

S → iSeS•

goto(I_5, i) = I_2

goto(I_5,a) = I_3

The LR parsing table for the grammar is:

Table 3.13

State	Action				Goto
	i	e	a	$	S
0	S_2		S_3		1
1				Acc	
2	S_2		S_3		4
3		R_3		R_3	
4		S_5		R_2	
5	S_2		S_3		6
6		R_1		R_1	

Example 3.3: *Generate LALR parsing table for the following grammar.*

E → E + E | E ↑ E | id

Also show the parsing of the string a+b ↑d ↑e

Solution: The grammar after removing ambiguity is:

E → E + T

E → T

T → F↑T

T → F

F → id

The canonical collection of LR(1) items is:

I_0:

E' → •E, $

E → •E+T, $

E → •T, +

T → • F↑T, +

T → • F, +

F → • id, $

I_1 = goto(I_0, E)

E' → E•, $

E → E•+T, $

I_2 = goto(I_0, T)

E → T•, +

I_3 = goto(I_0, T)

T → F•T, +

T → F•, +

I_4 : goto(I_0,id)

F → id•, $

I_5 = goto(I_1, +)

E → E+•T, $

T → •F↑T, $

T → •F, $

F → •id, ↑

I_6 = goto(I_3, ↑)

T → F↑• T, +

T → •F↑T, +

T → •F, +

F → •id, ↑| +

I_7 = goto(I_5,T)

E → E + T•, $

I_8 = goto(I_5,F)

T → F•↑T, ↑|$

T → F•, $

I_9 = goto(I_5,id)

F → id•, ↑

I_{10} = goto(I_6,T)

T → F↑T•, +

I_{11} = goto(I_6,T)

F → id•, ↑ | +

I_{12} = goto(I_8, ↑)

T → F↑•T, ↑|$

T → •F↑T, ↑|$

T → •F, ↑|$

F → •id, ↑|$

I_{13} = goto(I_{12}, T)

T → F↑T•, ↑|$

Following LR states can be merged:

$I_{38}=I_3 \cup I_8$

$I_{4911} = I_4 \cup I_9 \cup I_{11}$

$I_{612} = I_6 \cup I_{12}$

$I_{1013} = I_{10} \cup I_{13}$

The LALR parsing table is:

Table 3.14

state	action				goto		
	+	↑	id	$	E	T	F
0			S_{4911}		1	2	38
1	S_5			acc			
2	R_2						
38	R_4	S_{612}		R_4			
4911	R_5	R_5		R_5			
5			S_{4911}			7	38
612			S_{4911}			1013	38
7				R_1			
1013	R_3	R_3		R_3			

Example 3.4: *Consider the grammar G, given by the following production (where S is the start symbol):*

$S \rightarrow a\,S \mid S\,b \mid \varepsilon$

(a) What is the language generated by G? Justify your answer.

Solution: The language consisting of zero or more a's is followed by zero or more b's. (This includes the string with zero a's and zero b's – the empty string.)

Justification: When deriving a string with this grammar, any intermediate string has exactly one S. This is because, using the first alternative (a S), we eliminate one S (the one expanded) and introduce one S, for no net gain in the number of S's. Likewise, using the second alternative (S b) results in no net gain in the number of S's; using the third alternative terminates the derivation. Think of the unique S in an intermediate string as the growing point. Using the first alternative introduces an a to the left of the growing point; using the second alternative introduces a b to the right.

Therefore, just before the third alternative is used to terminate the derivation, all the a's are to the left side of the growing point and all the b's are to the right side. Using the third alternative eliminates the growing point without introducing anything and hence, all the a's are to the left of all the b's. The number of a's is the number of times the first alternative was used, and the number of b's is the number of times the second alternative was used. Each of the first two alternatives may be used any number (including zero) of times.

(b) Is G ambiguous? Justify your answer.

Solution: It is ambiguous as can be seen from the following two parse trees for the string ab:

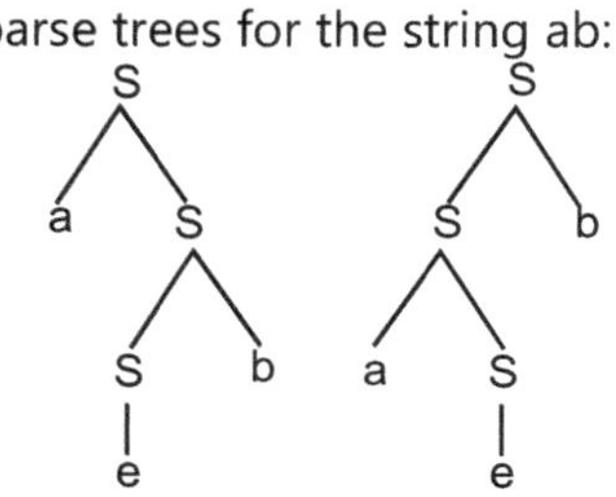

Fig. 3.19

Example 3.5: *Consider the grammar G′, given by the following productions (where S is the start symbol):*

$$T \rightarrow T \clubsuit a \mid (S) \mid a$$
$$S \rightarrow T \heartsuit S \mid T$$

(a) Which binary operator has higher precedence, ♥ or ♣?

Solution: ♣ has higher precedence than ♥. ♥ is introduced by the S-production and ♣ is introduced by the T-production. Since a T is a derivation tree for this grammar and is below an S, a ♣ is below a ♥, hence has higher precedence.

(b) What is the associativity of ♥ ?

Solution: Right associative (right-to-left) since the S-production is right-recursive.

(c) What is the associativity of ♣?

Solution: Left associative (left-to-right) since the T-production is left-recursive.

(d) Draw the parse tree for (a ♥ a) ♣ a.

Solution: See Fig. 3.20

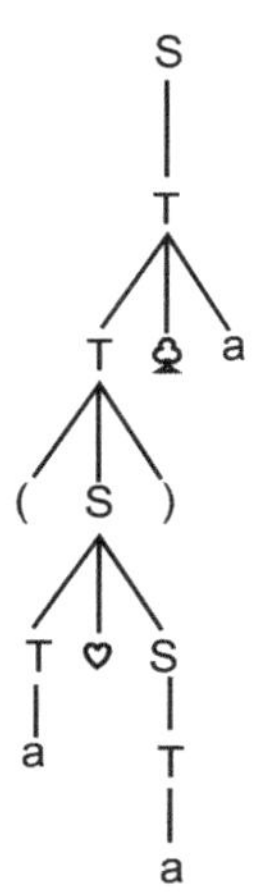

Fig. 3.20

Example 3.6: *Consider the grammar*

$$S \rightarrow (L) \mid a$$
$$S \rightarrow L, S \mid S$$

(a) Find the parse trees for the following sentences.

(i) (a, a)

Solution:

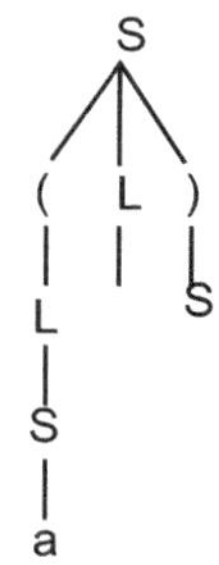

Fig. 3.21

(ii) (a, (a, a))

Solution:

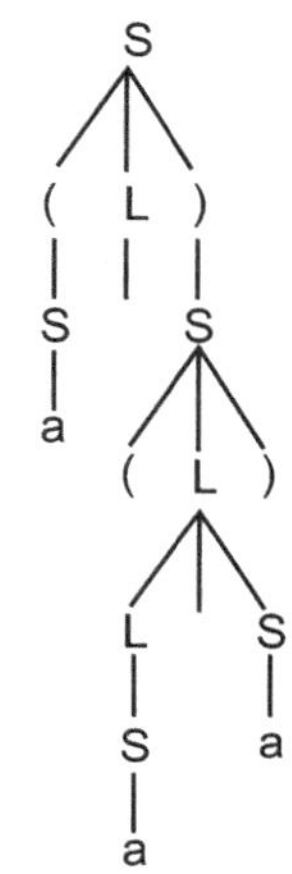

Fig. 3.22

(iii) (a, ((a, a), (a, a)))

Solution :

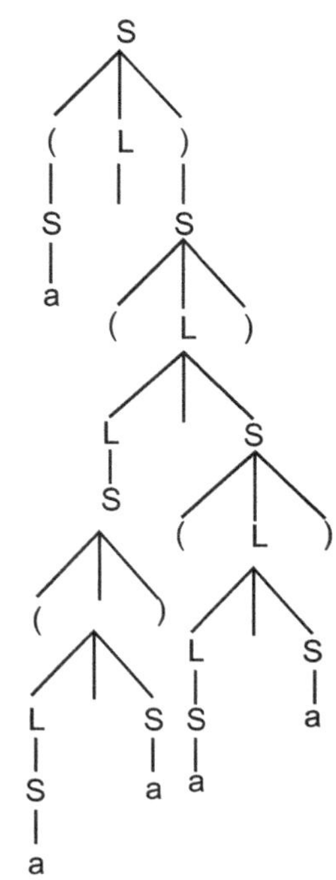

Fig. 3.23

Example 3.7: *Consider the grammar*

$S \rightarrow a\ B\ C\ d \mid d\ C\ B\ e$

$B \rightarrow b\ B \mid \varepsilon$

$C \rightarrow c\ a \mid a\ c \mid \varepsilon$

(a) *What are the terminals, non-terminals, and the start symbol for the grammar?*

(b) *Give the parse tree for the input string abbcad.*

(c) *Compute the First sets and Follow sets for each of the non-terminals in the grammar.*

Solution:

(a) terminals: { a, b, c, d, e}, non-terminals: {S, B, C}, start symbol : S.

(b)

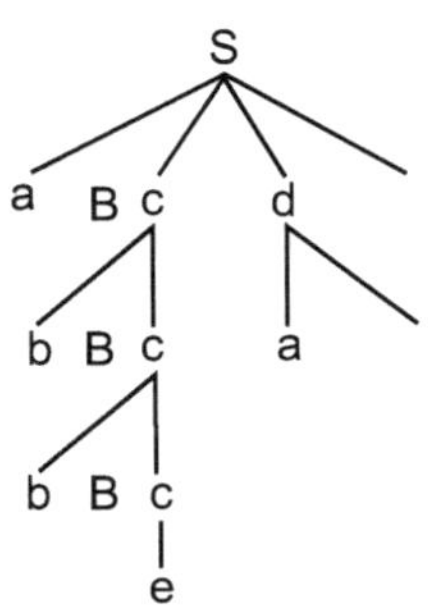

Fig. 3.24

(c) FIRST(S) = { a, d }, FIRST(B) = { b, ε }, FIRST(C) = { a, c, ε }.

FOLLOW(S) = { $ }, FOLLOW(B) = { a, c, d, e }, FOLLOW(C) = { b, d, e }.

Example 3.8: *Construct a recursive descent parser in C for the grammar in Example 3.7. You may assume that functions match( ) and error( ) are already available and global variable token is used to store the current token read by function match( ).*

Solution: void

```
S( )
{ switch(token) {
    case a: match(a); B( ); C( ); match(d); break;
    case d: match(d); C( ); B( ); match(e); break;
    default: error( );
    }
    }
    void B( ) {
    switch(token) {
    case b: match(b); B( ); break;
    case a: case c: case d: case e: break;
    default: error( );
    }
    }
    void C( ) {
    switch(token) {
    case c : match(c); match(a); break;
    case a : match(a); match(c); break;
    case b: case d: case e: break;
    default: error( );
    }
}
```

Example 3.9: *Construct an LL(1) parsing table for the grammar in the above Example.*

Solution:

Table 3.15

	a	b	c	d	e	$
S	S → a B C d			S → d C B e		
B	B → ε	B → b B	B → ε	B → ε	B → ε	
C	C → a c	C → ε	C → c a	C → ε	C → ε	

Example 3.10: *Consider the following grammar:*

$S \rightarrow a\ A\ d \mid a\ c\ e \mid b\ A\ e$

$A \rightarrow c$

(a) (25%) Construct the SLR(1) parsing table for this grammar. Is this grammar SLR(1)?

(b) (25%) Construct the LR(1) parsing table for this grammar. Is this grammar LR(1)?

(c) (20%) Construct the LALR(1) parsing table for this grammar. Is this grammar LALR(1)?

Solution:

(a)

(0) $S' \rightarrow S$

(1) $S \rightarrow a\ A\ d$

(2) $S \rightarrow a\ c\ e$

(3) $S \rightarrow b\ A\ e$

(4) $A \rightarrow c$

Follow(S) = {$}, Follow(A) = {d, e};

$I_1 = \{S' \rightarrow \bullet S, S \rightarrow \bullet a\ A\ d, S \rightarrow \bullet a\ c\ e, S \rightarrow \bullet b\ A\ e\}$,

$I_2 = goto(I_1, S) = \{S' \rightarrow S \bullet\}$,

$I_3 = goto(I_1, a) = \{S \rightarrow a \bullet A\ d, S \rightarrow a \bullet c\ e, A \rightarrow \bullet c\}$

$I_4 = goto(I_1, b) = \{S \rightarrow b \bullet A\ e, A \rightarrow \bullet c\}$

$I_5 = goto(I_3, A) = \{S \rightarrow a\ A \bullet d\}$

$I_6 = goto(I_3, c) = \{S \rightarrow a\ c \bullet e, A \rightarrow c \bullet\}$

$I_7 = goto(I_4, A) = \{S \rightarrow b\ A \bullet e\}$

$I_8 = goto(I_4, c) = \{A \rightarrow c \bullet\}$

$I_9 = goto(I_5, d) = \{S \rightarrow a\ A\ d \bullet\}$

$I_{10} = goto(I_6, e) = \{S \rightarrow a\ c\ e \bullet\}$

$I_{11} = goto(I_7, e) = \{S \rightarrow b\ A\ e \bullet\}$

Table 3.16

	a	b	c	d	e	$	S	A
I_1	s3	s4					g2	
I_2						accept		
I_3			s6					g5
I_4			s8					g7
I_5				s9				
I_6				r4	s10/r4			
I_7					s11			
I_8				r4	r4			
I_9						r1		
I_{10}						r2		
I_{11}						r3		

Since there is a shift/reduce conflict at state I_6, this grammar is not SLR(1) grammar.

(b)

I_1 = {[S' → • S, $], [S → • a A d, $], [S → • a c e, $], [S → • b A e, $]},

I_2 = goto(I_1, S) = {[S' → S •, $]},

I_3 = goto(I_1, a) = {[S → a • A d, $], [A → • c, d], [S → a • c e, $]}

I_4 = goto(I_1, b) = {[S → b • A e, $], [A → • c, e]}

I_5 = goto(I_3, A) = {[S → a A • d, $]}

I_6 = goto(I_3, c) = {[A → c •, d], [S → a c • e, $]}

I_7 = goto(I_4, A) = {[S → b A • e, $]}

I_8 = goto(I_4, c) = {[A → c •, e]}

I_9 = goto(I_5, d) = {[S → a A d •, $]}

I_{10} = goto(I_6, e) = {[S → a c e •, $]}

I_{11} = goto(I_7, e) = {[S → b A e •, $]}

Table 3.17

	a	b	c	d	e	$	S	A
I_1	s3	s4					g2	
I_2						accept		
I_3			s6					g5
I_4			s8					g7
I_5				s9				
I_6				r4	s10			
I_7					s11			
I_8					r4			
I_9						r1		
I_{10}						r2		
I_{11}						r3		

Since there is no conflict in the parsing table, this grammar is LR(1) grammar. (c)Since there are no two states with the same core in the LR(1) parsing table, the LALR(1) table is the same as LR(1) table, and the grammar is LALR(1) grammar.

SOLVED QUESTIONS AND ANSWERS

Question 1 : Write a short note on Operator Precedence Grammar.

Answer : Operator Grammar: The grammar with the property that no production right side is ε or has two adjacent non-terminals, is called operator grammar.

Example of Operator Grammar:

$E \rightarrow E + E \mid E - E \mid E * E \mid E / E \mid E \uparrow E \mid (E) \mid -E \mid id$

Precedence Relations:

In operator precedence parsing, three disjoint precedence relations,

$<\cdot$, $\doteq$, and $\cdot>$ are defined between certain pairs of terminals.

These precedence relations guide the selection of handles and have the following meaning.

Table 3.18

Relation	Meaning
$a <\cdot b$	a yields precedence to b
$a \doteq b$	a has the same precedence as b.
$a \cdot> b$	a takes precedence over b.

Parsing using Operator Precedence Relations:

Precedence relations are used to delimit the handle of a right sentential form in the following way.

$<\cdot$ - marking left end

$\doteq$ - appearing in the interior of the handle.

$\cdot>$ - marking the right end.

Right sides of productions cannot have adjacent non-terminals. Hence, the right sentential form will not have two adjacent non-terminals.

Thus, the right sentential form can be written as:

$\beta_0 \alpha_1 \beta_1 \alpha_2 \ldots\ldots \alpha_n \beta_n$.

where each β_i is either ∈ or a single non-terminal, and each a_i is a single terminal.

Let us assume that between a and a exactly one of the relations $<\cdot$, $\doteq$, and $\cdot>$ holds true. Let us use $ to mark each end of the string and define $ $<\cdot$ b and b $\cdot>$ $ for all terminals b.

Now consider that the non-terminals are removed from the string and correct relation <·, ≐ , and ·> between each pair of terminals, and between the endmost terminals and $'s marking the ends of the string.

Example :

Right sentential form is:

id + id * id

The precedence relations are:

Table 3.19

	id	+	*	$
id		·>	·>	·>
+	<·	·>	<·	·>
*	<·	·>	·>	·>
$	<·	<·	<·	

Then the string with the precedence relations inserted is:

$ <· id ·> + <· id ·> * <· id ·> $

The handle can be found by the following process.

1. Scan the string from the left end until the first ·> is encountered for the above string.

   $ <· id ·> + <· id ·> * <· id ·> $

   ↑

   First ·> is found

2. Then scan backwards (to left) over any ≐ 's until a < · is encountered

   In the above string, scan backwards to $.

   $ <· id ·> + <· id ·> * <· id ·> $

   ↑

3. The handle sometime contains things to the left of the first ·> and to the right of the <· encountered in step 2, including any intervening or surrounding non-terminals. In the above string.

   $ <· id ·> + <· id ·> * <· id ·> $

   ↑ ↑

   The handle is id.

Example:

Consider the string with precedence relations inserted.

$ <· id ·> + <· id ·> * <· id ·> $

The first handle is first id, which is reduced to E. Then the right sentential form is E + id * id. The string with precedence relations for this right sentential form can be written as:

$ <· + <· id ·> * <· id ·> $

Then the handle can be found by following the three steps given below.

1. $ <· + <· id ·> * <· id ·> $

   ↑

   First ·> is encountered

2. $ <· + <· id ·> * <· id ·> $

   ↑

   First <· in left direction is found

3. Hence the handle is id.

Then id is reduced to E. Similarly the third id is reduced to E, and we get the right sentential form.

E + E * E

The string with precedence relations inserted is:

$ <· + <· * ·> $

By following the three steps we get the handle * i.e. E * E, which is reduced to E. The right sentential form is

E + E

The string with precedence relations inserted is:

$ <· + ·> $

Hence the handle is + i.e. E + E which is reduced to E.

Question 2 : Define the role of Parser

Answer : The position of a syntax analyzer or parser in the compilation process is shown in Fig. 3.25.

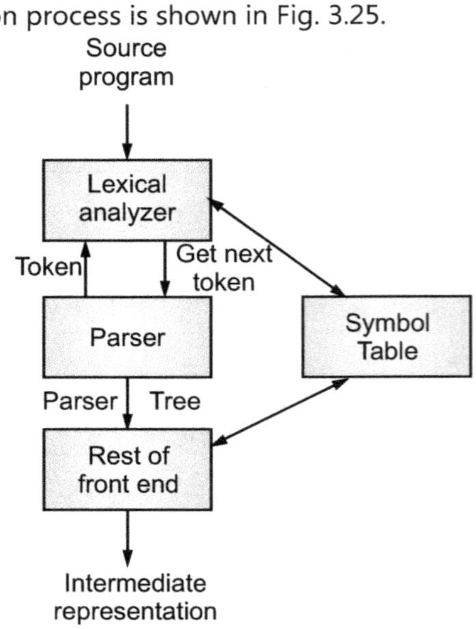

Fig. 3.25: Parser in Compiler Model

- In a compiler model, the parser obtains a string of tokens from the lexical analyzer, and verifies that the string can be generated by the grammar for the source language.
- If a syntax error occurs, the parser should be able to report it properly. It is also necessary that it should recover from commonly occurring errors so that the processing of the remaining input can proceed uninterrupted.
- The following section explains the nature of syntactic errors and general strategies for error recovery.

Question 3 : Define Context-Free Grammar (CFG)

Answer : It is a four-tuple denoted by: G = (V, T, P, S)

where,

(i) V is a finite set of symbols called as non-terminals or variables.

(ii) T is a set of symbols called as terminals.

(iii) P is set of productions. Each production consists of a non-terminal on the left-hand side, and a string of terminals and non-terminals on the right-hand side.

(iv) S is a member of V, and is called as start symbol.

An Example of CFG:

The grammar with the following productions defines simple arithmetic expressions.

expr → expr op

expr expr → (expr)

expr → expr

expr → id

op → id |+ |- |* |/

In this grammar,

the terminal symbols are Id + - * / ( ) the non-terminal symbols are expr, op, the start symbol is expr.

Question 4 : Define Terminals

Answer : Terminals are the basic symbols from which the strings are formed. The word "token" is a synonym for "terminal".

Question 5 : Define : Non-Terminals

Answer : Non-terminals are syntactic variables that denote sets of strings. In grammar, one non- terminal is distinguished as 'a'.

Question 6 : Define Productions

Answer : Productions of a grammar specify the manner in which the terminals and non-terminals can be combined to form strings. Each production consists of a non-terminal followed by an arrow, which is then followed by a string of non-terminals and terminals.

Question 7 : What is Ambiguous Grammar

Answer : A grammar is said to be ambiguous when it produces more than one parse tree for a sentence. In other words, it produces more than one leftmost derivation or more than one rightmost derivation for the same sentence.

Question 8 : Define Top down parsing

Answer : Top down parsing can be attempted to find the leftmost derivation for an input string, as well as, to construct a parse tree for the input starting from the root, and creating the nodes of the parse tree in preorder.

EXERCISE

1. Write a short note on Operator Precedence Grammar.
2. What is the necessary and sufficient condition for a grammar to be LL(1)? With respect to parsing, explain the following terms:
   a. Ambiguous Grammar
   b. Left Recursion
   c. Shift-Reduce Conflict
   d. Precedence Associativity
3. Differentiate between LR(0), Canonical LR and LALR items.
4. Discuss the various error recovery strategies that a parser can employ to recover from semantic errors.
5. Compare the top-down parsing and bottom-up parsing.
6. What is an operator precedence grammar? Explain how to construct precedence relations.
7. Comment on the following statements:
   a. The size of SLR(1) table and LALR(1) table for the same grammar if identical.
   b. The SLR(1) and LALR(1) tables have identical error entries for the same grammar.
8. Write an algorithm for constructing FOLLOW sets of a grammar.

9. Write the different rules for closure operation and then apply the same rules to compute the closure of the following grammar:

   E' → E

   E → E + T | T

   T → T – F | F

   F → (E) | id

10. Consider the following grammar:

    S → SAS |(S) | -S | id

    A → +|-|*

    Is the grammar operator a grammar? If yes, justify. If no, then correct it to operator grammar.

◈◈◈

UNIT IV

SYNTAX-DIRECTED TRANSLATION

4.1 SYNTAX-DIRECTED DEFINITIONS

1. Syntax-Directed Definition

- Syntax-directed definition is a generalization of a context-free grammar in which each grammar symbol has an associated set of attributes partitioned into two sets, the synthesized attributes and inherited attributes of that grammar.

2. Attribute

- An attribute can represent a string, a number, a type, a memory location. The value of an attribute at a parse tree node is defined by a semantic rule associated with the production used at that node.

3. Synthesized and Inherited Attributes

- The value of a synthesized attribute at a node is computed from the values of attributes at the children of that node in the parse tree. The value of an inherited attribute at a node is computed from the values of attributes at the siblings and parent of that node.

4. Semantic Rules

- Semantic rules set up dependencies between attributes that will be represented by a graph. From the dependency graph, we derive an evaluation order for the semantic rules.
- Evaluation of semantic rules defines the values of attributes at the nodes in the parse tree for the input string.
- Semantic rules may have side effects like
  - ➢ Printing a value
  - ➢ Updating a global variable

5. Annotated Parse Tree

- A parse tree showing the values of attributes at each node is called an annotated parse tree. The process of computing the attribute values at each node is called annotating or decorating the parse tree.

6. Syntax-Directed Definition

- In a syntax-directed definition, each grammar production A has a set of semantic rules of the following form associated with it.

$$b := f(c_1, c_2, \ldots\ldots, c_k)$$

where f is a function, and either of the following conditions holds good for b.

(i) b is a synthesized attribute of A and $c_1, c_2, \ldots\ldots, c_k$ are attributes belonging to the grammar symbols of the production OR

(ii) b is an inherited attribute of the grammar symbols on the right side of the production.

In both the cases, attribute b depends on attributes $c_1, c_2, \ldots\ldots, c_k$

Example:

Syntax-directed definition given in Table 4.1 for the grammar is:

$E \rightarrow E + T \mid T$

$T \rightarrow T * F \mid F$

$F \rightarrow (E) \mid id$

Table 4.1: Syntax-directed Definition

Production	Semantic Rules
$L \rightarrow En$	Print(E.val)
$E \rightarrow E_1 + T$	$E.val := E_1.val + T.val$
$E \rightarrow T$	$E.val := T.val$
$T \rightarrow T_1 * F$	$T.val := T_1.val - F.val$
$T \rightarrow F$	$T.val := F.val$
$F \rightarrow (E)$	$F.val := E.val$
F.digit	F.val := digit.lexval

- Synthesized attribute val is associated with each of the non-terminals E, T and F. The token digit has a synthesized attribute lexval whose value is assumed to be supplied by the lexical analyzer.

7. Attribute Grammar

- An attribute grammar is a context-free grammar where we define attributes of all symbols in the production group.
- These attributes can be divided into two types, synthesized attributes and inherited attributes. Evaluation of attributes occurs at the nodes of the abstract syntax tree.

8. Synthesized Attributes

- Syntax-directed definition that uses synthesized attributes exclusively is said to be an s-attributed definition.

- A parse tree for an s-attributed definition can always be annotated by evaluating the semantic rules for the attributes at each node, bottom-up from the leaves to the root.
- Syntax-directed definition given in Table 4.2 is the S-attributed definition for the desk calculator. Consider the expression 3 * 5 + 4 n. The annotated parse tree for the input 3 * 5 + 4 n is shown in Fig. 4.1.

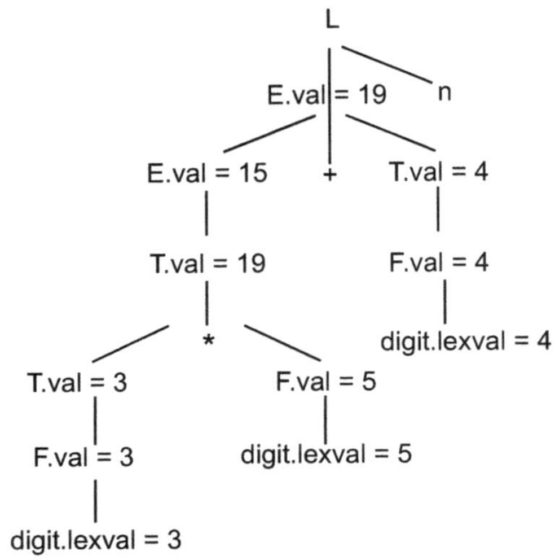

Fig. 4.1: Annotated Parse Tree for 3 * 5 + 4n

9. Inherited Attributes

- An inherited attribute is the one whose value at a node in a parse tree is defined in terms of attributes at the parent and/or siblings of that node.
- Inherited attributes are convenient for expressing the dependence of a programming language construct on the context in which it appears.

Example:

In the syntax-directed definition given in Table 4.2, L.in is the inherited attribute.

Table 4.2: Syntax-directed Definition

Production	Semantic Rules
$D \rightarrow T L$	L.in := T.type
$T \rightarrow$ int	T.type := integer
$T \rightarrow$ real	T.type := real
$L \rightarrow L_1$, id	L_1.in := L.in Addtype(id.entry, L.in)
$L \rightarrow$ id	Addtype(id.entry, L.in)

- The non-terminal T has synthesized attribute type whose value is determined by the keyword in the declaration. The annotated parse tree for the sentence real id_1, id_2, id_3 is shown in Fig. 4.2.

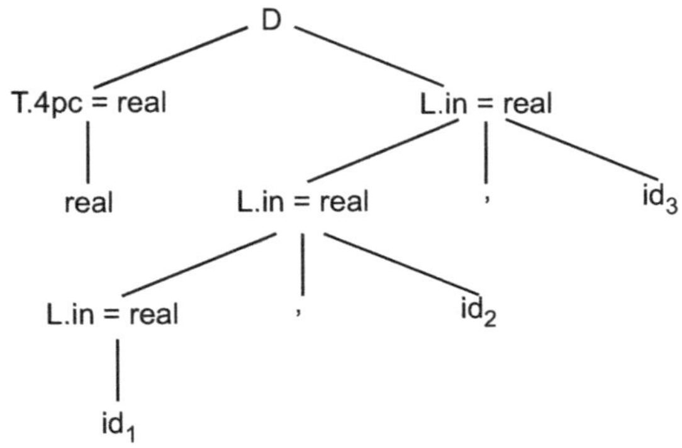

Fig. 4.2: Annotated Parse Tree

- The value of L.in at the three L-nodes gives the type of the identifiers id_1, id_2 and id_3.
- These values are determined by computing the value of the attribute T.type at the left child of the root, and then evaluating L.in top-down at the three L-nodes in the right subtree of the root.

10. Dependency Graph

- The interdependencies among the inherited and synthesized attributes at the nodes in a parse tree can be depicted by a directed graph called as dependency graph.
- To construct a dependency graph, we put each semantic rule into the form

$$b = f(c_1, c_2, \ldots\ldots, c_k)$$

by introducing a dummy synthesized attribute b for each semantic rule that consists of a procedure call.
- The graph has a node for each attribute, and in case attribute b depends on attribute c, it also has an edge to the node for b from the node for c.

Algorithm to Construct Dependency Graph:

```
for each node n in the parse tree do
    for each attribute a of the grammar symbol at n do
        construct a node in the dependency graph for a
for each node n in the parse tree do
for each semantic rule b:=f(c1,c2,.........,ck)
    associated with the production used at n do
for i:=1 tok do
    construct an edge from the node for ci to the node
    for b;
```

Example:

Consider that

The production is: $E \rightarrow E_1 + E_2$

and the associated semantic rule is :

$$E.val := E_1.val + E_2.val$$

- The dependency graph for the production is shown in Fig. 4.3.

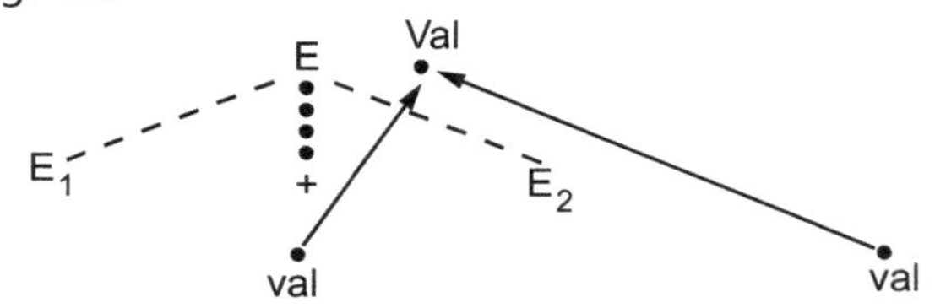

Fig. 4.3: Dependency Graph

- The three nodes of the dependency graph marked by • represent the synthesized attribute E.val, E_1.val, E_2.val at the corresponding nodes in the parse tree.

Example:

Consider the parse tree shown in Fig. 4.2. The dependency graph for the parse tree is shown in Fig. 4.4.

1. There is an edge to node 5 for L.in from node 4 for T.type because, the inherited attribute L.in depends on the attribute T.type according to the semantic rule

   L.in = t.type.

2. The two downward edges into nodes 7 and 9 arise because L1.in depends on L.in according to the semantic rule L1.in = L.in for the production L → L1.id.
3. Nodes 6, 8 and 10 are constructed for these dummy attributes.

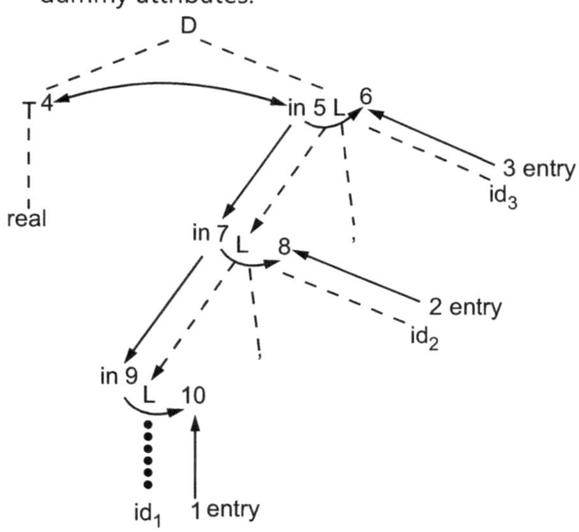

Fig. 4.4: Dependency Graph

11. Evaluation Order

- Topological Sort: A topological sort of a directed cyclic graph is any ordering $m_1, m_2, \ldots, m_k$ of the nodes of the graph, such that edges go from nodes earlier in the ordering, to later nodes.
- If $m_i \rightarrow m_j$ is an edge from m_i to m_j, then m_i appears before m_j in the ordering.
- Any topological sort of a dependency graph gives a valid order in which, the semantic rules associated with the nodes in a parse tree can be evaluated.
- In the topological sort, the dependency attributes $(c_1, c_2, \ldots, c_k)$ in the semantic rule

  $b = f(c_1, c_2, \ldots, c_k)$ are available at a node, before f is evaluated.
- For a given grammar we construct a parse tree. The dependency graph is constructed for the parse tree. From a topology of the dependency graph, we obtain an evaluation order for the semantic rules.
- Evaluation of the semantic rules in this order yields the translation of the input string.

Example:

Consider the dependency graph shown in Fig. 4.4.

From the topological sort, we get the following program:

```
a4 = real
a5 = real
addtype(id3.entry,a5);
a7 = a5
addtype(id2.entry,a7);
a9 = a7
addtype(id1.entry,a9);
```

Methods for Evaluating Semantic Rules:

1. **Parse Tree Methods:**
   - At compile time, these methods obtain an evaluation order from a topological sort of the dependency graph constructed from the parse tree for each input. These methods fail to find the evaluation order only if the dependency graph has a cycle.
2. **Rule-Based Methods:**
   - At the compiler construction time, the semantic rules associated with productions are analyzed. For each production, the evaluation order is predetermined at the compile time.
3. **Oblivious Methods:**
   - In this method, the evaluation order is chosen without considering the semantic rules. An oblivious evaluation order restricts the class of syntax-directed definitions that can be implemented.

- Rule based and oblivious methods need not explicitly construct the dependency graph at compile time. Hence, they are more efficient in the use of compile time and space.
- A syntax-directed definition is said to be circular, if the dependency graph for some parse tree generated by its grammar has a cycle.

4.2 CONSTRUCTION OF SYNTAX TREE

4.2.1 Syntax Tree

- A syntax tree is a condensed form of parse tree useful for representing language constructs.
- In a syntax tree, operators and keywords do not appear as leaves, they are associated with the interior node that would be the parent of those leaves.
- The syntax tree for the expression 3*5+4 is shown in Fig. 4.5.

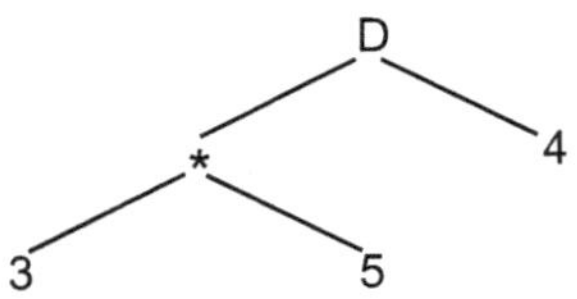

Fig. 4.5 : Syntax Three for 3*5+4

4.2.2 Construction of Syntax Tree

Syntax tree can be implemented as a record with several fields.

- **Operator Node:**

In the operator node, one field identifies the operator and the remaining fields contain pointers to nodes for the operands. The operator is often called the label of the node.

Functions to Create the Nodes of Syntax Tree:

1. **mknode(op, left, right)**

   It creates an operator node with label op and two fields containing pointers to left and right.

2. **mkleaf(id, entry)**

   It creates an identifier node with label id and a field containing entry, a pointer to the symbol table entry for the identifier.

3. **mkleaf(num,val)**

   It creates a number node with label num and a field containing val, the value of number.

Example:

Consider the following expression:

a – 4+c

The following sequence of function calls creates a syntax tree:

P_1 = mkleaf(id, entrya)

P_2 = mkleaf(num, 4)

P_3 = mknode('–', P_1,P_2)

P_4 = mkleaf(id, entryc)

P_5 = mknode('+', P_3,P_4)

Here P_1, P_2,........P_5 are pointers to nodes.

entrya and entryc are pointers to the symbol table entries for identifiers a and c.

The tree is constructed bottom-up as shown in Fig. 4.6.

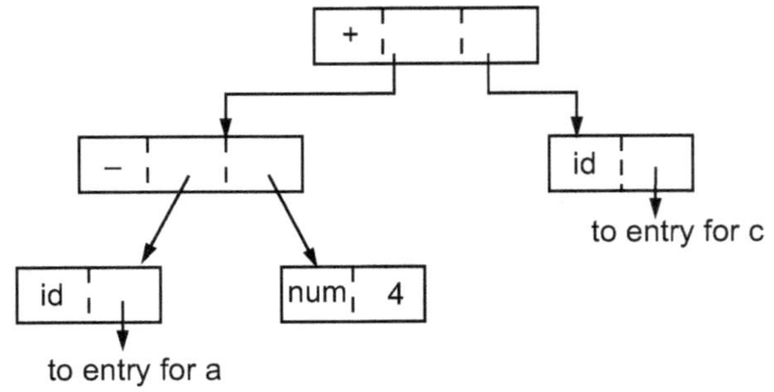

Fig. 4.6: Syntax Tree for a-4+c

Example:

Construct a syntax tree for 3*5+4

The following sequence of function calls creates a syntax tree:

P_1 = mkleaf(num, 3)

P_2 = mkleaf(num, 5)

P_3 = mknode('–', P_1,P_2)

P_4 = mkleaf(num, 4)

P_5 = mknode('+', P_3,P_4)

Syntax tree for the expression 3*5+4 is shown in Fig. 4.7.

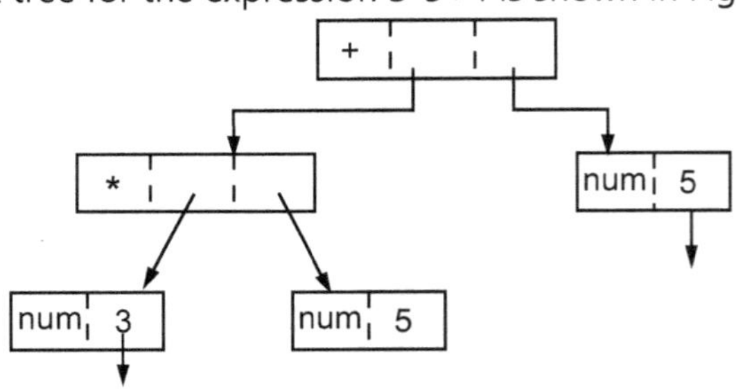

Fig. 4.7: Syntax Tree for 3*5+4

4.2.3 Syntax-Directed Definition for Constructing Syntax Tree

- Syntax-directed definition for constructing syntax tree is given by using the underlying productions of the grammar. It uses the productions to schedule the functions mknode and mkleaf to construct the tree.

Example:

Production	Semantic Rules
$E \rightarrow E_1 + T$	E.nptr:=mknode('+', E_1.nptr, T.nptr)
$E \rightarrow E_1 - T$	E.nptr:=mknode('-', E_1.nptr, T.nptr)
$E \rightarrow T$	E.nptr:=T.nptr
$T \rightarrow (E)$	T.nptr:=E.nptr
$T \rightarrow id$	T.nptr:=mkleaf(id, id.entry)
$T \rightarrow num$	T.nptr:=mkleaf(num, num.val)

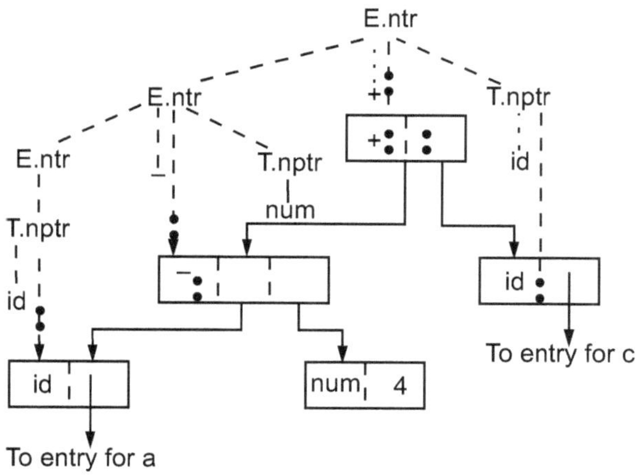

Fig. 4.8: Syntax Tree for a-4+c

- Annotated parse tree depicting the construction of the syntax tree for the expression a-4+c is shown in Fig. 4.8 using dotted lines.

4.2.4 Directed Acyclic Graph

- A directed acyclic graph called as DAG, for an expression, identifies the common sub- expressions in the expression. Just like a syntax tree:
    1. A DAG has a node for every sub-expression of the expression.
    2. An interior node represents an operator and its children represent its operands.

Difference Between DAG and Syntax Tree:

A node in DAG representing a common sub-expression has more than one parent. In syntax tree, the common sub-expression is represented as a duplicated subtree.

Example:

DAG for the expression

a+a* (b-c) (b-c)*d

Common sub-expressions are:

a and (b-c)

- a is common to sub-expressions:

  a

  a * (b-c)

- (b-c) is common to sub-expressions:

  a * (b-c)

  (b-c) * d

Hence a and (b-c) have a common "parent". DAG for this example is shown in Fig. 4.9.

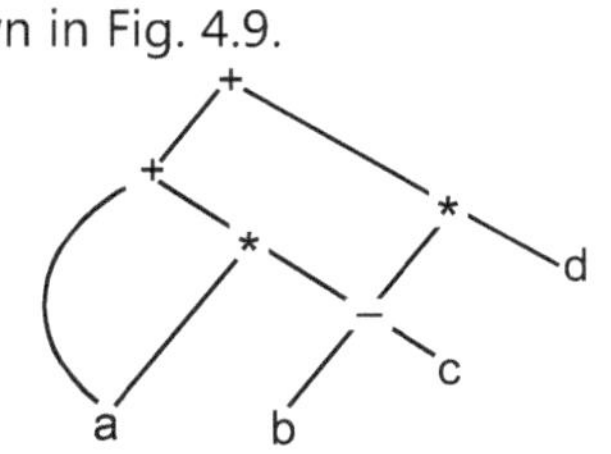

Fig. 4.9: DAG for a+a * (b-c) (b-c) * d

Instructions for Constructing DAG:

P_1 : = mkleaf(id,*a*)

P_2 : = mkleaf(id,*a*)

P_3 : = mkleaf(id,*b*)

P_4 : = mkleaf(id,*c*)

P_5 : = mknode('-',P_3,P_4)

P_6 : = mknode('*', P_2,P_5)

P_7 : = mknode('+', P_1,P_6)

P_8 : = mkleaf(id,*b*)

P_9 : = mkleaf(id,*c*)

P_{10} : = mknode('-',P_8,P_9)

P_{11} : = mkleaf(id,*b*)

P_{12} : = mknode('*', P_{10},P_{11})

P_{13} : = mknode('+', P_7,P_{12})

Here, the function constructing a node first checks to see whether an identical node already exists. If the node already exists, mknode(op,left,right) can return a pointer to the previously constructed node. The leaf constructing function mkleaf, can also behave similarly.

- When the call mkleaf(id,a) is repeated at step2, the node constructed by previous calls mkleaf(id,b) is returned so $P_1 = P_2$.
- When the calls mkleaf(id,b) and mkleaf(id,c) are repeated at step 8 and 9, the nodes constructed by previous calls mkleaf(id,b) and mkleaf(id,c) at step 3 and 4 are returned, so $P_3 = P_8$ and $P_4 = P_9$.
- Hence, the node returned at step 10 by function mknode, must be same as the node constructed by the function mknode at step 5.

4.2.5 Value Number

Nodes can be implemented as records stored in an array.

Example:

DAG for the expression i:=i +1 is shown in Fig. 4.10.

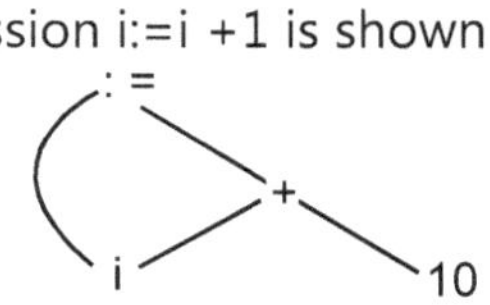

Fig. 4.10: DAG for i:=i +1

Node Representation:

1	id			→ To entry for i
2	num	10		
3	+	1	2	
4	: =	1	3	
5	………			

Each node can be referred by its index or position in the array. The integer index of a node is called as value number.

In the above example, node1 has label id, node2 has label num, node3 has +, and has two child nodes. Left child is node1 and right child is node2. Node4 has label := and its left child is node1 and right child is node3.

4.2.6 Value Number Method for Constructing a Node in a DAG

Consider that nodes are stored in an array and each node is referred by its value number. Let the signature of an operator node be a triple <op, l, r> consisting of its label op, left child 2 and right child r.

Algorithm for Constructing a Node in DAG:

Input: Label op, node l, node r

Output: A node with signature <op,l,r>

Method:

- Search the array for a node m with label op, left child l and right child r.
- If there is such a node, return m.
- Otherwise, create a new node n with label op, left child l, right child r, and return n.

The search for m can be made more efficient by using k lists, called buckets, and using a hashing function h to determine which bucket to search.

4.3 BOTTOM-UP EVALUATION

4.3.1 Evaluation of S-Attributed Definitions

- Synthesized attributes can be evaluated by a bottom-up parser while the input is being parsed. The parser can keep the values of the synthesized attributes associated with the grammar symbols, on its stack. When the reduction is done, the values of the new synthesized attributes are computed from the attributes appearing on the stack for the grammar symbols on the right side of the reducing production.
- A translator for an S-attributed definition can be implemented with the help of an LR parser generator.
- Bottom-up parser uses a stack to hold information about subtrees that have been parsed.
- An extra field is used in the parser stack to hold the values of the synthesized attributes.

Example:

	State	Val
	...	...
	X	X.x
	Y	Y.y
top →	Z	Z.z
	...	...

- The stack is implemented by a pair of arrays, state and val.
- Each state entry is a pointer to an LR(1) parsing table.
- State is referred by a unique grammar symbol.
- If the ith grammar symbol is A then val[i] will hold the value of attribute associated with the parse tree node corresponding to this A.
- The current top of the stack is indicated by the pointer top.
- Synthesized attributes are evaluated just before each reduction.
- If a symbol has no attribute, then the corresponding entry in the val array is undefined.
- After the reduction, top is decremented by 2, the state covering A is put in state[top] and the value of the synthesized attribute A.a is put in val[top].

Example:

Consider the syntax-directed definition for the desk calculator. The synthesized attributes can be evaluated by an LR parser during a bottom-up parse of the input line 3 * 5 + 4 n.

Production	Code Fragment
$L \rightarrow En$	Print(val[top])
$E \rightarrow E_1+T$	Val[ntop]:=val[top-2] + val[top]
$E \rightarrow T$	Val[ntop]:=val[top-2] * val[top]
$T \rightarrow T * F$	Val[ntop]:= val[top-1]
$T \rightarrow F$	
$F \rightarrow (E)$	
$F \rightarrow$ digit	

The code fragment is obtained from the semantic rules, by replacing each attribute by a position in the val array.

The sequence of moves made by the parser on the input 3 * 5 + 4 n is shown in Table 4.3.

Table 4.3

Input	State	VAL	Production Used
3 * 5 + 4 n	_	_	
* 5 + 4 n	3	3	
* 5 + 4 n	F	3	F → digit
* 5 + 4 n	T	3	T → F
5 + 4 n	T*	3 _	
+ 4 n	T * 5	3 _ 5	
+ 4 n	T * F	15	F → digit
+ 4 n	T	15	T → F
+ 4 n	E	15	E → T
+ 4 n	E+	15 _	
n	E + 4	15 _4	
n	E + F	15 _4	F → digit
n	E + T	15_4	T → F
n	E	19	E → E + T
	En	19_	
	L	19	L → E n

4.4 TOP-DOWN TRANSLATION

Elimination of Left Recursion from Translation Scheme:

Consider the translation scheme with the left-recursive grammar:

$E \rightarrow E_1 + T$ {E.val := E_1.val + T.val}

$E \rightarrow E_1 - T$ {E.val := E_1.val – T.val}

$E \rightarrow T$ {E.val := T.val}

$T \rightarrow (E)$ {T.val := E.val}

$T \rightarrow$ num {T.val := num.val}

The equivalent transformed translation scheme with right-recursive grammar is:

E →	T R	{R.i := T.val} {E.val := R.s}
R →	+ T R_1	 {R_1.i := R.i + T.val} {R.s := R_1.s}
R →	– T R_1	 {R_1.i := R.i – T.val} {R.s := R_1.s}
R →	ε	{R.s := R_1.s}
T →	(E)	 {T.val := E.val}
T →	num	{T.val = num.val}

Conti...

The annotated parse tree produced by this translation scheme for the expression 9 –5 +2 is shown in Fig. 4.11.

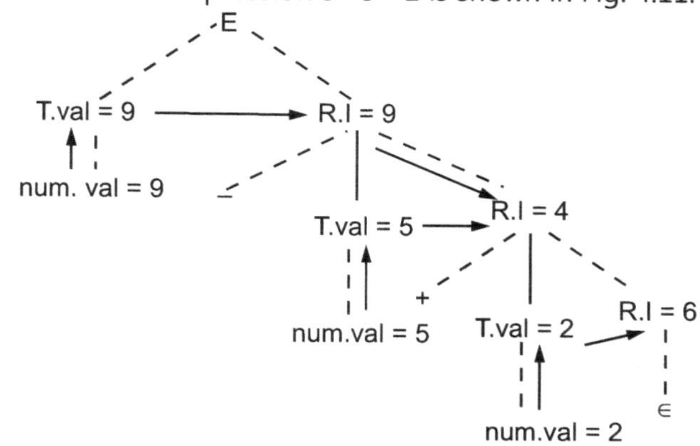

Fig. 4.11: Parse Tree for 9 – 5+2

4.5 BOTTOM-UP EVALUATION OF INHERITED ATTRIBUTES

4.5.1 Evaluation of L-Attributed Definitions

Depth-First Evaluation Order:

- The order of evaluation attributes is linked to the order in which the nodes of a parse tree are created by the parsing method.
- A natural order that characterizes top-down and bottom-up translation methods is the one obtained by applying the procedure dfvisit to the root of the parse tree. This evaluation order is called the depth-first-order. The procedure dfvisit is as follows:

```
procedure dfvisit(n:node);
begin
    for each child m of n, from left to right do begin
    evaluate inherited attributes of m dfvisit(m)
    end
    evaluate synthesized attributes of n
end
```

L-Attributed Definitions:

- L-attributed definition is a class of syntax-directed definitions, whose attributes can always be evaluated in the depth-first-order. Here, the 'L' is for left, because attribute information appears to flow from left to right.

- It is defined as follows.

  A syntax-directed definition is L-attributed if each inherited attribute of X_j, $i \le j \le n$ on the right side of $A \rightarrow X_1X_2.........X_n$ depends only on:

  1. the attributes of the symbols X_1 $X_2.........X_{j-1}$ to the left of X_j in the production and
  2. the inherited attributes of A.

Translation Scheme:

- A translation scheme is a context-free grammar in which attributes are associated with the grammar symbols, and semantic actions enclosed between braces { } are inserted within the right sides of productions.
- When only synthesized attributes are needed, we can construct the translation scheme by creating an action consisting of an assignment for each semantic rule, and placing this action at the end of the right side of the associated production.

Example:

Consider the following production and semantic rule.

Production: $T \rightarrow T_1 * F$

Semantic Rule: $T.val := T_1.val \times F.val$

Yield the following production and semantic action:

$T \rightarrow T_1 * F \{ T.val := T_1.val \times F.val\}$

- If we have both inherited and synthesized attributes, we must be more careful.
  1. An inherited attribute for a symbol on the right side of a production must be computed in an action before that symbol.
  2. An action must not refer to a synthesized attribute of a symbol, which is to the right side of the action.
  3. A synthesized attribute for the non-terminal on the left side can only be computed after all the attributes it references have been computed. The actions computing such attributes can usually be placed at the end of the right side of the production.
- A translation satisfying these three requirements can be implemented by a generalization of top-down and bottom-up parsers.

SOLVED EXAMPLES

Example 4.1: *Write the semantic rules to abstract syntax tree construction in Bison for these productions.*

You may use the type and functions implemented in tree.c:

*typedef struct tree *Tree;*

*Tree build_id(char * var);*

Tree build_program(Tree name, Tree decl, Tree stmt);

Tree build_while(Tree expr, Tree stmt);

Solution:

```
program → program Identifier is variables body
statements end
{syntax_tree = build_program(build_id($2), $4, $6);}
while_statement → while bool_expression do
statements end
{$$ = build_while($2, $4);}
```

Example 4.2: *Consider the following segment of productions for our course project.*

variable → integer Identifier;

arith_primary → Constant | Identifier | (arith_expression)

Write the semantic rules for type checking in Bison for these productions. You may use the functions implemented in symtab.c :

*void declare_variable_name(char *);*

*int is_declared(char *);*

Solution:

```
variable → integer Identifier ;
if (!is_declared($2)) { declare_variable_name($2);
} else {
fprintf(stderr, "semantic error: %d: Identifier %s
redeclared\n", yylineno, $2);
SEMANTIC_ERROR = 1;
}
arith_primary → Constant
{ Identifier
if (!is_declared($1)) {
fprintf(stderr,
"semantic error: %d: Identifier %s is not declared\n",
yylineno, $1);
SEMANTIC_ERROR = 1;
}
} ( arith_expression )
```

Example 4.3: *Consider the following grammar.*

$S \rightarrow L \,.\, L \mid L$

$L \rightarrow L\, B \mid B$

$B \rightarrow 0 \mid 1$

This represents the set of binary numbers. For example, the binary number 101.101 denotes the digital number 5.625. Give an S-attributed attribute grammar that computes the corresponding digital number value from the binary number representation.

Solution:

$S \rightarrow L_1 \,.\, L_2$ {S.val = L_1.val + L_2.val / L_2.mag;}

$S \rightarrow L$ {S.val = L.val;}

$L \rightarrow L_1\, B$ {L.val = L_1.val * 2 + B.val; L.mag *= 2;}

$L \rightarrow B$ {L.val = B.val; L.mag = 2;}

$B \rightarrow 0$ {B.val = 0;}

$B \rightarrow 1$ {B.val = 1;}

Example 4.4: *Consider the following attribute grammar.*

D → T	{L.in := T.type;} L	
T → int	{T.type := integer;}	
T → float	{T.type := float;}	

L → {L_1.in := L.in;} L_1 ',' id {addtype(id.entry, L.in);}

L → id {addtype(id.entry, L.in);}

that represents type declarations for variables. Write a top-down translator for this attribute grammar that installs the type information of variables into the symbol table.

Solution: Since this grammar is not LL(1), it is impossible to write a top-down translator for this attribute grammar. Assume that we transform the grammar into the following LL(1) grammar and attribute grammar.

D	→	T	{L.in := T.type;} L
T	→	int	{T.type := integer;}
T	→	float	{T.type := float;}
L	→	id	{L'.in := L.in;} L' {addtype(id.entry, L.in);}
L'	→	',' id	{L'1.in := L.in;}L'$_1$ {addtype(id.entry, L'.in);}
L'	→	ε	

```
void D( ) { int
   type;
   switch(token) {
      case INT: FLOAT:
         type = T( ); L(type); break;
      default: error( ); break;
   }
}

int T( ) { int
   type;
   switch(token) {
   case INT:
      type = yylval; match(INT); break;
   case FLOAT:
      type = yylval; match(FLOAT); break;
   default: error( ); break;
   }
   return type;
}

void L(int type) {
   char *entry;
   switch(token) {
      case ID:
      entry = yylval; match(ID); L'(type);
      addtype(entry, type); break;
   default: error( ); break;
   }
}

void L'(int type) {
   char *entry;
   switch(token) {
      case COMMA:
         match(COMMA); entry = yylval; match(ID);
         L'(type);
         addtype(entry, type); break;
   default: error( ); break;
   }
}
```

Example 4.5: *Construct a syntax-directed translation scheme that translates arithmetic expressions from infix notation into prefix notation. Give annotated parse trees for the inputs 9 – 5+2 and 9 – 5*2.*

Solution: Syntax-Directed Definition

Productions Semantic Rules

Productions	Semantic Rules
expr → expr1 + term	expr.t := '+' || expr1.t || term.t
expr → expr1 – term	expr.t := '–' || expr1.t || term.t
expr → term	expr.t := term.t
term → term1* factor	term.t := '*' || term1.t || factor.t
term → term1 / factor	term.t := '/' || term1.t || factor.t
term → factor	term.t := factor.t
factor → id	factor.t := id.lexeme
factor → num	factor.t := itoa(num.value)1
factor → (expr)	factor.t := expr.t

This syntax-directed definition is simple.

The string representing the translation of the non-terminal on the left-hand side of each production is the concatenation of the translations of the non-terminals on the right-hand side, in the same order as in the production, with some additional strings (perhaps none) interleaved.

Therefore, the translation scheme will have the actions that print the additional strings in the order they appear in the definition.

Syntax-Directed Translation Scheme

```
expr → expr + term {print('+')}
expr → expr – term {print('–')}
expr → term
term → term * factor {print('*')}
term → term / factor{print}('/')
term → factor
factor → id {print(id.lexeme)}
factor → num {print(itoa(num.value))}
```

Example 4.6: *Construct a syntax-directed translation scheme that translates integers into roman numerals.*

Solution: We partition a string of digits into four parts:

Everything left of the third digit from the right – non-terminal DThs (thousands) The third digit from the right – non-terminal DHu (hundreds)

The second digit from the right – non-terminal DTe (tens) The rightmost digit – DOn (ones)

Let the start symbol be Num. The grammar for decimal integers, which is designed to facilitate translation to roman numerals, is:

```
Num → DThs DHu DTe DOn
    | DHun DTe DOn //DHun doesn't allow '0', DHu does.
    | DTen Don // DTen doesn't allow '0', DTe does.
    | Don
DThs → first_digit DTh | ε
             //DThs doesn't allow an initial '0', DTh does.
DTh → DTh digit | ε
first_digit → 1 | 2 | 3 | 4 | 5 | 6 | 7 | 8 | 9
digit → 0 | 1 | 2 | 3 | 4 | 5 | 6 | 7 | 8 | 9
DHun → 1 | 2 | 3 | 4 | 5 | 6 | 7 | 8 | 9
DHu → 1 | 2 | 3 | 4 | 5 | 6 | 7 | 8 | 9
DTen → 1 | 2 | 3 | 4 | 5 | 6 | 7 | 8 | 9
DTe → 0 | DTen
DOn → 1 | 2 | 3 | 4 | 5 | 6 | 7 | 8 | 9
```

With all non-terminals except DThs and DTh, we associate a synthesized character string attribute t. With DThs, DTh, digit, and first_digit, we associate a synthesized integer attribute value. We assume a function string_of(n,c), where n is an integer and c is a character, which returns a string of n c's. Note that DThs.value can be used only after the non-terminal DThs is handled – we assume left-to-right evaluation.

```
first_digit → 1      first_digit.value := 1
...                  ...
first_digit → 9      first_digit.value := 9
digit → 1            digit.value := 1
...                  ...
digit → 9            digit.value := 9
DHun → 1             DHun.t := 'C'
```

...	...
DHun → 9	DHun.t := 'CM'
DHu → 0	DHu.t := ε
DHu → DHun	DHu.t := DHun.t
DTen → 1	DTen.t := 'X'
...	...
DTen → 9	DTen.t := 'XC'
DTe → 0	DTe.t := ε
DTe → DTen	DTe.t := DTen.t
DOn → 0	Don.t := ε
DOn → 1	Don.t := 'I'
...	...
DOn → 9	Don.t := 'IX'

From this, we construct a syntax-directed translation scheme. With respect to the attributes, the syntax-directed definition is simple. The value attributes don't introduce any difficulty. Since the recursion in the DThs- and DTh-productions is linear (only one recursive occurrence), we can use a global variable t-value for the values of the value attribute of all DThs and DTh nodes, and we can use a global variable d_value for the value attributes of all digit nodes. We must use a different global variable, first_value, for the first_digit node since this value must be remembered until all digits contributing to the thousands have been input.

Example 4.7: *In the programming language C, the for-statement has the form for*

(expr1 ; expr2 ; expr3) stmt

The meaning of the for-statement is similar to expr1 ; while (expr2) { stmt expr3 ; }

Construct a syntax-directed translation scheme to translate C for-statements into stack- machine code.

Solution: We write a stmt-production for the for-statement as follows, where we add a subscript to the stmt on the right-hand side since we intend to refer to stmt on both, the left-hand side and the right-hand side in a semantic rule.

stmt for (expr1 ; expr2 ; expr3) stmt1

The trick here is to notice that execution of expr3 occurs after execution of stmt1 although syntactically expr3 occurs before stmt1. The translation of expr3 must occur before the translation of stmt1, but we use goto's and label's so that execution jumps around in such a way that stmt1 is executed before expr3. If we attached labels to instructions, the translation we'd want would be

```
       code for expr1
test : code for expr2
       gofalse out goto end
mid :  code for expr3
       goto test
end :  code for stmt1
       goto mid
out :
```

In the code for the stack-machine, however, a label is an operand of a special label instruction. So the required translation has the form:

```
code for expr1
label test
code for expr2 gofalse out goto end
label mid
code for expr3
goto test label end
code for stmt1
goto mid label out
```

Suppose we have an attribute t of non-terminals stmt and expr that is the translation code associated with instances of these non-terminals. Given the above production, the required semantic rule is as follows, where we assume that test, mid, end, and out are unique labels. Here we don't worry whether each stack-machine instruction must be on a separate line.

```
stmt.t :=  expr1 . ||
           'label' || test ||
           expr2 . t ||
           'gofalse' || out ||
           'goto' || end ||
           'label' || mid ||
           expr3 . t ||
           'goto' || test ||
           'label' || end ||
           stmt1 . t ||
           'goto' || mid ||
           'label' || out ||
```

The production and semantic rule together give a simple syntax-directed definition. It is thus straightforward to obtain a translation scheme - we include semantic actions outputting the required translation within the production

as dictated by the order in which the translations appear in the semantic rule relative to the t attributes of the non-terminals. Following the text, we assume a function newlabel that generates a new label (number); variables test, mid, end, and out are set to values returned by newlabel calls just before these values are first used to produce labels. We also use a procedure emit to hide printing details. For example, emit can worry about whether each abstract-machine instruction needs to be on a separate
line. Then the translation scheme is:

```
stmt → for (
       expr1   {test := newlabel; emit('label, test);}
       ;
      expr2  {out := newlabel; end := newlabel; emit
             ('gofalse', out)
;
           emit('goto', end); }
    ;        { mid := newlabel; emit('label', mid);}
   expr3 )  {emit('goto', test); emit('label',
             end);}
   stmt1  {emit('goto', mid); emit('label, out);}
```

Example 4.8: *Implement a translator from roman numerals to integers based on the syntax- directed translation scheme. One character at a time is read and we take the transition from the current state labeled with that character. As long as the DFA can advance along a transition, it keeps reading characters. When a character is read and there is no transition from the current state labeled with that character, we push the character back into the input (use ungetc) and return the state name. (This is input retraction; since we only ever have to retract one character, we can get by with ungetc.) If the error state is entered, we output an error message and immediately exit.*

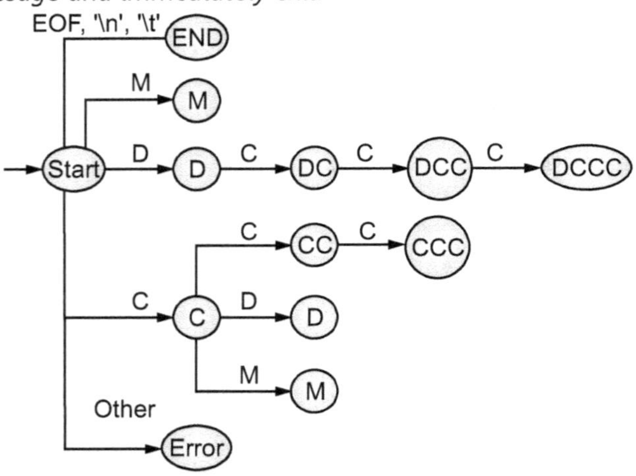

Fig. 4.12

Encode this Fig. 4.12 using switch statements

You should define symbolic constants for the tokens e.g.

```
# define I 1
# define II 2
# define III 3
# define IV 4
```

Produce a header file and separate files for the lexical analyzer and the parser.

Solution: Fig. 4.13 gives the entire transition diagram:

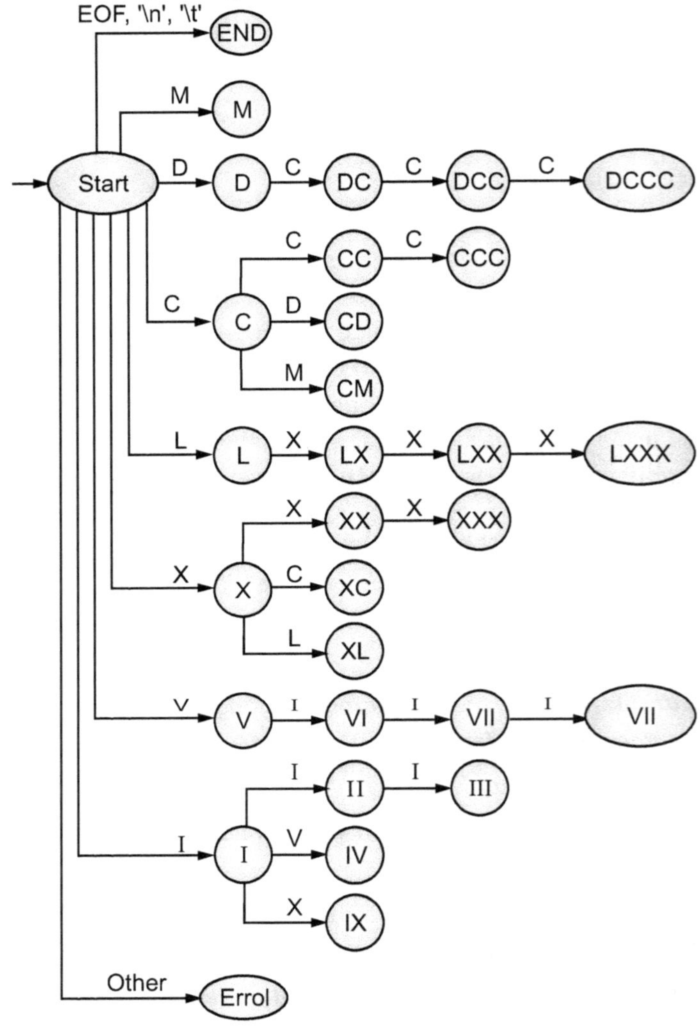

Fig. 4.13

The following is the header file:

```
# include <stdio.h>
# include <errno.h>
# define FALSE 0
# define TRUE 1
 # define END -2
# define ERROR -1
# define START 0
```

```
# define M 1000
# define CM 900
# define DCCC 800
# define DCC 700
# define DC 600
# define D 500
# define CD 400
# define CCC 300
# define CC 200
# define C 100
# define XC 90
# define LXXX 80
# define LXX 70
# define LX 60
# define L 50
# define XL 40
# define XXX 30
# define XX 20
# define X 10
# define IX 9
# define VIII 8
# define VII 7
# define VI 6
# define V 5
# define IV 4
# define III 3
# define II 2
# define I 1
typedef int Token ;
typedef int Boolean ;
 extern Boolean end_flag ;
void error ( char * m );
Token nexttoken ( void ) ;
void R ( void ) ;
void Th ( void ) ;
void Hu ( void ) ;
void Te ( void ) ;
void On ( void ) ;
void match ( int t ) ;
```

The following file, main.c, contains the main( ) function.

```
/****main.c**********************************/
# include "prob2-10.h"
int main ( void )
{
R ( ) ;
printf ( "\n" ) ;
exit ( 0 ) ; /* successful termination */
}
```

The following file, p2-10-lex.c, defines the lexical analyzer.

```
# include "prob2-10.h" Boolean end_flag = FALSE ;
Token nexttoken ( void )
{
int state = START ;
char c ;
while ( 1 ) {
c = getchar ( ) ; switch ( state ) { case START : switch ( c ) {
case EOF: case '\n': case '\t': case ' ':
end_flag = TRUE ; return END ;
case 'M' : return M ; case 'D' :
state = D ; break ;
case 'C' :
state = C ; break ;
case 'L' :
state = L ; break ;
case 'X' :
state = X ; break ;
case 'V' :
state = V ; break ;
case 'I' :
state = I ; break ;
default :
error ( "Lexical error" );
}
break ;
case D :
switch ( c ) { case 'C' :
state = DC ; break ;
default :
ungetc ( c , stdin ) ;
return state ;
```

```
}
break ; case DC : switch ( c ) { case 'C' :
state = DCC ; break ;
default :
ungetc ( c , stdin ) ; return state ;
}
break ; case
DCC : switch ( c )
{ case 'C'
:
return DCCC ;
default :
ungetc ( c , stdin ) ;
return state ;
}
break ; case C :
switch ( c ) { case 'C' :
state = CC ; break ;
case 'D' :
return CD ;
case 'M' :
return CM ;
default :
ungetc ( c , stdin ) ;
return state ;
}
break ;
case CC : switch ( c )
{ case 'C' : return CCC ; default :
ungetc ( c , stdin ) ;
return state ;
}
break ; case L : switch ( c ) { case 'X' :
state = LX ; break ;
default :
ungetc ( c , stdin ) ;
return state ;
}
break ;
case LX : switch ( c ) { case 'X' :
state = LXX ; break ;
default :
ungetc ( c , stdin ) ;
return state ;
}
break ; case LXX : switch ( c ) { case 'X' :
return LXXX ; break ;
default :
ungetc ( c , stdin ) ; return state ;
}
break ;
case X : switch ( c ) { case 'X' :
state = XX ; break ;
case 'C' : return XC ;
case 'L' : return XL ;
default :
ungetc ( c , stdin ) ;
return state ;
}
break ; case XX :
switch ( c ) { case 'X' : return XXX ; default :
ungetc ( c , stdin ) ;
return state ;
}
break ; case V : switch ( c ) { case 'I' :
state = VI ;
 break ;
default :
ungetc ( c , stdin ) ;
return state ;
}
break ; case VI :
switch ( c ) { case 'I' :
state = VII ;
break ;
default :
ungetc ( c , stdin ) ;
return state ;
}
break ; case VII : switch ( c ) {
case 'I' : return VIII ; default :
ungetc ( c , stdin ) ; return state ;
```

```
}
break ; case I : switch ( c ) { case 'I' :
state = II ; break ;
case 'V' : return IV ;
case 'X' : return IX ;
default :
ungetc ( c , stdin ) ;
return state ;
}
break ; case II :
switch ( c ) { case 'I' : return III ; default :
ungetc ( c , stdin ) ;
return state ;
}
break ;
default :
perror ( "Unknown state" ) ;
exit ( 1 ) ;
} /* End of outer switch */
} /* End of while */
} /* End of function nexttoken */
```

The following file, p2-10-par.c, implements the parser. Function R( ), called by main( ), corresponds to the start symbol.

```
# include "prob2-10.h"
int count ;
Boolean hu_flag , te_flag , hu_zero = FALSE ;
Token lookahead ;
void R ( void )
{
lookahead = nexttoken ( ) ;
Th ( ) ;
if ( count )
printf ( "%d" , count ) ;
hu_flag = count == 0 ? FALSE : TRUE ; Hu ( ) ;
te_flag = ( hu_zero && ! hu_flag ) ? FALSE : TRUE ;
Te ( ) ;
On ( ) ;
if ( ! end_flag )
error ( "Syntax error" ) ;
}
void Th ( void )
{
count = 0 ;
while ( lookahead == M ) {
match ( M ) ;
count ++ ;
}
}
void Hu ( void )
{
switch ( lookahead ) {
case CM :
match ( CM ) ;
printf ( "%c" , '9' ) ;
break ;
case DCCC :
match ( DCCC ) ;
printf ( "%c" , '8' ) ;
break ;
case DCC :
match ( DCC ) ;
printf ( "%c" , '7' ) ;
break ;
case DC :
match ( DC ) ;
printf ( "%c" , '6' ) ;
break ;
case D :
match ( D ) ;
printf ( "%c" , '5' ) ;
break ;
case CD :
match ( CD ) ;
printf ( "%c" , '4' ) ;
break ;
case CCC :
match ( CCC ) ;
printf ( "%c" , '3' ) ;
break ;
case CC :
match ( CC ) ;
```

```
printf ( "%c" , '2' ) ;
break ;
case C :
match ( C ) ;
printf ( "%c" , '1' ) ;
break ;
default :
hu_zero = TRUE ;
if ( hu_flag )
printf ( "%c" , '0' ) ;
}
}
void Te ( void )
{
switch ( lookahead ) {
case XC :
match ( XC ) ;
printf ( "%c" , '9' ) ;
 break ;
case LXXX :
match ( LXXX ) ;
 printf ( "%c" , '8' ) ;
break ;
case LXX :
match ( LXX ) ;
printf ( "%c" , '7' ) ;
break ;
case LX :
match ( LX ) ;
printf ( "%c" , '6' ) ;
break ;
case L :
match ( L ) ;
printf ( "%c" , '5' ) ;
break ;
case XL :
match ( XL ) ;
printf ( "%c" , '4' ) ;
break ;
case XXX :
match ( XXX ) ;
printf ( "%c" , '3' ) ;
break ;
case XX :
match ( XX ) ;
printf ( "%c" , '2' ) ;
break ;
case X :
match ( X ) ;
printf ( "%c" , '1' ) ;
break ;
default :
if ( te_flag )
printf ( "%c" , '0' ) ;
}
}


void On ( void )
{
switch ( lookahead ) {
case IX :
match ( IX ) ;
printf ( "%c" , '9' ) ;
break ;
case VIII :
match ( VIII ) ;
printf ( "%c" , '8' ) ;
break ;
case VII :
match ( VII ) ;
printf ( "%c" , '7' ) ;
break ;
case VI :
match ( VI ) ;
printf ( "%c" , '6' ) ;
break ;
case V :
match ( V ) ;
printf ( "%c" , '5' ) ;
break ;
case IV :
```

```
match ( IV );
printf ( "%c" , '4' );
break ;
case III :
match ( III );
printf ( "%c" , '3' );
break ;
case II :
match ( II );
printf ( "%c" , '2' );
break ;
case I :
match ( I );
printf ( "%c" , '1' );
break ;
default :
printf ( "%c" , '0' );
}
}
void match ( int t )
{
if ( lookahead == t ) lookahead = nexttoken ( ) ; else
error ( "Syntax error" );
}
```

Example 4.9: *Construct a syntax-directed translation scheme that translates arithmetic expressions from prefix to postfix. First give the grammar for prefix expressions involving only the operators '+' and '-'. Assume that the only primitive operands are single-digit numbers without signs. Next, give the syntax-directed definition for this translation (adding semantic rules associated with the productions of the grammar – be sure to identify the attribute(s) you need). Is this syntax-directed definition simple? Finally, give the syntax- directed translation scheme, which embeds semantic actions into the productions of the grammar.*

Also, draw the parse tree for the translation of + 9 – 5 2 into 9 5 2 - +.

Solution: We include two non-terminals, expr and term. Each has the same single attribute, t, the postfix translation of the substring matching it. Note that the recursive occurrences of the non-terminal expr in the RIGHT-HAND SIDEs of productions have been subscripted so that we may distinguish them in the semantic rules.

Production	Semantic Rule
expr → + $expr_1$ $expr_2$	expr.t := $expr_1$.t || $expr_2$.t || '+'
expr → – $expr_1$ $expr_2$	expr.t := $expr_1$.t || $expr_2$.t || '–'
expr → term	expr.t := term.t
term → 0	term.t := '0'
term → 1	term.t := '1'
...	...
term → 9	term.t := '9'

We could eliminate the non-terminal term, which would involve eliminating the production -

expr → term

and the corresponding rule, and replacing all productions of the form -

term → i, $0 \le i \le 9$,

with productions of the form -

expr → i,

and replacing their corresponding semantic rules with rules of the form -

expr.t := ' i '

This syntax-directed definition is simple since the attribute values for expr1 and expr2 appear in the same order in the translation for expr as non-terminals expr1 and expr2 appear in the production for expr.

Syntax-Directed Translation (Occurrences of expr on the right-hand sides are now not subscripted.)

```
expr → + expr expr print('+')
expr → - expr expr print('-')
expr → term
term → 0 print('0')
zterm → 1 print('1')
...
term → 9 print('9')
```

The parse tree for the translation of + 9 – 5 2 is:

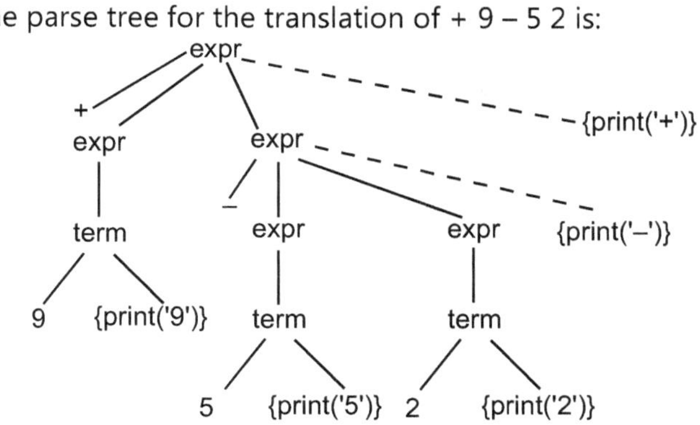

Fig. 4.14

SOLVED QUESTIONS AND ANSWERS

Question 1 : Briefly explain, what is syntax-directed translation?

Answer: In Syntax-directed translation, the translation of a language is guided by a context- free grammar, certain attributes are attached to each grammar symbol, values for attributes are computed via semantic actions, and attributes needed for translation are defined as record structures with fields for items like name, type, offset, etc.

Question 2 : What is Syntax-Directed Definition (SDD)?

Answer: It is a generalized context-free grammar that attaches attributes to each grammar symbol attribute values are defined by the semantic actions associated with each production.

Question 3 : What are the two varieties of attributes?

Answer:

1. **Inherited Attributes:** Computed from attributes of parent or siblings.
2. **Synthesized Attributes:** Computed from attributes of children.

Example: Consider a production X --> ALPHA B BETA X.a is considered synthesized if,

X.a = f (attributes of ALPHA, BETA, and/or B) B.a is considered inherited if,

B.a = f (attributes of ALPHA, BETA, and/or X)

Question 4 : How is attribute evaluation is done?

Answer: It is done by unrestricted syntax-directed definition, no restrictions on attribute dependency perform topological sort on attribute dependency graph, evaluation in the order of dependency, and is costly to evaluate.

S-attribute Definition: Restricted to synthesized attributes only, attributes may be evaluated bottom-up; it can be evaluated very efficiently.

L-attribute Definition: Allows both synthesized and some inherited attributes, restricted to inherit attributes from the left siblings, attributes may be evaluated by depth-first, left-to-right, it is possible to rewrite any L-attribute SDD to be S-attributed.

Questions 5 : What are intermediate forms for SDT?

Answer: Allows translation to be decoupled from parsing, alleviates some Examples, sometimes grammars do not reflect natural program structure, information may not be available when needed, and optimizations may depend on context.

Questions 6 : Give two examples of intermediate representation.

Answer: Postfix is a common intermediate representation for expressions.

E --> E

E1 op E2 --> E1' E2' op

(E) --> E' EG a+(b-x)*c-d --> abx-c*+d-

Abstract Syntax Tree

A condensed form of parse tree, abstracts away unnecessary terminals and non-terminals.

Questions 7 : What are S-attribute definitions?

Answer: S stands for synthesized attributes; all semantic actions follow the right-hand side of a grammar rule. Values of synthesized attributes are stored on a stack, Bison uses a value stack that parallels the LR parser's state stack, when a reduction is made, attributes of the children are on the stack, computes values for synthesized attributes, pops children's attributes and pushes synthesized attributes.

Questions 8 : What are L-attribute definitions?

Answer: L stands for Left, because attributes may be inherited from the Left, semantic actions may be placed throughout right-hand side of a grammar rule, a practical use of inherited attributes stmt --> DECLARE decl_list BEGIN stmt_list END ';', statements in stmt_list must reference declarations made in decl_list.

Questions 9 : How conversion of L-attribute to S-attribute is done?

Answer: Any L-attribute definition may be converted to an equivalent S-attribute definition, we replace the grammar rules containing L-actions, such as-

A --> B {print("hi");} C

with two rules.

1. Introduce a new non-terminal which goes to EPSILON followed by the L-action.
2. Replace the L-action in the old rule with the new non-terminal.

Questions 10 : What are recursive evaluators?

Answer: A multi-pass approach to evaluating attributes, build a parse tree in pass 1, make a pass over the parse tree to evaluate the attributes, allows more control over the order of evaluation and passing attributes, necessary for certain complicated languages.

Example: Distinguishing between array reference and function calls in Ada, performing type checking between public and private sections in C++ class declarations.

Questions 11 : Explain the concept of syntax-directed translation with example.

Answer: A syntax-directed translation is defined by augmenting the CFG, where a translation rule is defined for each production. A translation rule defines the translation of the left-hand side non-terminal as a function of -

- Constants
- Right-hand-side non-terminals' translations
- Right-hand-side tokens' values (e.g. the integer value associated with an INTLIT token, or the String value associated with an ID token)

Questions 12 : State and explain the translation rules that build an AST.

Answer: To define a syntax-directed translation so that the translation of an input is the corresponding AST, we first need operations that create AST nodes. And then apply the above rules (given in question 11).

Questions 13 : Comment on syntax-directed translation and predictive parsing with an example.

Answer: The semantic stack holds non-terminals' translations; when the parse is finished, it will hold just one value - the translation of the root non-terminal (which is the translation of the whole input).

Values are pushed onto the semantic stack (and popped off) by adding actions to the grammar rules. The action for one rule must do the followings:

(i) Pop the translations of all right-hand-side non-terminals.

(ii) Compute and push the translation of the left-hand side non-terminal.

Questions 14 : How does syntax-directed translation handle non-LL(1) grammars?

Answer: Recall that a non-LL(1) grammar must be transformed to an equivalent LL(1) grammar if it is to be parsed using a predictive parser. Also recall that the transformed grammar usually does not reflect the underlying structure, the way the original grammar did. For example, when left recursion is removed from the grammar for arithmetic expressions, we get grammar rules like this:

```
exp -> term exp' exp' -> epsilon
    -> + term exp'
```

Questions 15 : Briefly summarize the process of syntax-directed translation.

Answer: A syntax-directed translation is used to define the translation of a sequence of tokens to some other value, based on a CFG for the input. A syntax-directed translation is defined by associating a translation rule with each grammar rule. A translation rule defines the translation of the left-hand side non-terminal as a function of the right-hand-side non- terminals' translations and the values of the right-hand-side terminals. To compute the translation of a string, build the parse tree, and use the translation rules to compute the translation of each non-terminal in the tree, bottom-up; the translation of the string is the translation of the root non-terminal.

There is no restriction on the type of a translation; it can be a simple type like an integer, or a complex type list an abstract-syntax tree.

EXERCISE

1. Define the following terms with an example:
   (a) Synthesized attribute
   (b) Inherited attribute
   (c) S-attributed definition
   (d) L-attributed definition
2. Explain how to replace inherited attribute by synthesized attribute with an example.
3. Explain how to inherit the attributes on the stack with an example.
4. Define syntax-directed definition. Explain with an example.
5. Explain how a bottom-up parser stack can be used to implement L-attributed definition, with an example.

6. Consider the following grammar: E → E + T | T

   T → num.num

   T → num

   (i) Write syntax-directed definition to determine the type of each sub-expression. The resulting type is an integer if two integers are added, otherwise it is real.

   (ii) Construct an annotated parse tree for the input expression 10 + 20 + 15.2

7. Explain the bottom-up evaluation of synthesized attribute with an example.

8. What is the difference between a set of productions, syntax-directed definition and translation scheme?

9. State whether the following statements are true or false:

   (i) Every s-attributed definition is L-attributes

   (ii) Semantic rules for s-attributed grammar can be evaluated by a bottom-up parser as the input string is being parsed.

◈◈◈

INTERMEDIATE CODE GENERATION

5.1 INTERMEDIATE LANGUAGES

- As we have seen in the first chapter, the front-end of the compiler translates a source program into an intermediate representation from which, the back-end generates target code.
- Instead of converting the source program into the target code directly, the intermediate representation is used. Following are the advantages of using the intermediate representation:
  1. A compiler for a different machine can be created by attaching a back-end for the new machine to an existing front-end.
  2. A machine independent code optimization can be applied to intermediate representation.
- Position of the Intermediate Code Generator is shown in Fig. 5.1.

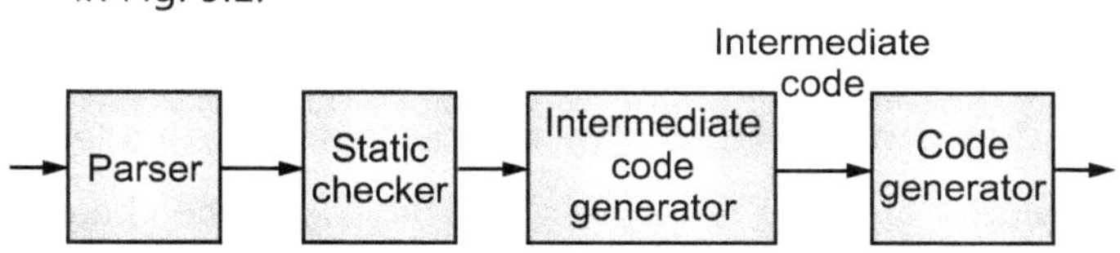

Fig. 5.1: Position of the Intermediate Code Generator

5.2 DECLARATIONS

- The storage details for names local to a procedure can be decided by examining the sequence of declarations in the procedure. For each local name, a symbol table entry is done with the information like the type and relative address of the storage for name. The relative address consists of an offset from the base of the static data area, or the field for local data in an activation record.

Declarations in a Procedure:

Consider the translation scheme:

```
P →                      {offset :=0}
D
D → D ; D
D → id : T               { enter(id.name, T.type,offset);
                           offset := offset + T.width}
T → integer              { T.type :=integer;
                           T.width :=4}
T → real                 { T.type :=real;
                           T.width :=8}
T → array [num] of T1    { T.type :=array(num.val,
                           T1.type);
                           T.width :=num.val → T1.width}
T → ↑ T1                 { T.type : =pointer(T1.type);
                           T.width :=4}
```

- The non-terminal P generates a sequence of declarations of the form id:T.
- Before the first declaration is considered, the offset is set to 0.
- Every new name is entered in the symbol table with the offset equal to the current offset value.
- offset is incremented by the width of the data object denoted by that name.
- The procedure enter(id.name, T.type, offset) creates a symbol table entry for name, type is T.type and relative address is set to offset.
- Synthesized attributes type and width are used to indicate the type and number of memory units taken by objects of that type.
- Type is constructed from the basic types - integer and real, by applying the type constructors, pointer and array.
- Integers have width 4 and real have width 8.
- The width of an array is obtained by multiplying the width of each element by the number of elements in the array. The width of each pointer is assumed to be 4.

Keeping Track of Scope Information

Consider the semantic rules:

```
P → D
D → D ; D | id : T | proc id ; D ; S
```

- The non-terminal S is for statements and T is for types.
- The semantic rules illustrate that when nested procedures are seen, processing of declarations in the enclosing procedure are suspended temporarily. Consider that there is a separate symbol table for each procedure in the language described by the semantic rules. A new symbol table is created when a procedure declaration:

D → proc id ; D ; S

- Entries for declarations in D are created in the new table. The new table points back to the symbol table of the enclosing procedure. The name represented by id is local to the enclosing procedure. The only change is that the procedure enter is told which symbol table to make an entry in.

Example:

Fig. 5.2 shows five symbol tables for the five procedures:

1. Sort,
2. readarray,
3. exchange,
4. quicksort and
5. partition

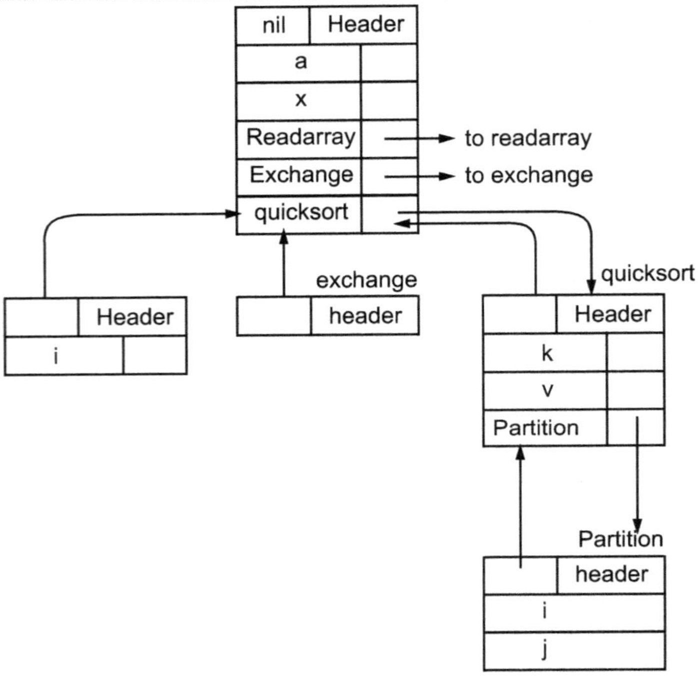

Fig. 5.2 : Symbol tables

The Procedure Sort Calls the Procedures: readarray, exchange, quicksort. Hence the symbol tables for these procedures points back to the symbol table for procedure sort.

The procedure quicksort calls the procedure partition. Hence, the symbol table for this procedure points back to the symbol table for procedure quicksort.

The Rules are Defined in Terms of the Following Operations:

1. **mktable (previous) :** It creates a new symbol table and returns a pointer to the new table. The argument previous, points to a previously created or enclosing procedure symbol table. The pointer previous, is placed in a header for the symbol table.
2. **enter (table, name, type, offset) :** It creates a new entry for name name in the symbol table pointed to by table, and enter places type type and relative address offset in the fields within the entry.
3. **addwidth (table, width) :** It records the cumulative width of all the entries in table in the header associated with the symbol table.
4. **enterproc (table, name, newtable) :** It creates a new entry for procedure name in the symbol table pointed to by table. The argument newtable points to the symbol table for this procedure name.

The translation scheme for nested procedures is:

P → M D	{addwidth(top(tblptr), top(offset)); pop(tblptr); pop(offset)}
M → ε	{ t := mktable(nil); push(t, tblptr); push(0, offset) }
D → D_1 ; D_2	
D → proc id ; N D_1 ; S	{ t:= top(tblptr); addwidth(t, top(offset)); pop(tblptr); pop(offset); enterproc(top(tblptr), id.name, t)}
D → id : T	{enter(top(tblptr),id.name, T.type, top(offset)) top(offset):= top(offset) + T.width }
N → ε	{ t :=mktable(top(tblptr)); push(t, tblptr); push(0, offset)}

Field Names in Records

The following production allows non-terminal T to generate records in addition to basic types, pointers and arrays.

$T \rightarrow$ record L D end

The translation scheme for the records is:

```
T → record L D end    {T.type := record(top(tblptr));
                       T.width:=top(offset);
                       pop(tblptr); pop(offset)}
L → ε                 { t :=mktable(nil);
                      push(t, tblptr); push(0, offset)}
```

When the keyword record is seen, the action associated with the marker L creates a new symbol table for the field names. A pointer to this symbol table is pushed onto the stack tblptr and relative address 0 is pushed onto stack offset. The top of stack offset will hold the width of all the data objects within the record, after the fields have been examined. The action following end returns the width as synthesized attribute T.width. The type T.type is obtained by applying the constructor record to the pointer to the symbol table for this record.

5.3 ASSIGNMENT STATEMENTS

- Three-address statements are formed by using names and it is considered that names represent the pointers to the symbol table entries. The translation scheme to produce the three-address code for assignment given below, shows how to find such symbol table entries.

```
S → id := E        { p:=lookup(id.name);
                     if p # nil then
                     emit(p ':=' E.place)
                     else error}
E → E1 + E2        {E.place := newtemp;
                     emit(E.place ':=' E1.place '+' E2.place)}
E → E1 * E2        {E.place := newtemp;
                     emit(E.place ':=' E1.place '*' E2.place)}
E → -E1            {E.place := newtemp;
                    emit(E.place ':=' 'uniminus' E1.place )}
E → ( E1 )         { E.place := E1.place}
E → id             {p :=lookup(id.name);
                    if p ≠ nil then
                    E.place:=p
                    else error}
```

- The lexeme for the name represented by id is given by attribute id.name.
- lookup(id.name) checks if there is an entry for the occurrence of name in the symbol table. If there is an entry, then it returns the pointer otherwise, it returns nil to indicate no entry.
- emit: the procedure emit is used to emit the three-address statements to an output file
- Suppose that the context in which the assignment appears is given by the grammar:

  $P \rightarrow M\ D$

  $M \rightarrow \varepsilon$

  $D \rightarrow D\ ;\ D \mid id : T \mid proc\ id\ ;\ N\ D\ ;\ S$

  $N \rightarrow \varepsilon$

- The non-terminal P becomes the new start symbol when these productions are added to those in the translation scheme given above.
- For each procedure generated by the grammar, the translation scheme sets up a new symbol table. Each such symbol table has a header containing a pointer to the table of the enclosing procedure.
- Consider the productions for non-terminal S given in the translation scheme. Names in the assignment generated by S must have been declared in the procedure in which S appears, or in the enclosing procedure.

5.4 BOOLEAN EXPRESSIONS

- Boolean expressions have two primary purposes:
  1. To compute logical values.
  2. They are used as conditional expressions.
- Boolean expressions are composed of Boolean operators (and,or,not) applied to elements that are Boolean variables or relational expressions.
- Here, we consider the Boolean expressions generated by the grammar: $E \rightarrow$ E or E | E and E| not E| (E)| id relop id | true |false
- Comparison operators represented by relop are $<, \leq, =, \neq, >, \geq$.
- We assume that or and and are left associative and or has lowest precedence then and, then not.

- Following are two methods for representing the value of Boolean expression:
  1. First method is to encode true and false numerically and to evaluate Boolean expression like an arithmetic expression. Generally, 1 is used to denote true value and 0 is used to denote false value.
  2. The method of implementation is by flow-of-control that is representing the value of a Boolean expression by position reached in a program. This method is useful in implementing Boolean expression in flow-of-control statements such as if-then and while-do statements.

5.4.1 Numerical Representation of Boolean Expressions

Consider that implementation of Boolean expressions is using 1 to represent true and 0 to represent false value. The Boolean expressions are evaluated from left to right like an arithmetic expression.

If we consider the expression

```
a or b and not c
```

The three-address code for the expression is:

```
t1 := not c
t2 := b and t1
t3 := a or t2
```

If we consider the relational expression

```
if a < b then 1 else 0
```

the three-address code for the expression is:

```
100:   if a < b goto 103
101:   t := 0
102:   goto 104
103:   t := 1
104:
```

The translation scheme for producing three-address code for Boolean expressions is:

```
E → E1 or E2          { E.place := newtemp;
                        emit ( E.place ':=' E1.place 'or'
                        E2.place ) }

E → E1 and E2         { E.place := newtemp;
                        emit ( E.place ':=' E1.place 'and'
                        E2.place ) }
E → not E1            { E.place := newtemp;
                        emit ( E.place ':=' 'not' E1.place ) }
E → ( E1 )            { E.place := E1.place }
E → id1 relop id2     { E.place := newtemp;
                        emit( ' if ' id1.place relop.op
                        id2.place 'goto' nextstate + 3);
                        emit (E.place ':=' '0');
                        emit('goto' nextstat + 2);
                        emit (E.place ':=' '1' ); }
E → true              {E.place :=newtemp;
                        emit (E.place ':=' '1' ) }
E → false             {E.place :=newtemp;
                        emit (E.place ':=' '0' ) }
```

Example:

The three-address code for the expression

```
a < b or c < d and e < f
100 : if a < b goto 103
101 : t1 := 0
102 : goto 104
103 : t1 := 1
104 : if c < d goto 107
105 : t2 := 0
106 : goto 108
107 : t2 := 1
108 : if e < f goto 111
109 : t3 := 0
110 : goto 112
111 : t3 := 1
112 : t4 := t2 and t3
113 : t5 := t1 or t4
```

Short-Circuit Code or Jumping Code is a method of evaluation in which, the Boolean expression is translated to three-address code without generating code for any of the Boolean operators and, or, and not, and without having the code to evaluate the entire expression.

5.4.2 Flow-of-Control Method of Evaluation

Here, we consider the translation of following flow-of-control statements:

```
S →    if E then S1
       |if E then S1 else S2
       |while E do S1
```

In these statements, E is the Boolean expression to be translated.

- Boolean expression E has two labels:
  1. E.true – it is the label to which control is transferred if E is true.
  2. E.false – it is the label to which control is transferred if E is false.
- The inherited attribute S.next is a label that is attached to the first three-address instructions to be executed after the code for S. Translation of if-then statement:

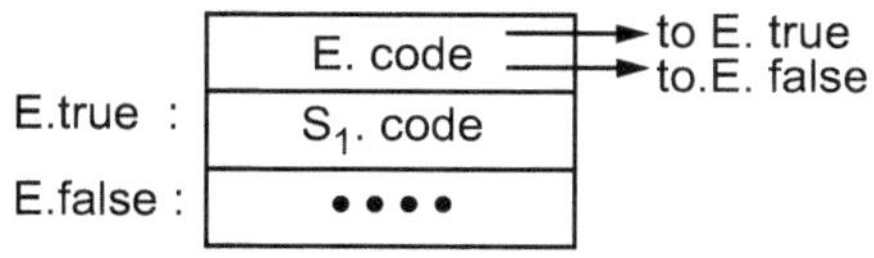

Fig. 5.3: Code for if-then

- In translating if-then statement $S \rightarrow$ if E then S_1
- A new label E.true is created and attached to the first three-address instruction generated for the statement S_1. The code for E generates a jump to E.true if E is true and a jump to S.next if E is false. Hence we set E.false to S.next. The code for if-then is shown in Fig. 5.3.
- In translating if-then-else statement $S \rightarrow$ if E then S_1 else S_2 Three labels E.true, E.false and S.next are used as shown in Fig. 5.4.
- The code for Boolean expression E has jump to label E.true i.e. first instruction of the code for S_1 if E is true, it has jump to label E.false i.e. first instruction of the code for S_2 if E is false. After completing the code for S_1 an explicit goto S.next is executed. The code for if-then-else is shown in Fig. 5.4.

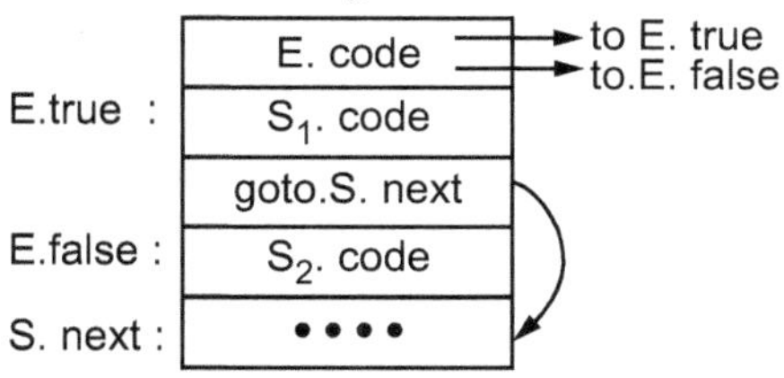

Fig. 5.4: Code for if-then-else

- In translating the while-do statement $S \rightarrow$ while E do S_1
- A new label S.begin is created and attached to the first instruction for E.
- The label E.true is attached to the first instruction for S_1.
- The label E.false is set to S.next.
- The code for E generates a jump to E.true if E is true, and generates a jump to E.false if E is false.
- After the code for S_1 the instruction goto S.begin is set. The code for while-do is shown in Fig. 5.5.

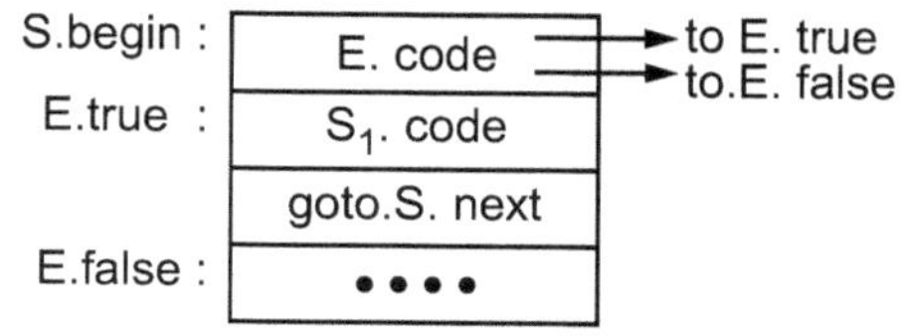

Fig. 5.5: Code for while-do

Syntax-Directed Definition For Flow-of-Control Statements:

Productions	Semantic Rules
$S \rightarrow$ if E then S_1	E.true := newlabel; E.false :=S.next; S_1.next := S.next; S.code :=E.code || gen(E.true ':') || S_1.code
$S \rightarrow$ if E then S_1 else S_2	E.true := newlabel; E.false := newlabel; S_1.next := S.next; S_2.next := S.next; S.code :=E.code || gen(E.true ':') || S_1.code|| gen('goto' S.next)|| gen(E.false ':') ||S_2.code
$S \rightarrow$ while E do S_1	S.begin :=newlable; E.true := newlabel; E.false :=S.next; S_1.next := S.begin; S.code := gen(S.begin ':') ||E.code|| gen(E.true ':') || S_1.code || gen('goto' S.begin)

Control Flow Translation of Boolean Expressions:

If E is of the form a < b, then the generated code is:

```
if a < b goto E.true
goto E.false
```

If E is of the form E_1 or E_2 then E is true if E_1 is true, therefore, E_1.true is the same as E.true. If E_1 is false, then E_2 must be evaluated. Hence E_1.false is the label for the first statement of E_2 code. If E_2 is true then E is set to be true.

Syntax-directed definition to produce three-address code for the Boolean expression is:

Productions	Semantic Rules
$E \rightarrow E_1$ or E_2	E_1.true := E.true; E_1.false := newlabel; E_2.true := E.true; E_2.false := E.false; E.code := E_1.code || gen(E_1.false ':') || E_2.code
$E \rightarrow E_1$ and E_2	E_1.true := newlabel; E_1.false := E. false; E_2.true := E.true; E_2.false := E.false; E.code := E_1.code || gen(E_1.true ':') || E_2.code
$E \rightarrow$ not E_1	E_1.true := E. false; E_1.false := E. true; E.code := E_1.code
$E \rightarrow (E_1)$	E_1.true := E. true; E_1.false := E. false; E.code := E_1.code
$E \rightarrow id_1$ relop id_2	E.code := gen ('if' id_1.place relop.op id_2.place ' goto' E.true) || gen ('goto' E.false)
$E \rightarrow$ true	E.code := gen('goto' E.true)
$E \rightarrow$ false	E.code := gen('goto' E.false)

Example:

Consider the expression

```
      a < b or c < d and e < f
      if a < b goto Ltrue
      goto L1
L1:   if c < d goto L2
      goto Lfalse
L2:   if e < f goto Ltrue
      goto Lfalse
```

5.5 CASE STATEMENTS

Consider the switch case statement

```
switch E
begin
    case V1     :   S1
    case V2     :   S2
    case Vn-1   :   Sn-1
    default     :   Sn
end
```

The syntax-directed translation scheme can be obtained as follows:

- For the keyword switch, generate two new labels test and next and new temporary t.
- Then parse the expression and evaluate E into t. After evaluating E, generate goto test.
- For each keyword case, create a new label Li and enter it into the symbol table. Each statement case Vi : Si is processed by emitting the label Li, followed by the code Si, followed by the jump goto next.
- When the keyword end is found, generate the code for n-way branch.

```
          code to evaluate E into t
          goto test
L1 :      code for S1
          goto next
L2 :      code for S2
          goto next
          .........
Ln-1 :    code for Sn-1
          goto next
Ln :      code for Sn
          goto next
test:     if t = V1 goto L1
          if t = V2 goto L2
          ........
          if t = Vn-1 goto Ln-1
          goto Ln
next:
```

Another translation scheme for the case statement can be given below.

```
          code to evaluate E into t
          if t ≠ V1 goto L1
          code for S1
          goto next
L1 :      if t ≠ V2 goto L2
          code for S2
          goto next
L2 :
          ......
Ln-2 :    if t ≠ Vn-1 goto Ln-1
          code for Sn-1
          goto next
Ln-1 :
next:
```

5.6 BACKPATCHING

- The problem with generating the code for Boolean expressions and the flow-of-control statements in a single pass is that during one pass, we may not know the labels that control 'must go to' at the time the jump statements are generated. This problem can be solved by generating a series of branching statements with targets of jumps temporarily unspecified. Each such 'go to' statement will get the label when the proper label can be determined. This subsequent filling in of the labels is called as backpatching.
- Following three functions are used to manipulate the lists of labels:
  1. **makelist (i) :** This creates a new list containing only i, an index into the array of quadruples. Makelist returns a pointer to the list it has made.
  2. **merge(p_1,p_2) :** This concatenates the lists pointed to by p_1 and p_2, and returns a pointer to the concatenated list.
  3. **backpatch(p, i) :** This inserts i as the target label for each of the statements on the list pointed to by p.

Consider the Grammar for Boolean Expressions:

(1) E → E_1 or M E_2asd
(2) |E_1 and M E_2 asd
(3) |not E_1 asd
(4) |(E_1)
(5) |id_1 relop id_2
(6) |true
(7) |false
(8) M → ε

- The translation scheme to produce quadruples for Boolean expressions is given below.

1. Synthesized attributes truelist and falselist for non-terminal E are used to generate jumping code for Boolean expressions.
2. Attribute M.quad records the number of first statement of E_2.code.
3. The variable nextquad holds the index of the next quadruple to follow.

E → E_1 or M E_2	{ backpatch (E_1.falselist, M.quad); E.truelist :=merge(E_1.truelist, E_2.truelist); E.falselist := E_2.falselist}
E → E_1 and M E_2	{ backpatch (E_1.truelist, M.quad); E.truelist := E_2.truelist; E.falselist :=merge(E_1. falselist, E_2. falselist)}
E → not E_1	{ E.truelist :=E_1.falselist; E.falselist := E_1.truelist}
E → (E_1)	{ E.truelist := E_1.truelist; E.falselist := E_1.falselist }
E → id_1 relop id_2	{ E.truelist := makelist (nextquad); E.falselist := makelist (nextquad+1); emit ('if' id_1.place relop.op id_2.place 'goto _') emit('goto _')
E → true	{ E.truelist := makelist (nextquad); emit('goto _') }
E → false	{ E.falselist := makelist (nextquad); emit('goto _') }
M → ε	{ M.quad := nextquad }

Consider the Grammar for Flow-of-Control Statements:

(1) S → if E then S
(2) |if E then S else S
(3) | while E do S
(4) | begin L end
(5) | A
(6) L → L ; S
(7) | S

- Here, S is a statement, L is a statement list, A is an assignment statement and E is a Boolean expression.
- Non-terminal E has two attributes E.truelist and E.falselist.
- The attributes L.nextlist and S.nextlist point to a list of unfilled quadruples that must be completed by backpatching.
- In while-do statement S.begin and E.true mark the beginning of the code for the complete statement S and the body S_1.
- The production M → ε is with an action setting attribute M.quad to the number of next quadruple.

S → if E then M_1 S_1 N else M_2 S_2

{backpatch (E.truelist, M_1.quad);
backpatch (E.falselist, M_2.quad);
S.nextlist := merge(S_1.nextlist, merge(N.nextlist, S_2.nextlist)) }

N → ε { N.nextlist :=makelist(nextquad);
emit ('goto _')

M → ε {M.quad := nextquad}

$S \rightarrow$ if E then M S_1

{backpatch (E.truelist, M.quad);

S.nextlist := merge(E.falselist, S_1.nextlist) }

$S \rightarrow$ while M_1 E do M_2 S_1

{backpatch (S_1.nextlist, M_1.quad);
backpatch (E.truelist, M_2.quad);

S.nextlist := E.falselist;

emit('goto' M_1.quad) }

$S \rightarrow$ begin L end

{S.nextlist := L.nextlist}

$S \rightarrow A$

{S.nextlist := nil }

$L \rightarrow L_1$; M S

{backpatch (L_1.nextlist, M.quad);
L.nextlist := S.nextlist }

$L \rightarrow S$ {L.nextlist : = S.nextlist }

5.7 PROCEDURE CALLS

When a procedure call occurs, following are essential.

- Space must be allocated for the activation record of the called procedure.
- The arguments of the called procedure must be evaluated and made available to the called procedure.
- Environment pointers must be established to enable the called procedure to access data in enclosing block.
- The state of the calling procedure must be saved so that it can resume execution after the call.
- A jump to the beginning of the code for called procedure must be generated.

The Grammar for Procedure Call is:

(1) $S \rightarrow$ call id (Elist)

(2) Elist$\rightarrow$ Elist , E

(3) Elist$\rightarrow$ E

Syntax-Directed Translation Scheme for Procedure Calls is:

```
S → call id (Elist)
    { for each item p on queue do
            emit('param' p);
            emit('call' id.place)}
Elist → Elist , E
        { append E.place to the end of queue }
Elist → E
        { initialize queue to contain only E.place}
```

SOLVED EXAMPLES

Example 5.1: *Generate the three-address code for the following C programs:*

```
main()
{
int i=1
int a[10]
while(i<=10)
a[i] = ;
}
```

Solution: The three-address code for the program is:

(1) i=1

(2) if i<=10 goto(4)

(3) goto(8)

(4) t_1 = i * width

(5) t_2 = addr(a) – width

(6) $t_2[t_1]$ = 0

(7) goto(2)

Example 5.2: *Generate the three-address code for the following program:*

```
while(A<C and B>D) do
    if A =1 then C = C + 1
        else
        while A <= D do
        A = A + 3
```

Solution: The three-address code for the program is:

(1) if A<C goto(3)

(2) goto (16)

(3) if B>D goto (5)

(4) goto(16)

(5) if a =1 goto(7)

(6) goto(10)

(7) t_1 = c +1

(8) c = t_1

(9) goto(1)

(10) if a <=d goto(12)

(11) goto(1)

(12) t_2 = a + 3

(13) a = t_2

(14) goto(10) (15) goto(1)

Example 5.3: *Generate the three-address code for the following program:*

```
begin
    add=0
    i=1
    j=1
    do
        begin
        add = add + a[i,j]
        i=i+1
        j=j+1
        end
    while i <=20 and j <=20
end
```

Solution: The three-address code is:

[1] add = 0

[2] i = 1

[3] j = 1

[4] t_1 = i * 20

[5] $t_1 = t_1$ + j

[6] $t_1 = t_1$ * 4

[7] t_2 = addr(a) – 84

[8] $t_3 = t_2[t_1]$

[9] t_4 = j * 20

[10] $t_4 = t_4$ + i

[11] $t_4 = t_4$ * 4

[12] t_5 = addr(b) – 84

[13] $t_6 = t_5[t_4]$

[14] $t_7 = t_3 * t_6$

[15] t_7 = add +t_7

[16] t_8 = i + 1

[17] i = t_8

[18] t_9 = j + 1

[19] j = t_9

[20] if i<=20 goto(22)

[21] goto NEXT

[22] if j<=20 goto(4)

[23] goto NEXT

Example 5.4: *For the following program fragment, generate three-address code:*

```
sum =0
for(i = 1; i<=20; i++)
sum = sum +a[i] +b[i]
```

Solution:

The three-address code is:

(1) sum = 0

(2) i = 1

(3) if i<= 20 goto(8)

(4) goto NEXT

(5) t_1 = i + 1

(6) i = t_1

(7) goto(3)

(8) t_2 = i * 4

(9) t_3 = addr(a) – 4

(10) $t_4 = t_3[t_2]$

(11) t_5 = i * 4

(12) t_6 = addr(b) – 4

(13) $t_7 = t_6[\,t_5]$

(14) t_8 = sum + t_4

(15) $t_8 = t_8 + t_7$

(16) sum = t_8

(17) goto(5)

Example 5.5: *Consider the following piece of code in the source language –*

```
if x > 0 then x = 3 * (y + 1) else y = y + 1
```

Construct the syntax tree.

Solution: The syntax tree for this is shown in Fig. 5.6

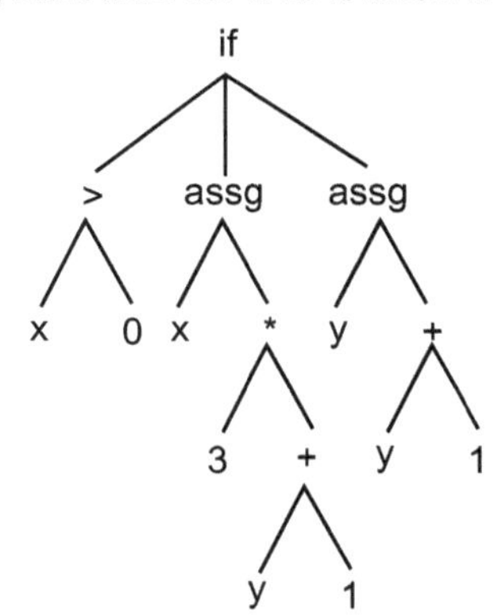

Fig. 5.6: Syntax tree

Example 5.6: *Consider the statement*

X:= (y + z) * (-w + v)

Construct the annotated parse tree for the statement and then show the reduction actions.

Solution: The annotated parse tree for the statement is shown in Fig. 5.7. The reduction sequence for a bottom-up parser is marked with the encircled numbers in Fig. 5.7. The actions at various stages of reductions encircled in Fig. 5.7 are as shown in Fig. 5.7.

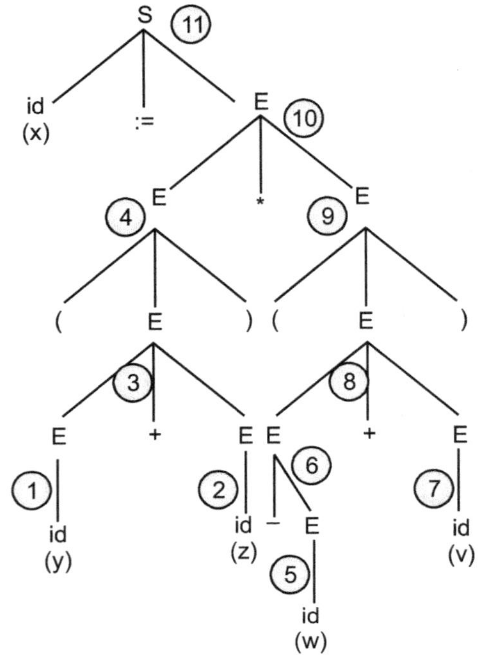

Fig. 5.7: Parse tree

Table 5.1 shows the reduction actions.

Table 5.1 : Code Generation

Reduction No.	Action
1.	E.place = y
2.	E.place = z
3.	E.place = t_1
4.	E.code = {t_1 : = y + z}
5.	E.place = t_1
6.	E.code = {t_1 : = y + z}
7.	E.place = w
8.	E.place = t_2
9.	E.code = {t_2 := uminus w}
10.	E.place = v
11.	E.place = t_3
12.	E.code = {t_2 := uminus w, t_3 := t_2 + v}
13.	E.place = t_4
14.	E.code = {t_2 := uminus w, t_3 •= u + v}
15.	E.place = t_4
16.	E.code = {t_1 : y + z, t_2 : uminus w, t_3 = t_2 + v, t_4 = t_1 * t_3}
17.	E.code = {t_1 : y + z, t_2 : uminus w, t_3 = t_2 + v, t_4 = t_1 * t_3, x = t_3}

Example 5.7: *Consider the following assignment statement-*

X[I,j]:= Y[I+j,k] + Z[k,l]

Construct an annotated parse tree.

Solution: Assume the arrays to be of dimensions X[di,d2], Y[da,d] and Z[d5,de] and each element of all the arrays to be of width w. The annotated parse tree for the statement is shown in Fig. 5.8. The code generation has been explained in Table 5.2.

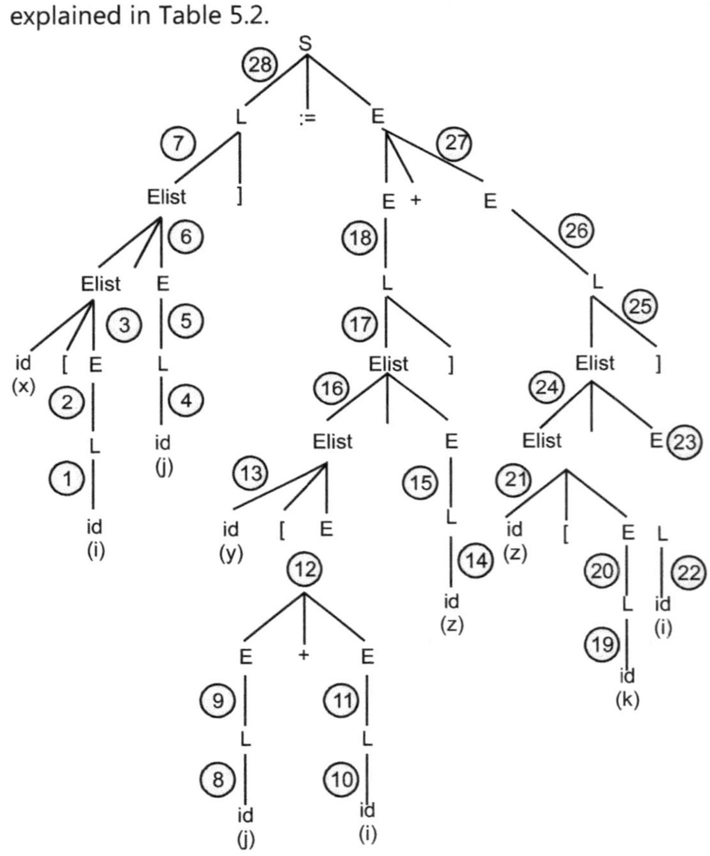

Fig. 5.8: Parse tree

Table 5.2: Code Generation Process

Step No.	Attribute Assignment	Code Generated
1.	L.place = i, L.offset = null	
2.	E.place = i	
3.	Elist.array = X, Elist.place = i, Elist.dim = 1	

4.	L.place = j, L.offset = null	
5.	E.place = j	
6.	Elist.array – X, Elist.place = ij, Elist.dim = 2	t\ = i; * d_2, ti := ti + i
7.	L.place = t_2, L.offset = £3	ti := C(X), t_3
8.	L.place = i, L.offset = null	
9.	E.place = i	
10.	L.place – j, L.offset = null	
11.	E.place = j	
12.	E.place = £4	U :– i + j
13.	Elist.array = Y, Elist.place = <4, Elist.dim = I	
14.	L.place = k, L.offset = null	
15.	E.place – k	
16.	Elist.array = Y, Elist.place – £5, Elist.dim = 2	t$:– t_4 * d_4, t$:= t5 + k
17.	L.place = *6; L.offset – £7	t_6 := C(Y), t_r := t_5 * w
18.	E.place = t$	ts ~ t_a[t_7]
19.	L.place = k, L.offset = null	
20.	E.place = k	
21.	Elist.array = Z, Elist.place = k, Elist.dim = 1	
22.	L.place = I, L.offset = null	
23.	E.place – I	
24.	Elist.array = Z, Elist.place – tg, Elist.dim = 2	tg : = k * d_6, tg := tg + I
25.	L.place – tio, L.offset = tn	tiz — C(Z), tn '·— tg * w
26.	E.place = ti2	tiz := <io *n
27.	E.place – ti3	t^ := t_S + ti_2
28.		*2^s] := *13

Example 5.8: *Consider the Boolean expression*

x > y or z > k and not r < s

Construct the parse tree and generate the code.

Solution: The corresponding parse tree has been shown in Fig. 5.9. Assuming that code generation starts* from quadruple number 1, that is, nextquad is initialized to 1, actions at various reduction*! are as follows:

Red. 1: B.truelist = {1}

B.falselist = {2}

Following lines of codes are generated:

1: if x > y goto ... 2:

goto ...

Red. 2: M.quad = 3

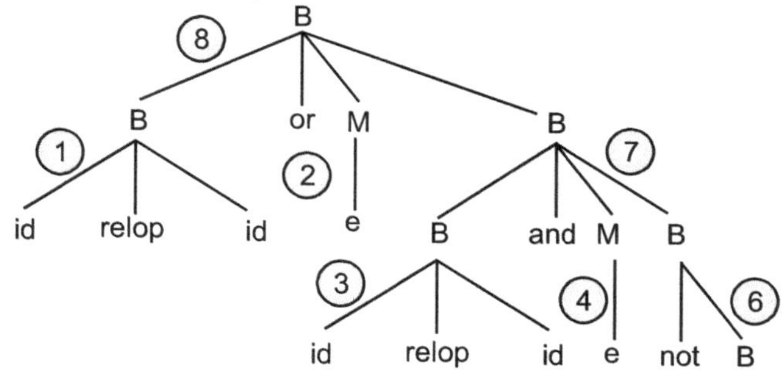

Fig. 5.9 : Parse tree for Boolean expression

Red. 3: B.truelist = {3}

B.falselist = {4}

Codes generated are as follows :

5: if r < s goto ... 6:

goto ...

Red. 6: B.truelist = {6}

B.falselist — {5}

Red. 7: It first backpatches the list {3} with 5. Thus, quadruple 3 is modified as : 3 : if z > fc goto 5 Red. 8: It backpatches the list {2} with 3. Thus, quadruple 2 is modified as :

2 : goto 3

B.truelist = {1,6}, B.falselist = {4,5}

Thus, the full code generated is as follows:

```
1: if x > y goto ...
2: goto 3
3: if z > k goto 5
4: goto ...
5: if r < s goto ...
6: goto ...
```

The branch target of 1 and 6 is the true exit point and that of 4 and 5 is the false exit point of the entire Boolean expression.

Example 5.9: *Consider the following piece of code:*

```
Begin
    While a>b do
    Begin
    X = y + z
    A= a - b
    End
    X= y - z
    end
```

Construct the parse tree and generate code.

Solution: The parse tree for the code segment has been shown in the following diagram:

The activities at various stages of reduction are as shown in Table 5.3. The final code generated is as follows:

```
1:  if a > b goto
2:  3 goto 8
3:  t i = y + z
4:  x = ti
5:  t2 = a — b
6:  a = t2
7:  goto 1
8:   t3 = y, - z
9:  x = t3
```

Table 5.3 : Code Generation Actions

Hed. No.	Action
1.	M.quad = 1
2.	B.truelist = {1}, B.falselist ={2} Code generated : 1 : if a > b goto ... 2 : goto ...
3.	M.quad = 3
4.	E.place = y
5.	E.place = z
6.	E.place = t_1 Code generated : 3 : t_1 = v + z
7.	Code generated : 4 : z ='t_1'
8.	S.nextlist = '{}
9.	L.nextlist = '{}'
10.	M.quad '= '5
11.	E.place = a
12.	E.place = b
13.	E.place – t_1 Code generated : 5 : t_2 = a – b
14.	Code generated : 6 : a = t_2
15.	S.nextlist = '{} '
16.	Backpath('{}', 5) L.nextlist '=' '{}'
17.	S.nextlist = '{} '
18.	backpatch('{}', 1) backpatch({1}, 3} = *Code modified as : 1 : if a > b goto 3 S.nextlist = {2} Code generated 7 : goto ...
19.	L.nextlist - {2}
20.	M.quad = 8
21.	E.place = y
22.	E.place = z
23.	E.place = t_3 Code generated : 8 : t_3= y – z
24.	Code generated : 9: x = t_3
25.	S.nextlist = '{}'
26.	Batchpatch ({2}, 8) => Code modified as : 2: goto 8 L.nextlist '= {} '
27.	S.nextlist = '{}'

SOLVED QUESTIONS AND ANSWERS

Question 1: What is intermediate code representation?

Answer: Let's think of code generation in two parts:

1. One or more machine-independent transformations from an abstract syntax tree to intermediate representations of the program, followed by
2. One or more machine-dependent transformations from the final intermediate representation to machine code.

To sum up, intermediate transformations enable us to retarget the compiler to different machines more easily, and to optimize the code in machine-independent ways, without having to manipulate a complex target language.

Question 2: Comment on choosing an intermediate representation.

Answer: Strictly speaking, a syntax tree is itself an intermediate representation of a source program on the way to a target program. We could use a variation of the syntax tree as the next level of representation.

Question 3: What are the types of three-address statements?

Answer: These usually correspond to source language instructions,

Binary assignments:	x := y op z ;
Unary assignments:	x := op y ;
Copy assignments:	x := y ; Jump
statement:	goto L ; Conditional
jumps:	if x relop y goto L ;
Load arguments and call a subroutine:	load x ; load y ; call p, n ;
Indexed assignment:	x := y[i] ;x[i] := y
Address and pointer assignments:	x := &y ;x := *y ;*x := y ;

Question 4: How are expression trees represented?

Answer: Represented by a DAG or a tree.

```
arguments: expr_tree_list;
    END CASE;
END RECORD;
```

Question 5: What are the issues in processing higher-level control structures?

Answer: Most source languages have high-level control structures such as if..then..else.. and for..to..do... Three-address code can represent such statements using code labels and jumps.

Question 6: What are implementation issues related to three-address code generation?

Answer: A three-address statement is an abstraction that the compiler writer must implement in code. In practice, each statement will be a record with fields for its parts. What might each three-address code statement look like? There are at least two options.

There is one other issue that can arise. When the compiler generates code for a Boolean expression or a conditional statement, it may not yet know where the target of a jump is. The result is a label with no corresponding code in the target program. This can also occur when the compiler generates code "out of order", say, by generating code for local chunks of the AST independently and then stitching the pieces together at the end.

One solution is to generate code in two passes, first pass to generate the framework of the target program and the second pass to compute the jumps and labels. Another approach is to make only a single pass over the whole program. When the compiler generates a branch whose jump target is undefined, it adds the statement to a list of "jumps to be completed". As soon as the correct label is known, the compiler fills in the slot and removes the statement from the to-do list. This technique is known as backpatching. Note that for simple languages, this problem may not arise.

EXERCISE

1. Write the syntax-directed translation scheme for:

   i. if E then S

   ii. if E then S else S

   iii. while E do S
2. What is an intermediate code? Discuss advantages of writing the intermediate code.
3. Write quadruples, triples, and indirect triples for the following expression: (x+y)*(y+z)+(x+y+z)
4. Draw a syntax tree for the following expression:

   ```
   a * (b+c) - d/2
   ```

   Also write the expression in its postfix form.
5. Translate the following program code into three-address code.

```
int i
i = 1
while a < 10 do
    if x>y then a=x+y
    else a=x-y
```

6. Give the syntax-directed definition to produce a three-address code for:
   i. Assignment statement.
   ii. While statement.
   iii. Flow-of-Control Statements.
   iv. Boolean expressions.
7. Explain the methods to implement three-address statements.
8. Write a note on backpatching.
9. Give the syntax-directed translation scheme for:
   i. Assignment statement
   ii. Boolean expression
   iii. Case statement
   iv. Nested procedures
   v. Procedure call.

◈◈◈

UNIT VI

CODE GENERATION

6.1 INTRODUCTION

Code generation is the final phase in the compiler design. The input given to the code generator is the intermediate representation of the source program, which is then converted to the target code by the code generator and given as output. The position of the code generator is shown in Fig. 6.1.

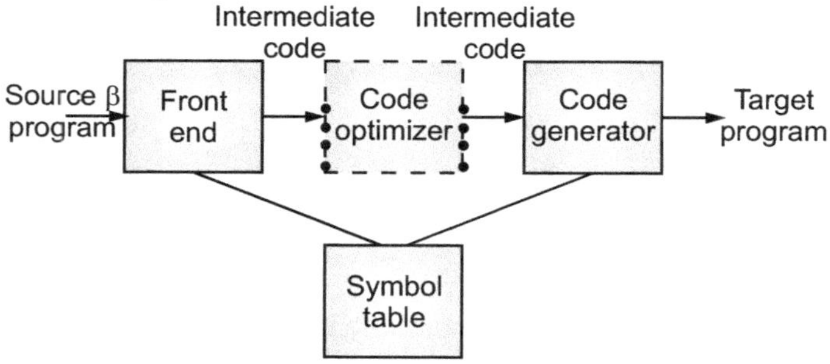

Fig. 6.1: Position of Code Generator

6.2 ISSUES IN CODE GENERATION

Issues that are usually encountered in code generation are given below.

1. **Input to the Code Generator**

- The input to the code generator is the intermediate representation of the source program produced by the front end of the compiler with the symbol table information.
- There are various choices for intermediate representations.
  (i) Linear representation, such as postfix representation or three-address code representation.
  (ii) Virtual machine representation, such as stack machine code.
  (iii) Graphical representation, such as syntax tree and DAGs.
- It is assumed that before code generation, the front end of the compiler has taken care of following issues:
  (i) The source program is scanned, parsed, and translated to a detailed intermediate representation.
  (ii) Necessary type checking is done.
  (iii) The input is free of errors.

2. **Output of Code Generator**

- The output of the code generator is the target code. This target code may take on a variety of forms.
  (i) Absolute machine language
  (ii) Relocatable machine language
  (iii) Assembly language
- The advantage of producing absolute machine language is that it can be placed in a fixed location in the memory and immediately executed.
- The advantage of producing relocatable machine language is that it allows sub-programs to be compiled separately. A set of relocatable object modules can be linked and loaded for execution by a linking loader. If the target machine does not handle relocation automatically, the compiler must provide explicit relocation information to the loader, to link the separately compiled program segments.
- The advantage of producing assembly language is that the process of code generation becomes easier. We can generate symbolic instructions and use the macro facility of the assembler to help in code generation.

3. **Memory Management**

- The front end of the compiler and the code generator does the mapping of names in the source program to addresses of the data objects in run-time memory, cooperatively.
- In the intermediate code generation, it is assumed that a name in three-address statement refers to a symbol table entry for the name. These symbol table entries are created as the declaration of the name is examined.
- The type in the declaration determines the width i.e. the amount of storage needed for the declared name. From the symbol table entry, a relative address can be determined for the name in a data area for the procedure.
- The intermediate representation can be converted to the addresses in the target code by using the implementations of static and stack allocation of data areas.

4. Instruction Selection

- The set of instructions for the target machine determines the level of difficulty in the selection of instructions. The uniformity and completeness of the instruction set are the important factors in determining the instruction set.
- If the target machine does not support each data type in a uniform manner, then each exception to the general rule requires special handling. Instruction speeds and machine idioms are also important factors. If the efficiency of the target program is not considered, then the instruction selection is easy and straightforward.
- For each three-address statement, we can design a code skeleton that outlines the target code to be generated for that construct. A three-address statement like x := y + z, code generated is:

```
MOV y, R0
ADD z, R0
MOV R0, x
```

But this kind of statement-by-statement code generation often produces a poor code.

Example:

```
a := b + c
d := a + e
```

- The code generated is:

```
MOV b, R0
ADD c, R0
MOV R0, a
MOV a, R0
ADD e, R0
MOV R0, d
```

Here, the fourth instruction is redundant and so is the third, if a is not subsequently used. The quality of the generated code is determined by its speed and size.

5. Register Allocation

- Efficient utilization of registers is important in code generation because the instructions utilizing register operands, are shorter and faster than those using operands in memory.
- The use of registers is divided into two sub-tasks.

  (i) Register Allocation: During register allocation, a set of variables that will reside in the registers at a given point in the program is decided.

  (ii) Register Assignment: During register assignment, a specific register in which the variable will reside is decided.

- An optimal assignment of registers to variables is difficult even with single-register values. Consider the given three-address code statements in the optimal machine code sequences with the following representations.

L	:	Load
A	:	Add
ST	:	Store
M	:	Multiplication
D	:	Division

SRDA: shift the dividend into R_1 and clear R_0 so that all bits are equal to sign bit.

- Three-address code statement 1:

```
t := a + b
t := t * c
t := t / d
```

- Optimal machine code sequence is:

```
L   R1, a
A   R1, b
M   R0, c
D   R0, d
ST  R1, t
```

- Three-address code statement 2:

```
t := a + b
t := t + c
t := t / d
```

- Optimal machine code sequence is:

```
L      R0, a
A      R0, b
A      R0, c
SRDA   R0, 32
D      R0, d
ST     R1, t
```

6. Choice of Evaluation Order

- The order in which the computations are performed, affects the efficiency of the code generator. Deciding a best order of evaluation is a difficult problem. It can be said that deciding the best order of evaluation is a NP-complete problem.

6.3 TARGET MACHINE DESCRIPTION

Knowing the target machine and its instruction set, is a prerequisite for designing a good code generator. The details of the target machine are given here.

- The target machine is a byte-addressable machine with four bytes to a word, and n general purpose registers R_0, R_1,.......... R_{n-1}.
- It has two address instructions
  - (i) op (op-code)
  - (ii) source, destination (data fields)
- Target machine has the following op-codes

  MOV - move source to destination

  ADD - add source to destination

  SUB - subtract source from destination
- Source and destination fields are not long enough to hold memory addresses
- The address modes together with their assembly language forms and associated costs are given here :

Table 6.1

MODE	FORM	ADDRESS	COST
Absolute	M	M	1
Register	R	R	0
Indexed	c(R)	c + contents(R)	1
Indirect register	*R	contents(R)	0
Indirect Indexed	*c(R)	contents(c+contents(R))	1
literal	#c	c	1

- A memory location M or a register R represents itself when used as a source or destination.

  Example : MOV R_0, M

  It stores the contents of register R_0 into the memory location M.
- An address offset c from the value in register R is written as c(R).

  Example : MOV 4(R_0), M

  It stores the value contents(4+contents(R_0)) into the memory location M.
- The instruction MOV *4(R_0), M stores the value contents(contents (4+contents(R_0))) into the memory location M.
- The final address mode allows the source to be constant. The instruction MOV R_0, M loads the constant 1 into the register R_0.

How to Find the Instruction Cost:

- The cost of instruction is taken to be one, plus the cost associated with the source and destination address modes. Address modes involving registers have the cost as zero, while those involving memory have the cost as one.

Some Examples are Given in the Following Table 6.2 :

Table 6.2

Instruction	Destination Cost	Source Cost	Total Cost
MOV R_0,R_1	0	0	1
MOV R_0,M	1	0	2
ADD #1,R_3	0	1	2
SUB 4(R_0), *12 (R_1)	1	1	3

Consider the following sequence of instructions to find the total cost.

1.

   MOV b, R_0
   ADD c, R_0
   MOV R_0, a

   The total cost is (2 + 2 +2) 6

2.

   MOV b, a
   MOV c, a

   The total cost is (3 + 3) 6

3.

   MOV *R_1, *R_1
   ADD *R_2, *R_0

The total cost is (1 + 1) 2

4.

   ADD R_2, R_1
   MOV R_1, a

The total cost is (1 + 2) 3

6.4 RUN-TIME STORAGE MANAGEMENT

6.4.1 Subdivision of Run-Time Memory

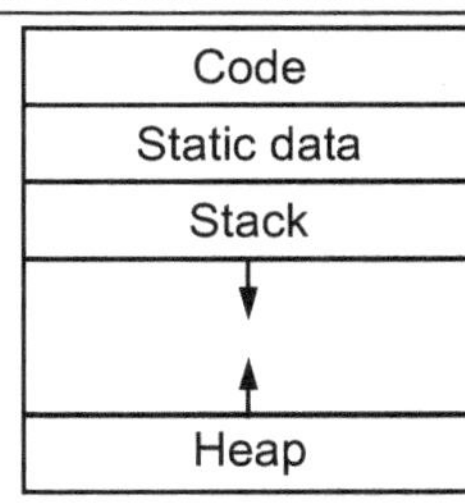

Fig. 6.2 : Subdivision of Runtime Memory

- Run-time storage can be subdivided to hold :
  1. The generated target code
  2. Data objects
  3. A counterpart of the control stack to keep track of procedure activations.
- The size of the target code is fixed at compile time, so the compiler can place it in a statically determined area. Similarly, the size of some of the data objects may also be known at compile time, and these also can be placed in a statically determined area.
- A separate area of run time memory, called a *heap*, holds all other information.
- As shown in Fig. 6.2 the sizes of the stack and the heap can change as the program executes. By convention, stacks grow down, i.e. the top of the stack is drawn towards the bottom of the stack.

6.4.2 Activation Records

Information needed by a single execution of a procedure is managed using a contiguous block of storage called an activation record or frame. It consists of following fields :

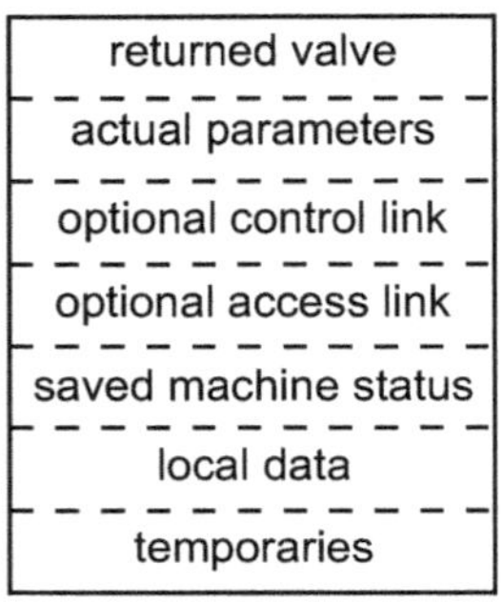

Fig. 6.3 : Activation Record

The purpose of fields of activation record is as follows :

- Temporary values, such as those arising in the evaluation of the expression are stored in the field for temporaries.
- The field for local data holds data that is local to an execution of a procedure.
- The field for saved machine status holds information about the state of the machine just before the procedure is called. This information includes values of the program counter and machine registers.
- The optional access link is used to refer to nonlocal data held in other activation records.
- The optional control link points to the activation record of the caller.
- The field for actual parameters is used by the calling procedure to supply parameters to the called procedure.
- The field for returned value is used by the called procedure to return a value to the calling procedure.

All the languages or all the compilers do not use all these fields. But, registers can take place of one or more of these fields. The sizes of these fields can be determined at the time a procedure is called.

6.5 BASIC BLOCKS AND FLOW GRAPHS

6.5.1 Basic Block

A basic block is a sequence of consecutive statements in which flow of control enters at the beginning, and leaves at the end without halt or possibility of branching, except at the end. The following sequence of three-address code statements forms a basic block:

$$t_1 : = a * a$$
$$t_2 : = a * b$$
$$t_3 : = 2 * t_2$$
$$t_4 : = t_1 + t_3$$
$$t_5 : = b * b$$
$$t_6 : = t_4 + t_5$$

A three-address statement x := y + z is said to define x and use y and z.

A name in a basic block is said to be live at a given point if its value is used after that point in the program.

Steps to Partition a Sequence of Three-Address Statements into Basic Blocks:

1. Determine the set of leaders, the first statements of the basic blocks.
   (i) The first statement is a leader.
   (ii) Any statement that is the target of a conditional or unconditional goto is a leader.
   (iii) Any statement that immediately follows a goto or conditional goto statement is a leader.
2. For each leader, find its basic block which consists of the leader and all statements up to, but not including the next leader, or the end of the program.

Example :

Consider the fragment of source code to compute dot product.

```
    begin
        prod := 0;
i :=0
do begin
prod := prod + a[i] *b[i];
i := i + 1;
end
while i<=20 end
```

The three-address code for this code is:

```
(1) prod := 0
(2) i := 1
(3) t1 := 4*i
(4) t2 := a [t1]
(5) t3 := 4*i
(6) t4 := b [t3]
(7) t5 := t2 * t4
(8) t6 := prod + t5
(9) prod := t6
(10)t7 := i + 1
(11)i := t7
(12)if i <= 20 goto (3)
```

By applying the above steps to find basic block leaders, the leaders in the above three- address code are :

1. statement (1) is leader by rule i
2. statement (3) is leader by rule ii
3. statement (12) is leader by rule iii

Basic blocks in the code:

The code has two basic blocks.

1. First basic block is of statement(1) and statement(2)
2. Second basic block is from statement(3) to statement(12)

6.5.2 Transformations on Basic Blocks

- A basic block computes a set of expressions. These expressions are values of the names live on exit from the block. Two basic blocks are said to be equivalent if they compute the same set of expressions.
- A number of transformations can be applied to a basic block without changing the set of expressions computed by the block. There are two important classes of local transformations that can be applied to basic blocks.

1. Structure Preserving Transformations

The primary structure preserving transformations are:

(i) Common sub-expression elimination

(ii) Dead code elimination

(iii) Renaming of temporary variables

(iv) Interchange of two independent adjacent statements

Let us now examine these transformations in detail. Here we assume that basic blocks have no arrays, pointers, or procedure calls.

(i) Common Sub-Expression Elimination

Consider the basic block

```
a := b + c
b := a - d
c := b + c
d := a - d
```

Here, the second and fourth statements compute the same expression. Hence, the basic block can be transformed into:

```
a := b + c
b := a - d
c := b + c
d := b
```

Note that the first and third statements appear to have same expression on right. But the second statement redefines b. Hence, the value of b in the third statement is different from the value of b in first statement, and the two statements do not compute the same expressions.

(ii) Dead Code Elimination

x is said to be dead, if it is never subsequently used from the point where the statement x := y + z appears in a basic block. Then the statement can be safely removed without changing the value of the basic block.

(iii) Renaming Temporary Variables

Consider a statement t:=b+c, where t is a temporary variable. If the statement is changed to u:=b+c, where, u is a new temporary variable, and all the uses of t are changed to u, then the value of this basic block is not changed.

(iv) Interchange of Statements

Consider the basic block

```
t1 := b + c
t2 := x + y
```

The two statements can be interchanged without affecting the value of the block if and only if x and y are not t_1, and b and c are not t_2.

2. Algebraic Transformation

Number of algebraic transformations can be applied to change the set of expressions into algebraically equivalent expressions. Few of them are discussed here,

(i) Consider the Statements:

```
x :=x + 0
or
x := x * 1
```

These statements can be eliminated from the basic block without changing the set of expressions it computes.

(ii) Consider the Statement Using Exponentiation Operator:

x := y ** 2

It requires a function call to implement the exponentiation operator.

Using algebraic transformation, this statement can be replaced by an optimized but equivalent statement:

x := y * y

6.5.3 Flow Graph

A graphic representation of a three-address statement is called a flow graph. It is useful for understanding the code generation algorithms even when the graph is not constructed by a code generation algorithm. Nodes in the flow graph represent computations, and the edges represent the flow of control.

Features of a Flow Graph

- Flow-of-control information can be added to the set of basic blocks which constitute a program, by constructing a directed graph, that is, the flow graph.
- The nodes of a flow graph are the basic blocks.
- One node is distinguished as initial, which is the block whose leader is the first statement.
- There is a directed edge from block B_1 to block B_2 in case B_2 can immediately follow B_1 in some execution sequence. This happens in the following situations.
- There is a conditional or unconditional jump from the last statement of B_1 to the first statement of B2. B_2 immediately follows B1 in the order of the program, and B_1 does not end in an unconditional jump.
- B_1 is said to be a predecessor of B_2 if B_2 is a successor of B_1.

Example:

Consider the three-address code:

```
(1) prod := 0
(2) i := 1
(3) t1 := 4*i
(4) t2 := a [t1]
(5) t3 := 4*i
(6) t4 := b [t3]
(7) t5 := t2 * t4
(8) t6 := prod + t5
(9) prod := t6
(10) t7 := i + 1
(11) i := t7
(12) if i <= 20 goto (3)
```

Flow graph for the program is given in Fig. 6.4.

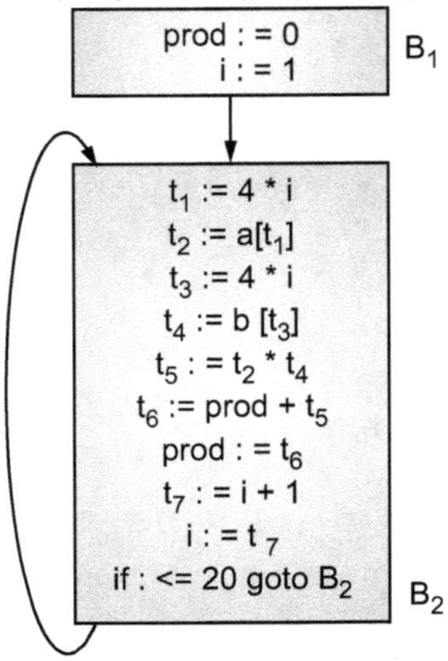

Fig. 6.4 : Flow Graph

Representation of Basic Blocks

Basic blocks can be represented by a variety of data structures.

- Representing a basic block by a set comprising of -
  - ➢ A record consisting of a count of the number of quadruples in the block
  - ➢ A pointer to the leader of the block.
  - ➢ The lists of predecessors and successors of the block.
- Making a linked list of the quadruples in each block.

  In this case, explicit references to quadruple numbers in the statements at the end of the basic blocks can cause problems if the quadruples are moved during code optimization.

Loops

- A Loop in a flow graph is a collection of nodes in the flow graph such that
- All nodes in the collection are strongly connected, i.e. there is a path of length one or more, from one node to another node in the loop.
- The collection of nodes has a unique entry point. If it is desired to reach a node within the loop from a node that is outside the loop, the only way is to go through this entry.

6.6 NEXT USE INFORMATION

- In this section we explain the use of a name in a three-address statement. Suppose a three- address statement i assigns a value to x. If
  1. The statement j has x as an operand and
  2. The control can flow from statement i to j along a path that has no intervening assignments to x then we say that j uses the value of x computed by i.

- Let us determine the next uses of x, y, and z for each three-address statement x := y op z. For doing this, the algorithm uses a backward scan. When the end of the block is found, the algorithm scans backward to the beginning. For each name x it will record whether x has a next use in the block or not. If not, then it checks whether it is live on exit from that block.
- Consider that a three-address statement i: x := y op z is reached in the backward scan. The algorithm executes the following steps:
  1. Attach to statement i, the information currently found in the symbol table regarding the next use and liveness of x, y, and z.
  2. In the symbol table, set x to "not live" and "no next use".
  3. In the symbol table, set y and z to "live" and the next uses of y and z to i. Here the order of statements (2) and (3) cannot be interchanged because x may be y or z.
  4. If the three-address statement is of the form x := y or x := op y, the steps are the same as above, and z is ignored.

Storage for Temporaries

- In an optimizing compiler, it is useful to create a distinct name each time a temporary is needed. However, space has to be allocated each time, to hold the values of these temporaries. The size of the field for temporaries in the general activation record grows with the number of temporaries.
- Two temporaries can be packed into the same location if they are not live simultaneously. The next use information can be used to pack temporaries.
- Storage location for temporaries can be allocated by examining each in turn. The assigning a temporary to the first location in the field for temporaries, which does not contain a live temporary. If a temporary cannot be assigned to any previously created location, add a new location to the data area for the current procedure.

Example:

The six temporaries in the basic block can be packed into two locations. These locations correspond to t_1 and t_2.

```
t1:= a * a
t2:= a * b
t2:= 2 * t2
t1:= t1 * t2
t2:= b * b
t1:= t1 + t2
```

6.7 SIMPLE CODE GENERATOR

- Here, a fixed translation to the target code is selected for each possible node type. During code generation, the nodes in the AST are rewritten to their translations, and the AST is scheduled by following the data flow inside expressions and the flow of control in a different place.
- When the correctness of this composition of translations depends very much on the interface conventions between each of the translations, it is important to keep these interface conventions simple but, as typical, more complicated interface conventions allow more efficient translations.
- Simple code generation requires local decisions only, and is therefore especially suitable for narrow compilers. With respect to machine types, it is particularly suitable for two somewhat similar machine models, the pure stack machine and the pure register machine.
- A pure stack machine uses a stack to store and manipulate values; it has no registers. It has two types of instructions, those that move or copy values between the top of the stack and in a different place, and those that do operations on the top element or elements of the stack.
- The stack machine has two important data administration pointers: the stack pointer SP, which points to the top of the stack, and the base pointer BP, which points to the beginning of the region on the stack where the local variables are stored;. It may have other data administration pointers, for example a pointer to the global data area and a stack area limit pointer, but these play no direct role in simple code generation.
- Data administration in a simple stack machine interrupt, which allows the operating system to increase the stack size.

6.8 REGISTER ALLOCATION AND ASSIGNMENT

Instructions involving only register operands are shorter and faster than those involving memory operands. Hence efficient utilization of registers is necessary for good code generation. This section explains the various strategies to determine what values should reside in the registers and in which register these should reside.

6.8.1 Global Register Allocation

- Registers are assigned to frequently used variables and these registers are kept consistent across block boundaries i.e. globally. A natural approach to global register allocation is to keep a frequently used value in a fixed register throughout a loop.
- One of the strategies for global register allocation is to assign a fixed number of registers to hold the most active values in each inner loop. These selected values may be different in different loops. Registers which are not already allocated may be used to hold values that are local to a block.
- This method is simple to implement but it has a disadvantage. One cannot decide or fix the number of registers that should be made available for global register allocation.
- Usage Count's various benefits of global register allocations are as follows:
  - ➢ One unit of cost is saved for each reference to x, if x is stored in a register.
  - ➢ After x has been computed in a block, x remains in the register if there are subsequent uses of x in that block. Here we count a savings of one for each use of x in loop L that is not preceded by an assignment to x in the same block.
  - ➢ Two unit costs can be saved if we can avoid a store of x at the end of a block.
  - ➢ If x is live on entry to the loop header, x needs to be loaded into the register before it enters loop L. This load results in a cost of two.
  - ➢ For each exit block B of loop L, at which x is live on entry to some successor of B outside of L, x must be stored at a cost of two.

Thus, a formula for the benefit to be realized from allocating a register to x within loop L can be devised as follows:

$$\sum_{\text{blocks B in L}} (\text{use}(x, B) + 2*\text{live}(x, B))$$

where,

use(x, B) is the number of times x is used in B prior to any definition of x.

live(x, B) is 1 if x is live on exit from B and is assigned a value in B.

live(x, B) is 0 otherwise.

Example:

Consider the basic blocks in Fig. 6.5 given below.

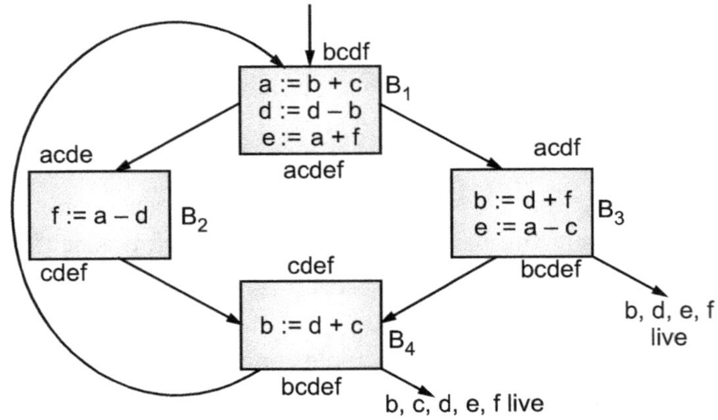

Fig. 6.5 : Flow Graph

Here it is assumed that registers R_0, R_1, and R_2 are allocated to hold values throughout the loop.

Variables live on entry into, and exit from each block, are shown in Fig. 6.5.

To evaluate x = a

a is live on exit from B_1 but it is not live on exit from B_2, B_3, B_4.

Hence,

$$\sum_{\text{blocks B in L}} (2*\text{live}(x, B)) = 2$$

Similarly, use(a,B_1) = 0, use(a,B_2) = 1, use(a,B_3) = 1, use(a, B_4) = 0,

Hence,

$$\sum_{\text{blocks B in L}} (\text{use}(x, B))$$

Therefore,

$$\sum_{\text{blocks B in L}} (\text{use}(x, B) + 2*\text{live}(x, B))$$

That is, four units cost can be saved by selecting a for one of the global registers.

For x = b

$$\sum_{\text{blocks B in L}} (\text{use}(x, B) + 2*\text{live}(x, B)) = 6$$

For x =c

$$\sum_{\text{blocks B in L}} (\text{use}(x, B) + 2*\text{live}(x,B)) = 3$$

For x =d

$$\sum_{\text{blocks B in L}} (\text{Use}(x, B) + 2*\text{live}(x,B))= 6$$

For x =e

$$\sum_{\text{blocks B in L}} (\text{use}(x, B) + 2*\text{live}(x,B)) =4$$

For x =f

$$\sum_{\text{blocks B in L}} (\text{use}(x, B) + 2*\text{live}(x,B))=4.$$

6.8.2 Register Assignment for Outer Loops

- If an outer loop L_1 contains an inner loop L_2, the registers with names allocated that in L_2 need not be the allocated registers in $L_1 - L_2$.
- If name x is allocated a register in loop L_1 but not L_2, x must be stored on entrance to L_2 and load x if we leave L_2 and enter a block of $L_1 - L_2$.
- If we choose to allocate x a register in L_2 but not L_1 we must load x on entrance to L_2 and store x on exit from L_2.

6.8.3 Register Allocation by Graph Coloring

- When a register is needed for some computation but all the available registers are in use, then the contents of one of the used register must be stored or spilled into a memory location in order to free up a register.
- Graph coloring is the simple technique for allocating registers and managing register spills. This method uses two passes.
  1. **First Pass:** Target machine instructions are selected by considering that there are an infinite number of symbolic registers, which are in effect. The names used in the intermediate code become names of registers, and three-address statements become machine language statements.

     If access to variables requires instructions that use stack pointers, display pointers, base registers or other quantities, then we assume that these quantities are held in registers reserved for each respective purpose.
  2. **Second Pass:** For each procedure, a register interference graph is constructed in which the nodes are symbolic registers. An edge connects two nodes if one is live at a point where the other is defined.
- Graph coloring colors the register interference graph using k-colors where, k is the number of assignable registers. A graph is said to be colored if each node has been assigned a color in such a way that no two adjacent nodes have the same color. A color represents a register, and the coloring makes sure that no symbolic registers that can interfere with each other are assigned the same physical register.

6.9 DAG REPRESENTATION OF BASIC BLOCKS

6.9.1 Directed Acyclic Graph (DAG)

- DAGs are useful data structures for implementing transformations on basic block.
- DAG gives a picture of how the value computed by each statement in a basic block is used in subsequent statements of the block.
- Constructing a DAG from three-address statements is a good way of -
  - ➢ Determining common sub-expressions within the block.
  - ➢ Determining which names are used inside the block but evaluated outside the block
  - ➢ Determining which statements of the block can have their computed value used outside the block.

DAG for a Basic Block

It is a directed acyclic graph with the following labels on nodes:

- Leaves are labeled by unique identifiers, either variable names or constants. From the operator applied to a name, we determine whether the l-value or r-value of a name is needed or not. Most leaves represent r-values.
- Interior nodes are labeled by an operator symbol.
- Nodes are optionally given a sequence of identifiers for the labels. The reason being that the interior nodes represent computed values and the identifiers which label a node, are supposed to have that value.

Example:

Consider the three-address code given below:

```
(1) t1 := 4*i
(2) t2 := a [t1]
(3) t3 := 4*i
(4) t4 := b [t3]
(5) t5 := t2 * t4
(6) t6 := prod + t5
(7) prod := t6
(8) t7 := i + 1 (9)     i := t7
(10)if i <= 20 goto (1)
```

The DAG corresponding to this basic block is shown in Fig. 6.6.

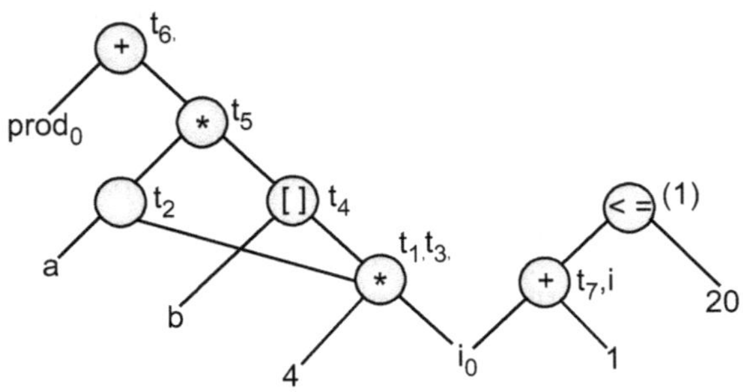

Fig. 6.6 : DAG for the Three-address Code

6.9.2 DAG Construction

To construct a DAG for a basic block, we process each statement of the block. When a statement of the form x := y + z occurs, we find the values of y and z. Then create a node labeled + and give it two children, the left child is y and the right child is z. However, if there is already a node denoting the same value as y + z, we do not add the new node to the DAG but rather give the existing node, an additional label x.

Algorithm for DAG Construction

DAG constructed by the algorithm has the following information:

- A label for leaves which is an identifier and a label for interior nodes, which is an operator symbol.
- For each node, a list of identifiers is attached.

Considerations in the algorithm:

- node(identifier) is a function which returns the most recently created node associated with identifier.
- Following are the three-address statements :

(i) x := y op z

(ii) x := op y

(iii) x := y

These statements are referred as (i), (ii) and (iii).

Steps for DAG Construction:

1. If node (y) is undefined, create a leaf labeled y, and let node(y) be this node. In case (i) node (z) is undefined, create a leaf labeled z and let that leaf be node (z).
2. a. In case (i), determine if there is a node labeled op, whose left child is node(y) and whose right child is node (z). If not, create such a node. In both the events let n be the node found or created.

   b. In case (ii), determine whether there is a node labeled op, whose only child is node(y). If not, then create such a node and let n be the node found or created.

   c. In case (iii), let n be node(y).
3. Delete x from the list of attached identifiers for node (x). Append x to the list of attached identifiers for the node n found in (2), and set node (x) to n.

6.9.3 Applications of DAG

- Common sub-expressions can be automatically detected using DAG.
- We can determine which identifiers have their values used in the block, they are exactly those for which leaf is created in the previous step (1) at some time.
- We can determine which statements compute values that could be used outside the block. They are those statements S whose node n is constructed or found in step (2) and which still has node(x) = n at the end of the DAG construction, where x is the identifier assigned by statement S.
- Simplified list of quadruples can be reconstructed by taking the advantage of common sub-expressions, and not performing assignments of the form x:=y unless absolutely necessary.

Example:

Consider the DAG given in Fig. 6.6. The basic block for the DAG can be reconstructed as follows.

- Begin with the node representing 4 * i. The node has two identifiers t_1 and t_2. Take t_1 to hold the value 4 * i. The first reconstructed statement is

t_1 : = 4 * i

- The second node considered is t_2. The reconstructed statement is

t_2 : = a [t_1]

- The next node considered is t_4. The reconstructed statement is

t_4 : = b [t_1]

- The next node considered is t_5. The reconstructed statement is

t_5 := t_2 * t_4

- The next node considered is prod. The reconstructed statement is

prod := prod + t_5

- The last two statements generated are

i : =i + 1

if i<=20 goto (1)

Thus, ten statements are reduced to seven statements by taking advantage of the common sub-expressions and by eliminating unnecessary assignments.

6.10 GENERATING CODE FROM DAG

1. Rearranging the Order

- The order in which computations are done can affect the cost of the resulting target code. For example, consider the following basic block:

```
t1 := a + b
t2 := c + d
t3 := e - t2
t4 := t1 - t3
```

- The DAG representation of the code is given in Fig. 6.7. The order of evaluation can be obtained from the syntax directed translation of the expression (a + b) – (e – (c + d)).

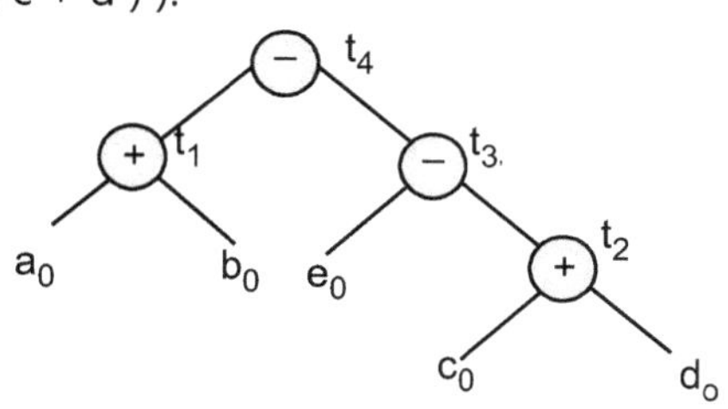

Fig. 6.7: DAG for the Basic Block

- If we generate a code for the three-address statements using the algorithm, we get the following code sequence.

```
MOV a, R0
ADD b, R0
MOV c, R1
ADD d, R1
MOV R0, t1
MOV e, R0
SUB R1, R0
MOV t1, R1
SUB R0, R1
MOV R1, t4
```

- On the other hand, we can rearrange the order of statements as follows:

```
t2 := c + d
t3 := e - t2
t1 := a + b
t4 := t1 - t3
```

- Using code generation algorithm, we get the code sequence as:

```
MOV c, R0
ADD d, R0
MOV e, R1
SUB R0, R1
MOV a, R0
ADD b, R0
SUB R1, R0
MOV R0, t4
```

2. Heuristic for Ordering Nodes of DAG:

The algorithm for heuristic ordering is given below.

- It lists the nodes of a DAG in such a way that the reverse listing of the node results in the computation order.

```
while unlisted interior nodes exists do
begin
   select an unlisted node n, all of whose parents have
   been listed
   list n;
   while the leftmost child m of n has no unlisted parents
   and is not a leaf do
      begin
      list m
      n :=m
      end
end
```

Example:

Consider the DAG given in Fig. 6.8.

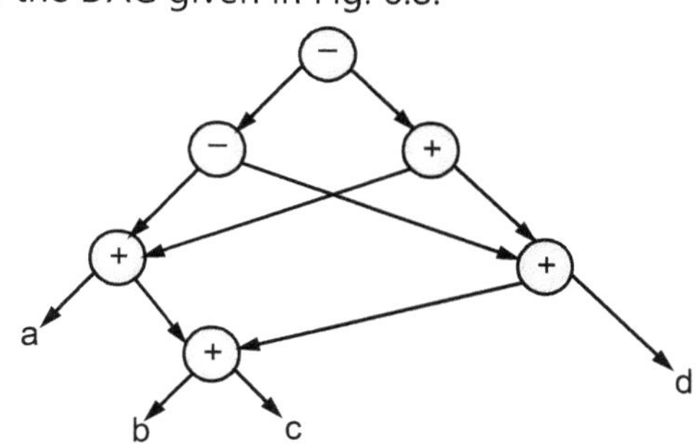

Fig. 6.8 : DAG Representation

The order in which the nodes are listed by the heuristic ordering is shown in Fig. 6.9. Hence, the computations order is:

```
t6 := b + c
t5 := t6 + d
t4 := a + t6
t3 := t4 + t5
t2 := t4 - t5
t1 := t2 - t3
```

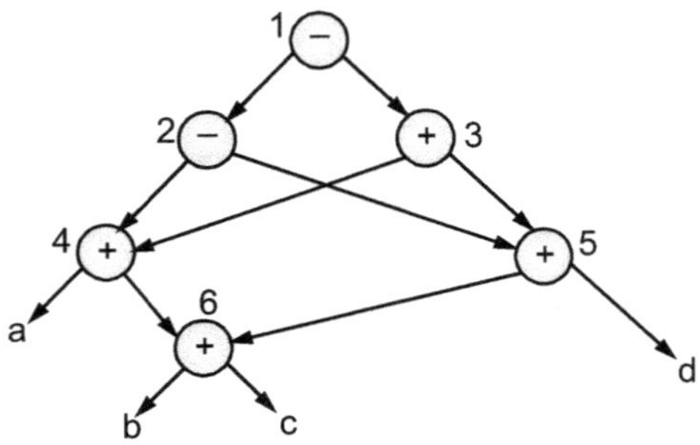

Fig. 6.9: DAG Representation with Heuristic Ordering

3. Labeling Algorithm

- This algorithm works on the tree representation of a sequence of three-address statements. The algorithm has two parts -
  1. The first part labels the tree, each node of the tree is labeled from the bottom to top with an integer that denotes the minimum number of registers required to evaluate the tree and with no storing of intermediate results.
  2. The second part of the algorithm is the tree traversal that travels the tree in an order governed by the computed labels in the first part, and which generates the code during the tree traversal.
- The Labeling algorithm is given below.

```
    if n is a leaf node then
    if n is the leftmost child of its parent then
        label(n) := 1
    else label(n) := 0
else begin
    let n1, n2,........... nk be the children of n ordered by
    label, so label(n1) ≥ label(n2) ≥ .............. ≥ label(nk)
    max
    label(n) :=   1<i<j label(ni)+I -1)
    end
```

Example:

Consider the following basic block:

```
t1 := a + b
t2 := c + d
t3 := e - t2
t4 := t1 - t3
```

The DAG representation of the code is given in Fig. 6.7. The tree after labeling is shown in Fig. 6.10.

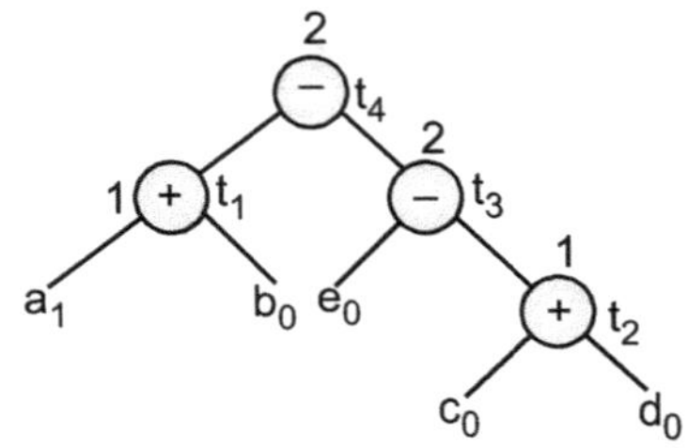

Fig. 6.10 : DAG Representation with Labeling

4. Code Generation by Traversing a Labeled Tree

- This section explains the algorithm that traverses the labeled tree and generates machine code to evaluate the tree in register R_0. The algorithm uses a recursive procedure gencode(n) to produce the machine code for evaluating the subtree of T with root n into a register.
- The procedure uses a stack rstack to allocate registers. Initially rstack contains all the available registers, which we assume are R_0, R_1,..........$R_{(r-1)}$.
- The function swap(rstack) interchanges the top two registers on rstack.
- The procedure gencode uses a stack tstack to allocate temporary memory locations. We assume tstack initially contains T_0, T_1, ...
- Depending upon the type of node n, gencode(n) works as follows.

Case I: When n is a leaf node and is the left most child of its parent In this case, gencode generates a load instruction for loading the top register of rstack by the label of node n

```
MOV name, rstack[top]
```

Case II: When n is an interior node (it will be an operator node labeled by op with the children n_1 and n_2) and n is a simple operand and not the root of the subtree as shown in Fig. 6.11.

In this case, gencode will -

1. First generate the code to evaluate the subtree rooted at n_1 in the rstack[top].
2. Then generate the instruction: op name, rstack[top]

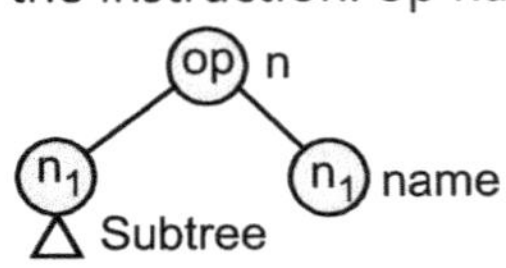

Fig. 6.11: Node n is an Operand

Case III: When n is an interior node (it will be an operator node labeled by op with the children n_1 and n_2) and both n_1 and n_2 are roots of the subtrees, as shown in Fig. 6.12.

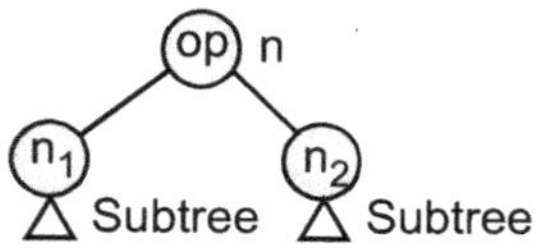

Fig. 6.12: Node n is an Operator and n_1 and n_2 are roots

In this case, there are three possibilities.

1.. label(n_2) > label(n_1)

Here, n_2 requires a greater number of registers than n_1, to evaluate without storing the intermediate results. Therefore, gencode checks whether the total number of available registers r is greater than the label(n_1). If it is, then the subtree rooted n_1 can be evaluated without storing the intermediate results.

Here, gencode performs the following steps.

(i) It first swaps the top two registers of rstack.

(ii) Then generates the code for evaluating the subtree rooted at n_2.

(iii) It removes the top most register from rstack and stores it in R.

(iv) Then generate the code for evaluating the subtree rooted at n_1 in rstack[top].

(v) An instruction OP R rstack[top] is generated, which pushes R into rstack.

(vi) The top two registers are swapped so that the register holding the value of n will be in the top register of rstack.

2. label(n_2) <= lable(n_1)

Here, n_1 requires a greater number of registers than n_2, to evaluate without storing the intermediate results. Therefore, gencode checks whether total number of available registers r is greater than the label(n_2). If it is, then the subtree rooted n_2 can be evaluated without storing the intermediate results.

Here, gencode performs the following steps.

(i) It first generates the code for evaluating the subtree rooted at n_1.

(ii) It removes the top most register from rstack and stores it in R,

(iii) Then generate the code for evaluating the subtree rooted at n_2 in rstack[top].

(iv) An instruction OP R rstack[top] is generated, which pushes R into rstack.

In this case, after pushing R onto rstack, the top register holds the value of n. Therefore, swapping and re-swapping is needed.

3. label(n_1) and label(n_2) are greater than equal to r

In this case, a temporary memory location is required. Here, gencode performs the following steps.

(i) It first generates the code for evaluating n_2, in a temporary memory location.

(ii) Then generates the code to evaluate n_1,

(iii) It gives instruction to evaluate the root n in the top register of rstack.

Algorithm for Implementing gencode(n) :

```
procedure gencode(n)
    begin
    /* case 1 */
    if n is a left leaf representing operand name and n
    is the leftmost child of its parent then
    print 'MOV' || name || ',' || top(rstack)
else if n is an interior node with operator op, left child
n1, and right child n2 then
    /* case 2 */
    if label(n2) = 0 then begin
    let name be the operand represented by n2
    gencode(n1)
    print op || name ||',' || top(rstack)
end
else if 1 ≤label(n1) < label(n2) and label(n1) < r then
begin
    /* case 3 */
swap(rstack) gencode(n2)
    R := pop(rstack)
    gencode(n1)
    print op ||R ||',' || top(rstack)
    push(rstack,R)
    swap(rstack)
end
else if 1 ≤ label(n2) ≤ label(n1) and label(n2) < r
    then begin
    /* case 4 */
    gencode(n1)
    R := pop(rstack)
    gencode(n2)
    print op || top(rstack) ||',' ||R
    push(rstack,R)
end
    else begin
    /* case 5 */
```

```
        gencode(n2)
        T := pop(rstack)
        Print 'MOV' ||top(rstack) || ',' || T
        gencode(n1)
        push(tstack,T)
        print op || T || ',' ||top(rstack)
        end
    end
```

The algorithm given above can be used when the DAG represented is a tree. However, when there are common sub-expressions in the basic block, the DAG representation is no longer a tree, because the common sub-expressions will correspond to nodes with more than one parent. These nodes are called shared nodes. In this case we can apply the labeling and gencode( ) algorithm by partitioning the DAG into subtrees.

Example :

Consider the DAG shown in Fig. 6.13.

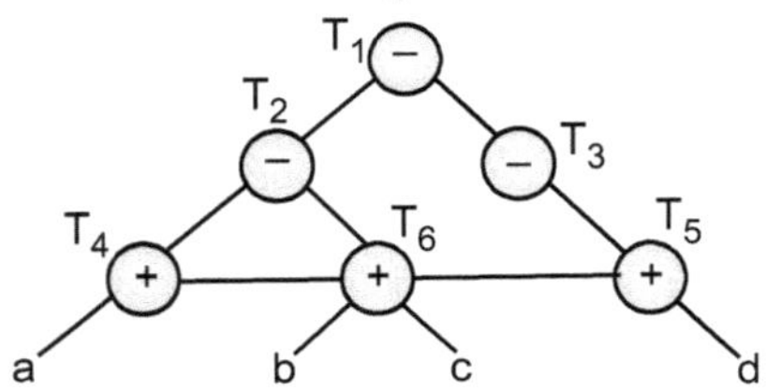

Fig. 6.13: Non-tree DAG

The DAG is not a tree but it can be partitioned into the set of trees shown in Fig. 6.14. The procedure gencode( ) can be applied each of this tree.

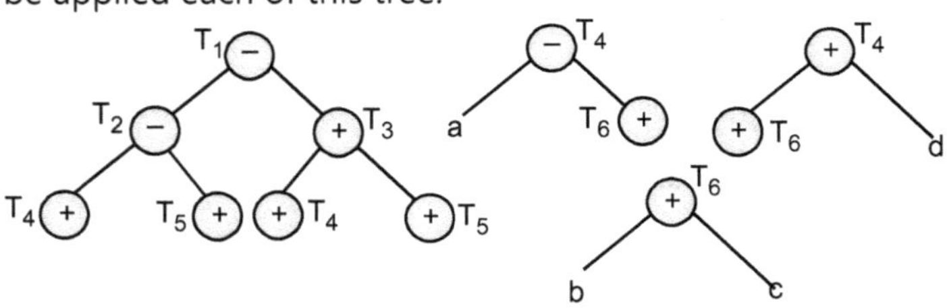

Fig. 6.14: DAG Partitioned into Subtrees

Example :

Consider the labeled expression tree shown in Fig. 6.15.

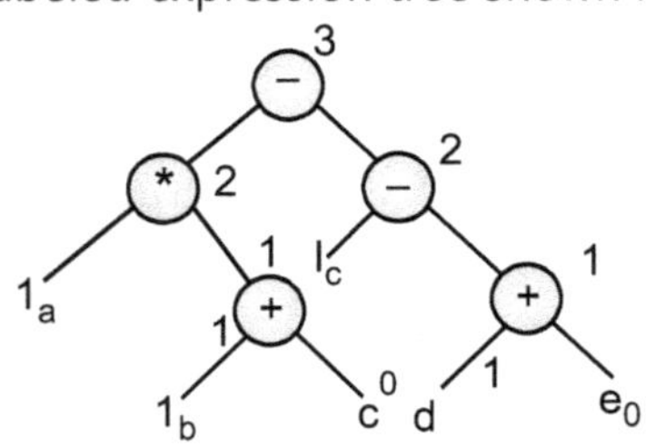

Fig. 6.15: Labeled Expression Tree

The trace of gencode( ) is shown in Fig. 6.16.

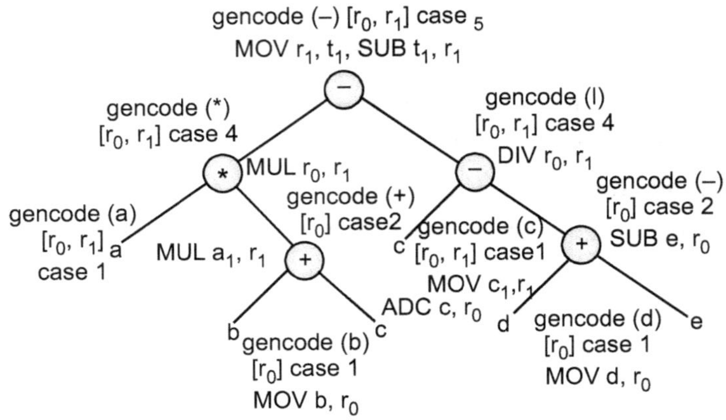

Fig. 6.16 : Trace of gencode

The code generated is:

```
MOV c, R1
MOV d, R0
SUB e, R0
DIV R0, R1
MOV R1, t1
MOV a, R1
MOV b, R0
ADD c, R0
MUL R0, R1
SUB t1 R1
```

Example :

Consider the labeled expression tree shown in Fig. 6.17.

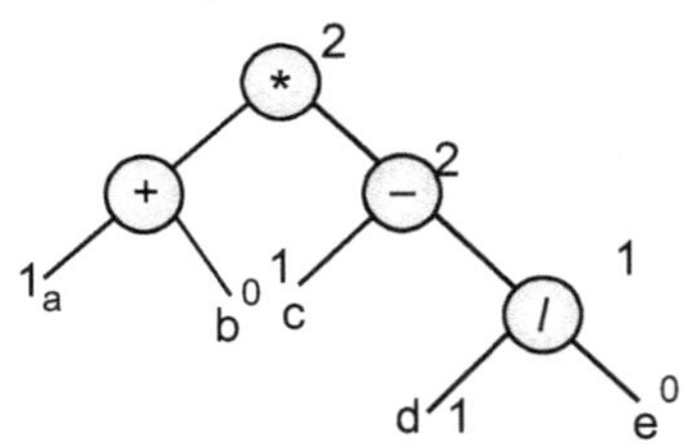

Fig. 6.17 : Labeled Expression Tree

The code generated is:

```
MOV c, R0
MOV d, R1
DIV e, R1
SUB R1, R0
MOV a, R1
ADD b, R1
MUL R0, R1
```

The trace of gencode( ) is shown in Fig. 6.18.

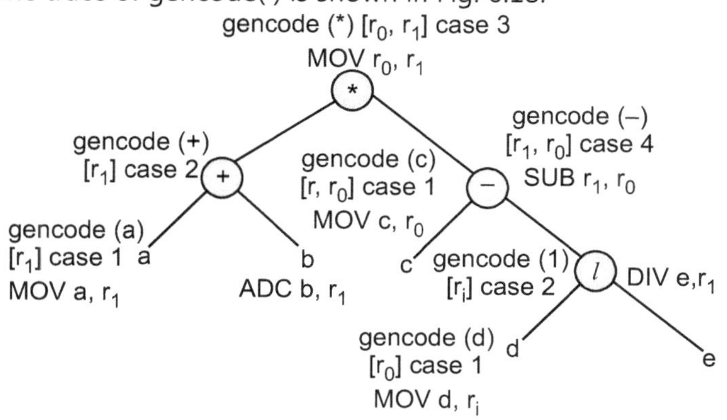

Fig. 6.18: Trace of gencode

6.11 DYNAMIC PROGRAMMING CODE GENERATION ALGORITHM

An algorithm based on the principle of dynamic programming can be used to extend the class of machines, for which optimal code can be generated from expression trees in linear time. The algorithm applies to a broad class of register machines with complex instruction sets.

Class of Register Machines:

- The dynamic programming algorithm can be applied to generate code for any machine with r interchangeable registers R_0, R_1,..........R_{r-1}, and instructions of the form R_i := E, where E is any expression containing operators, registers and memory locations. If E involves one or more registers, then R_i must be one of those registers.

Principle of Dynamic Programming:

- The dynamic programming algorithm partitions the problem of generating optimal code for an expression into sub-problems of generating optimal code for the sub-expressions of the given expression.
- For example, consider that the expression E is of the form $E_1 + E_2$. An optimal program for E is formed by combining the optimal programs for E_1, E_2 followed by the code to evaluate the operator +.
- An optimal program produced by the dynamic programming algorithm has the property that it evaluates an expression E = E_1 op E_2 "contiguously".

Contiguous Evaluation:

- We say that program P evaluates a tree T contiguously if it first evaluates those subtrees of T that need to be computed into memory. Then it evaluates the remainder of T either in the order T_1, T_2, and then the root, or in the order T_2, T_1, and then the root. In either case, it uses the previously computed values from the memory, whenever necessary.
- For the register machine class, it can be proved that given any machine language program P to evaluate an expression tree T, we can find an equivalent program P′ such that:
  1. P′ is no higher cost than P, and
  2. P′ uses no more registers than P, and
  3. P′ evaluates the tree in a contiguous fashion.
- This result implies that every expression tree can be evaluated optimally by a contiguous program.

Dynamic Programming Algorithm:

The algorithm proceeds in three phases.

1. **First Phase:**
   - Compute an array C of costs, bottom-up, for each node n of the expression tree T. The ith component C[i] of array C is the optimal cost of computing the subtree S, which is rooted at n into a register. Here it is assumed that I registers are available for computation for $1 \leq i \leq r$. The cost includes the following components.
     (i) All loads and stores necessary to evaluate S in the given number of registers.
     (ii) The cost of computing the operator at the root of S.
2. **Second Phase:**
   - Traverse T by using the cost vectors to determine which subtrees of T must be computed into the memory.
3. **Third Phase:**
   - Traverse each tree using cost vectors and associated instructions, to generate the final target code. The code for the subtrees computed into memory locations is generated first.

6.12 CODE GENERATORS

- Code generation involves the following steps:
  1. Picking an order of evaluation for the operations
  2. Assigning registers to hold values
  3. Selecting the appropriate target language instructions to implement the operators in intermediate representation
- Tree-rewriting is the technique which can be used to construct the instruction selection phase of a code generator, automatically from a high level specification of the target machine.

Code Generation by Tree Rewriting:

- Target code is generated during a process in which the input tree is reduced to a single node by applying a sequence of tree rewriting rules, to the tree. Each tree rewriting rule is of the form:

replacement ← template { action }

where,

replacement – is a single node

template – is a tree

action – is a code fragment.

- A set of tree rewriting rules is called a tree translation scheme. Each tree template represents a computation performed by the sequence of machine instruction generated by the associated action. Usually a tree corresponds to a single machine instruction. The leaves of the template are attributes with subscripts, as in the case of input tree. Often certain restrictions apply to the values of the subscripts in the templates. These restrictions are specified as semantic predicates that must be specified before the template is said to match.
- A tree translation scheme is a convenient way to represent the instruction selection phase of a code generator.
- Following are some of the tree rewriting rules for some target machine instructions:
- First two rules correspond to load instructions; the next two rules correspond to store instructions, and the remainder to indexed loads and additions.

1 { MOV #c, R_i }

$reg_i \leftarrow const_c$

2 { MOV a, R_i }

$reg_i \leftarrow mem_a$

3 { MOV R_i, a }

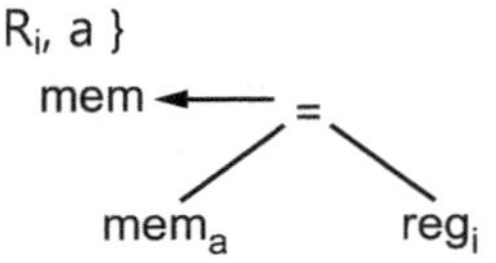

4 { MOV R_j, *R_i }

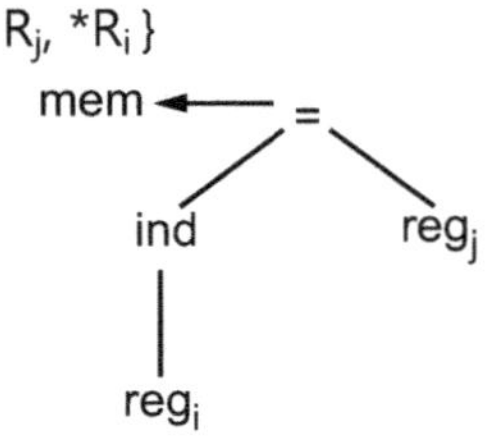

5 { MOV c(R_j),R_i }

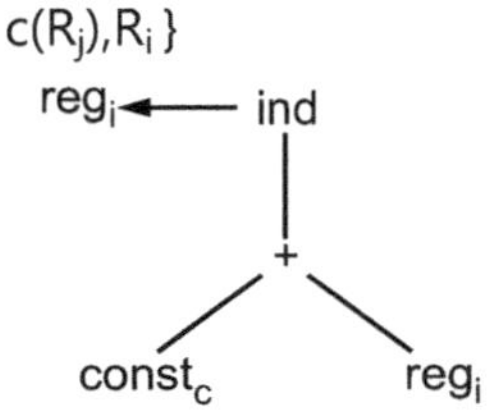

6 { ADD c(R_j), R_i }

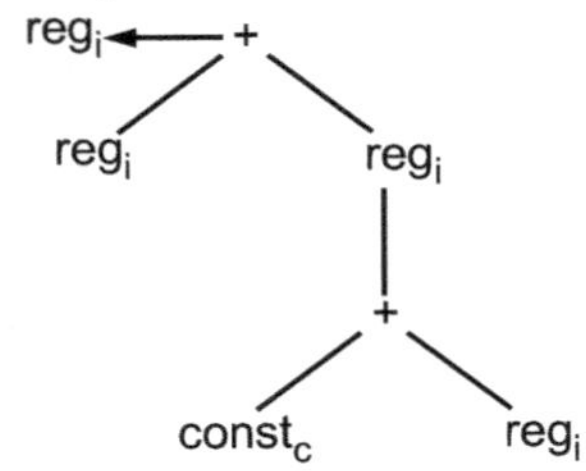

7 { ADD R_j,R_i }

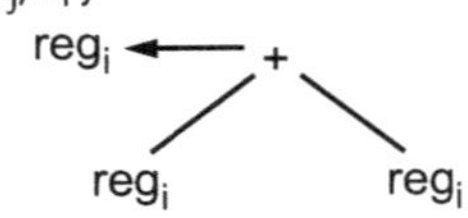

8 { INC R_i }

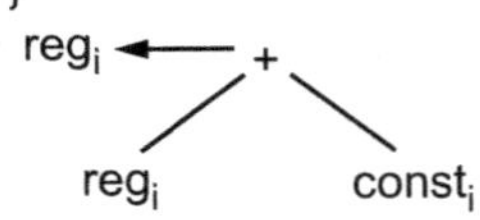

A tree translation scheme for a given input tree works in the following way.

- The templates in the tree rewriting rules are applied to its subtrees.
- If template matches, the matching subtree in the input tree is replaced with the replacement node of the rule, and the action associated with the rule is done.
- If the action associated contains a machine instruction, the instructions are emitted.
- This process is repeated until the tree is reduced to a single node, or until no more templates match.
- The sequence of machine instructions generated as the input tree is reduced to a single node and this constitutes the output of the tree translation scheme on the given input tree.

SOLVED EXAMPLES

Example 6.1: *In a sentence, define what is meant by each of the following terms. Give an example of a short program fragment in Java or C that illustrates each term.*

Solution:

1. Structural equivalence of types: In structural equivalence, two type expressions are either the same basic type or formed by applying the same constructor to structurally equivalent types.

   int a;

   int b;

   float c;

   a and b have structurally equivalent types but a and c do not.

2. Call graph: A call graph is a directed graph that represents calling relationships among the procedures in a computer program. The nodes represent procedures and the edges procedure calls.

```
int fib(n) {
if (n == 0)
    return 0;
else if (n == 1)
    return 1;
else
    return fib(n-1) + fib(n-2);
}
    int main( ) {
    fib(3);
}
```

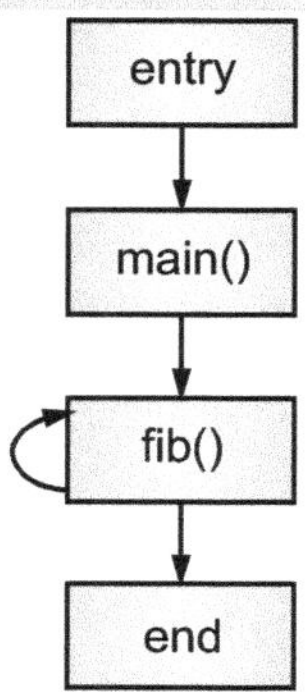

Fig. 6.19: Call graph

3. Basic Block: A basic block is a sequence of statements in which flow of control always enters at the beginning and leaves at the end, without halt or possibility of branching except at the end.

```
int a = 1;
int b = 2;
int c;
c = a + b;
```

4. Flow graph: A flow graph is a directed graph in which nodes represent the basic blocks and edges, the flow of control.

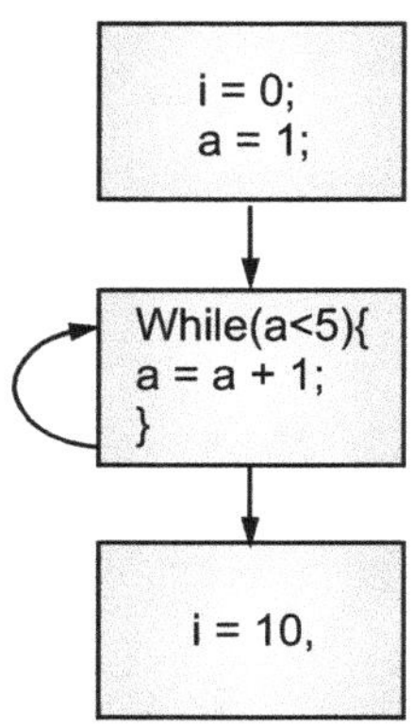

Fig. 6.20

5. Peephole optimization: Peephole optimization is a method for improving the performance of a program by examining a short sequence of instructions, called the peephole, and replacing these instructions by an equivalent shorter or faster sequence, whenever possible.

   Example of eliminating redundant load:

   a = b + c;

   d = a + e;

   generates

```
MOV b, R0
ADD c, R0
MOV R0, a
MOV a, R0 #redundant load, can be removed
ADD e, R0
MOV R0, d
```

Example 6.2 : *Mapping ASTs into DAGs*

1. Write an algorithm in pseudo code that takes as input an abstract-syntax tree (AST) and produces as output a DAG that merges common sub-expressions in the AST. Describe the data structures used to represent the input and output.

Solution: We represent the nodes in AST and DAG with the following data structure:

```
struct node {
    int value;
    struct node *left;
    struct node *right;
}
```

A leaf is a node in which the left and right pointers are both null. For convenience, we will assume that all interior nodes have binary operators.

To create the DAG, we call the following routine createDAG on the root of the AST to make the DAG. createDAG uses a hash table to determine whether a DAG node has been previously created.

```
createDAG(node) {
    if (node is a leaf in the AST with
        fields (null, id, null)) {
            if (DAGleaf is an existing node with
            fields (null, id, null))
                return pointer to DAGleaf;
                else {
                make a new DAGleaf with fields
                (null, id, null);
            enter DAGleaf in hash table;
```

```
            return a pointer to DAGleaf;
            }
        }
        elseif (node is an interior node in AST with
            fields (left, op, right)) {
                leftPtr = createDAG(left);
                rightPtr = createDAG(right);
                if (DAGnode is an existing node with
                fields (leftPtr, op, rightPtr))
                return a pointer to DAGnode;
        else {
        make a new DAGnode with fields
            (OP, left, right);
        enter DAGnode in hash table;
        return pointer to DAGnode;
            }
        }
    }
```

2. Using your input data structure, show an AST for the assignment statement x = a*b + c - a*b + d.

Solution:

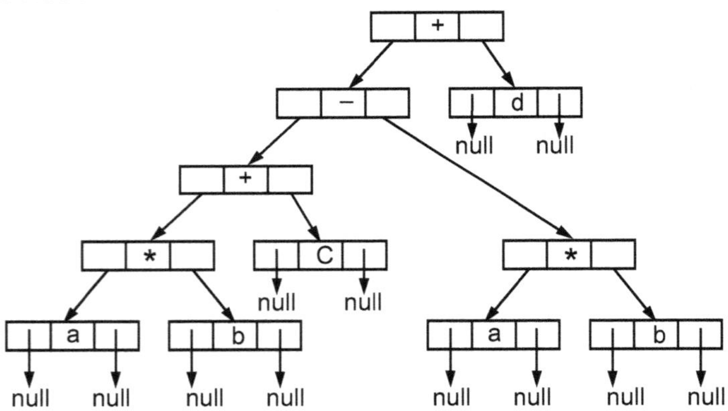

Fig. 6.21

3. Show the output data structure produced by your algorithm with this AST as input.

Solution:

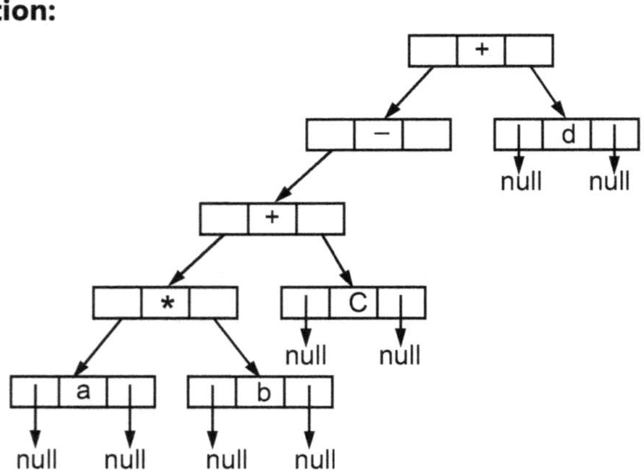

Fig. 6.22

Hash Values	Left Ptr	Value	Right Ptr
1	null	a	null
2	null	b	null
3	ptr(a) (1)	*	ptr(b) (2)
4	null	c	null
5	ptr(*) (3)	+	ptr(c) (4)
6	ptr(+) (5)	-	ptr(*) (3)
7	null	d	null
8	ptr(-) (6)	+	ptr(d) (7)

4. What is the running time of your algorithm as a function of the number of nodes in the AST?

Solution: Running time of this algorithm is 0(n), where n is the number of nodes in the AST. Each node of the AST is visited exactly once. We are assuming we can determine whether a node is already in the hash table in 0(1) time.

Example 6.3 : *Translate the following C fragment into three-address code. State all the assumptions about your run-time environment.*

```
int i;
    int a[10][10];
    i = 0;
    while (i < 10) {
    a[i][i] = 1;
    i++;
}
```

Solution:

Assumptions about run-time environment:

1. 2-dimensional arrays are stored in row-major form.
2. 4 bytes per word: a[i][j] is found at location addr(a) + (10*i+ j)*4.
3. a[i][i] is found at location addr(a) + 44*i.
4. Declarations are assumed to be taken care of in the symbol table.

Three-address Code:

```
i = 0
L0: if i < 10 goto L1
t1 = 44*i
a[t1] = 1
t2 = i+1
i = t2
 goto L0
L1:
```

Example 6.4 : *Let fib(n) be the function*

```
int fib(n) {
if (n == 0)
 return 0;
else if (n == 1)
 return 1;
 else
return fib(n-1) + fib(n - 2);
}
```

1. Show the activation tree for fib(3).

Solution:

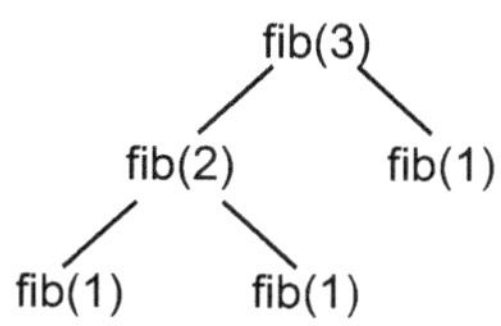

Fig. 6.23

2. Show the activation records that get placed on the run-time stack when fib(3) is invoked. Just show the return value, actual parameters, and the caller's frame pointer of each activation record.

Solution:

Position in the Activation Tree

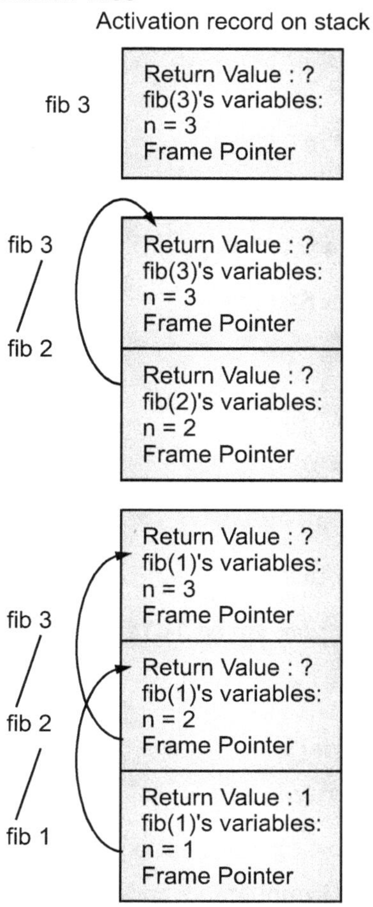

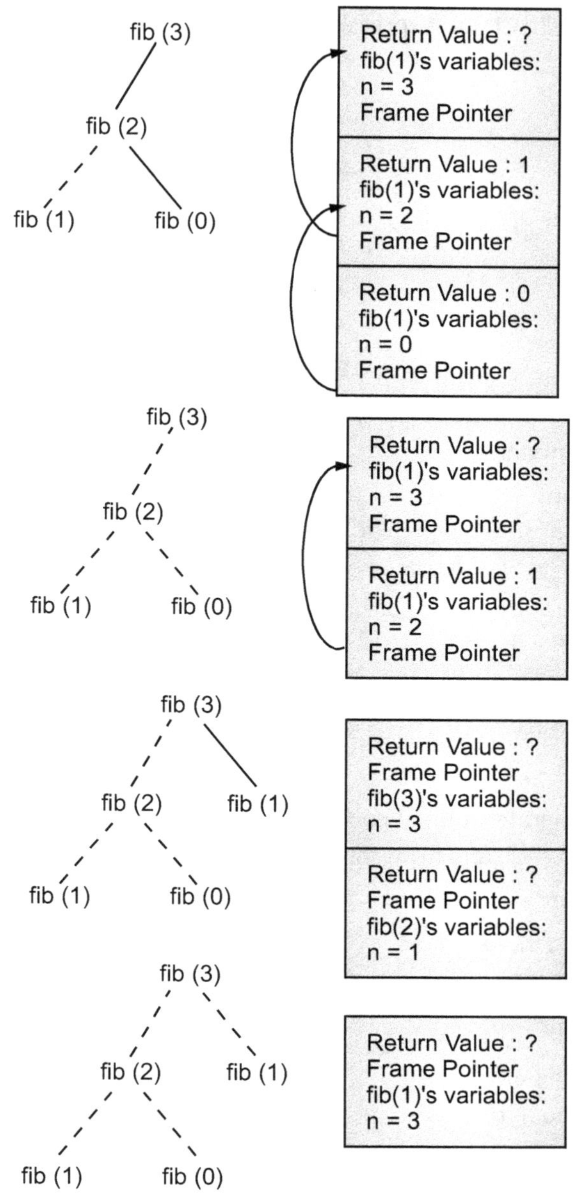

Fig. 6.24

Example 6.5 : *Optimal code generation using Sethi-Ullman numbers*

1. Construct the three-address code for the following arithmetic expression: (a+b)-(c-(d+e))

Solution:

The corresponding three-address code is:

$t_1 = a + b$

$t_2 = d + e$

$t_3 = c - t_2$

$t_4 = t_1 - t_3$

2. Construct an expression tree for your three-address code.

Solution:

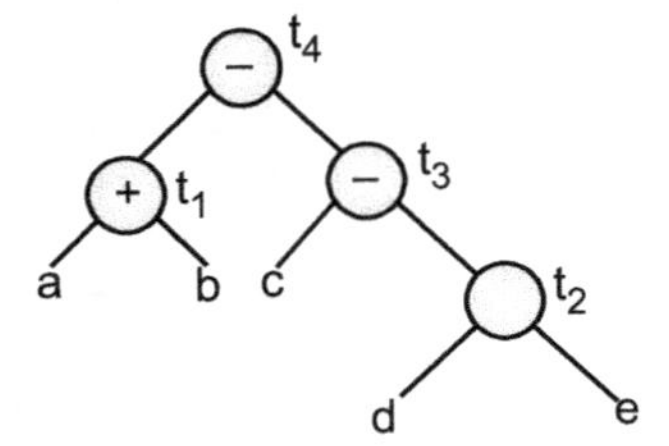

Fig. 6.25

3. Label the nodes of your expression with Sethi-Ullman numbers.

Solution:

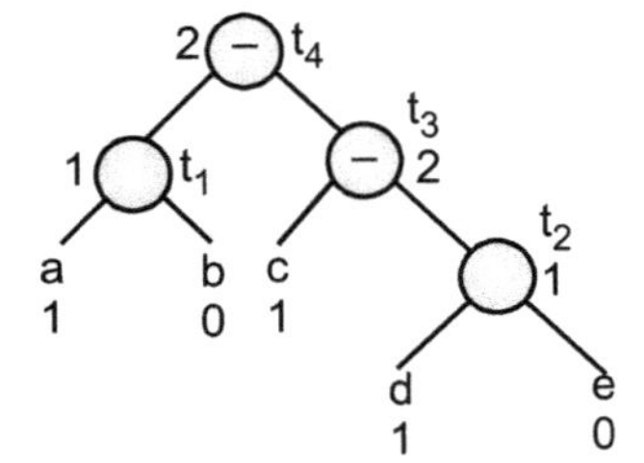

Fig. 6.26

4. Generate optimal code for a two-address machine with two registers from this labeled expression tree.

Solution:

```
MOV d, R0
ADD e, R0
MOV c, R1
SUB R0,R1
MOV a, R0
ADD b, R0
SUB R1,R0
```

5. Generate optimal code for a two-address machine with one register from this labeled expression tree.

Solution:

```
MOV d, R0
ADD e, R0
MOV R0,t2
MOV c, R0
SUB t2,R0
MOV R0,t3
MOV a, R0
ADD b, R0
SUB t3,R0
```

Example 6.6: *We consider the following C-program to calculate the factorial function:*

```
main(){
int n, fact, i;
    scanf("%d", &n);
    fact = 1;
    for (i = 1; i <= n; i = i + 1)
    fact = fact * i;
    printf("%d\n", fact);
}
```

Solution:

The corresponding three-address code is:

```
0 param_string %d
1 param_l_val n
2 call scanf
3 fact = 1
4 nop
5 i = 1
6 nop
7 if i <= n goto 9
8 goto 16
9 t0 = fact * i
10 fact = t0
11 nop
12 t0 = i + 1
13 i = t0
14 nop
15 goto 7
16 param_string %d\n
17 param_r_val fact
18 call printf
19 return
```

The following information can be computed / obtained from the symbol table and the target code:

The stack size (activation record) which includes the following:

Variables, and

Return address and Saved registers

Offset of the variables from stack pointer,

Associate labels to format string : "%d" (LC0) and "%d\n" (LC1), Associate labels to three-address code indices : 9 ($L7) and 16 ($L3)

The generated MIPS-32 Assembly code and the assembler directives will be :

```
# GNU C 2.7.2.3 [AL 1.1, MM 40] SGI running IRIX 5.x
compiled by GNU C
# Cc1 defaults:
# -mabicalls
# Cc1 arguments (-G value = 0, Cpu = 3000, ISA = 1):
# -quiet -dumpbase -O -o gcc2_compiled.:
 gnu_compiled_c:
.rdata
        .align  2
    $LC0:
        .byte   0x25,0x64,0x0
        .align  2
    $LC1:
        .byte   0x25,0x64,0xa,0x0
        .text
        .align  2
        .globl  main
        .ent    main
main:
        .frame  $sp,40,$31 # vars= 8, regs= 2/0, args= 16,
                extra= 8
        .mask   0x90000000,-4
        .fmask  0x00000000,0
        .set    noreorder
        .cpload $25
        .set    reorder
        subu    $sp,$sp,40
        .cprestore 16
        sw      $31,36($sp)
        sw      $28,32($sp)
        la      $4,$LC0
        addu    $5,$sp,24
        jal     scanf
        li      $5,0x00000001 # 1
        li      $3,0x00000001 # 1
        lw      $2,24($sp)
        #nop
        .set    noreorder
        .set    nomacro
        blez    $2,$L3
        move    $4,$2
        .set    macro
        .set     reorder
        mult    $5,$3
    $L7:
        mflo    $5
        #nop
        addu    $3,$3,1
        slt     $2,$4,$3
        .set    noreorder
        .set    nomacro
        beq     $2,$0,$L7
        mult    $5,$3
        .set    macro
        .set    reorder
    $L3:
        la      $4,$LC1 jal printf
        lw      $31,36($sp)
        addu    $sp,$sp,40
        j       $31
        .end    main
        .globl  printf .text
        .globl  scanf .text
```

Example 6.7: *Consider the following C-program to recursively calculate the factorial function:*

```
main( ) {
    int n, factn;
    scanf("%d", &n);
    factn = fact(n);
    printf("%d\n", factn);
    }
    int factn(int n){
    if (n <= 1) return n;
    else return n * factn(n-1);
    }
```

Solution:

The corresponding three-address code is given below. The three-address code corresponding to main:

```
0  param_string %d
1  param_1_val n
2  call scanf
3  param_r_val n
4  call_assign t0 = fact
5  factn = t0
6  nop
7  param_string %d\n
8  param_string %d\n
9  param_r_val factn
10 return
```

The three-address code corresponding to fact:

```
0  read n
1  if n <= 1 goto 3
2  goto 5
3  return_place n
4  t0 = n - 1
5  param_r_val t0
6  call_assign t0 = fact
7  t0 = n * t0
8  return_place t0
```

Stack size, offsets and associated labels can be computed/inferred from the symbol tables of main and fact functions.

The generated MIPS-32 assembly code and the assembler directives will be:

```
# GNU C 2.7.2.3 [AL 1.1, MM 40] SGI running IRIX 5.x
compiled by GNU C
# Cc1 defaults:
# -mabicalls
# Cc1 arguments (-G value = 0, Cpu = 3000, ISA = 1):
# -quiet -dumpbase -O -o gcc2_compiled.:
gnu_compiled_c:
.rdata
        .align   2
    $LC0:
        .byte    0x25,0x64,0x0
        .align   2
    $LC1:
        .byte    0x25,0x64,0xa,0x0
        .text
        .align   2
        .globl   main
        .ent     main
    main:
        .frame   $sp,40,$31 # vars= 8, regs= 2/0, args=
                 16, extra= 8
        .mask    0x90000000,-4
        .fmask   0x00000000,0
        .set     noreorder
        .cpload  $25
        .set     reorder
        subu     $sp,$sp,40
        .cprestore 16
        sw       $31,36($sp)
        sw       $28,32($sp)
        la       $4,$LC0
        addu     $5,$sp,24
        jal      scanf
        lw       $4,24($sp)
        jal      fact
        la       $4,$LC1
        move     $5,$2
```

```
    jal      printf
    lw       $31,36($sp)
    addu     $sp,$sp,40 j     $31
    .end     main
    .align   2
    .globl   factn
    .ent     factn factn:
    .frame   $sp,40,$31
    # vars= 0, regs= 3/0, args= 16, extra= 8
    .mask    0x90010000,-8
    .fmask   0x00000000,0
    .set     noreorder
    .cpload  $25
    .set     reorder
    subu     $sp,$sp,40
    .cprestore 16
    sw       $31,32($sp)
    sw       $28,28($sp)
    sw       $16,24($sp)
    move     $16,$4
    slt      $2,$16,2
    .set     noreorder
    .set     nomacro
    bne      $2,$0,$L3
    move     $2,$16
    .set     macro
    .set     reorder
    addu     $4,$16,-1
    jal      factn
    mult     $16,$2
    mflo     $2
$L3:
    lw       $31,32($sp)
    lw       $16,24($sp)
    addu     $sp,$sp,40
    j        $31
    .end     factn
    .globl printf .text
    .globl fact .text
    .globl scanf .text
```

Example 6.8 : *Consider the following piece of code. Generate the three-address code. repeat {*

```
p = p + x[i]/y[i]
until i > 100
```

Solution: The block corresponding to the code consists of the following three-address code statements:

(1) : ti = 4* i

(2) : t_a = x[ti]

(3) : t_3 = 4* I

(4) : t_4 = yftgj

(5) : t_s = t_2/t_4

(6) : t_6 — p + t_s

(7) : p = t_6

(8) : t_7 = i + 1

(9) : i = t_7

(10) : if i > 100 goto (3)

SOLVED QUESTIONS AND ANSWERS

Question 1 : What is Target Code generation?

Answer: If we translate the AST of the source program into an intermediate representation, then the code generator must include a second stage that translates the intermediate program into target code.

Whether we translate an intermediate program into target code, or the AST directly into target code, or even generate target code immediately during the parsing phase, we will use a similar process.

```
generateCode( AST tree )
{
if ( tree != null )
{
generate code to prepare for code of left subtree
generateCode( tree.leftChild( ) );
generate code to prepare for code of right subtree
generateCode( tree.rightChild( ) );
generate code to implement tree's behavior
}
}
```

The best sort of intermediate representation as input to a code generator has data objects that map directly onto the primitives of the target machine. This includes the insertion of type conversion operators.

The output of the generator can be absolute or relative. Absolute code has all of its addresses already computed and placed in the code. A program in this form can be loaded anywhere and executed immediately. The downside is that it requires compiling the whole program at the same time, which limits the flexibility available to programmers who use the compiler. Relative code with addresses computed only as offsets to be resolved at the time the program is loaded to execute, offers the flexibility of separate compilation but requires the cost of linking the modules and loading each time the program is run.

Question 2 : What are the tasks of Code generator?
Answer: Code generation consists of two critical tasks:

1. Target instruction selection
2. Register usage.

Selecting target instructions is the essential element of code generation. The size, and thus the completeness of the target machine's instruction set drive the selection process, and the uniformity with which it treats data and control determines its complexity.

Question 3: What is the use of Registers?

Answer: The use of registers has a large effect on the target program's efficiency, because the instructions that work with the data in the registers are typically shorter and much faster than those that work only with the data in the memory. The difficulty in using them well usually arises from the fact that most machines provide only a small set of registers.

Question 4: What are the techniques for Generating Target Code?

Answer: Generating efficient target code is a difficult task. To do so, the compiler must take into account, the speed of each target instruction and implement the idioms of the target machine. Unfortunately, accurate data about instruction speed is usually hard to come by.

If the efficiency of the generated code doesn't matter, then selecting instructions can be done in a straightforward way using code skeletons. The generator associates such a template with each instruction in the intermediate language. You can probably see how this would lead to inefficient code: target code for each statement in the input would be generated independent of the statements around it.

Question 5: What is peephole optimization?

Answer: A statement-by-statement code-generation strategy often produces a target code that contains redundant instructions and sub-optimal constructs. The quality of such target code can be improved by applying "optimizing" transformations to the target program. The term "optimizing" is somewhat misleading because there is no guarantee that the resulting code is optimal under any mathematical measure Nevertheless, many simple transformations can significantly improve the running time or space requirement of the target program. Therefore, it is important to know what kinds of transformations are useful in practice.

A simple but effective technique for locally improving the target code is peephole optimization, a method for trying to improve the performance of the target program by examining a short sequence of target instructions (called the peephole) and replacing these instructions by a shorter or faster sequence, whenever possible. Although we discuss peephole optimization as a technique for improving the quality of the target code, the technique can also be applied directly after intermediate code generation to improve the intermediate representation.

Question 6: What are the characteristics of peephole optimization?

Answer: The peephole is a small, moving window on the target program. The code in the peephole need not be contiguous, although some implementations do require this. It is characteristic of peephole optimization that each improvement may spawn opportunities for additional improvements. In general, repeated passes over the target code are necessary to get the maximum benefit. Some of the examples of program transformations that are characteristic of peephole optimizations are:

- Redundant-instruction elimination
- Flow-of-control optimizations
- Algebraic simplification
- Use of machine idioms

EXERCISE

1. Define the term basic block. Explain any two transformations that can be performed on basic block.
2. Consider a machine with three registers, R_1, R_2, R_3 and the following instructions :

```
LOAD Ri, M
STORE M, Ri
ADD Ri,Rj
MULT Ri,Rj
```

   Give the optimal code for this machine for the expression

   ((a + b) + (c + d) * (e + f) + (g + h))
3. For the following code, construct the basic block, three-address code, flow graph and DAG.

```
main ()
{
    int prod, i, a[20];
    prod = 0;
    i =1;
    do
    {
        prod = prod + a[i] & b[i]
        i = i + 1
    }
    while(i< 20)
}
```

4. Consider the following code-

```
void sort_array(int m, int n)
{
    int i, j;
    int temp, s; if(n<=m) return i = m-1
    j = n
    temp = a[n]
    while(1)
    {
        do
        i = i +1
        while(a[i] < temp)
        do
        j = j+1
        while (a[j] > temp)
        if(i>=j) break s = a[i]
        a[i] = a[j]
        a[j] = s
    }
    s=a[i]
    a[i] = a[n] a[n]
    = s
    sort_array(m,j)
    sort_array(i+1,n)
}
```

   For this code:

   i. Generate the three-address code.

   ii. Draw a flow graph.

   iii. Apply the possible sources of optimization.
5. What are the issues in code generation?
6. With examples, explain how to decide the cost of instructions.
7. Give steps to partition a sequence of three-address statements into basic blocks.
8. Which are the structures preserving transformations?
9. Explain the algebraic transformations with example.
10. With an example, explain how to find the usage count.
11. Give an algorithm for DAG construction.
12. What are the applications of DAG?
13. Write a note on peephole optimization.
14. With an example, explain how the computation order can affect the cost of object code.
15. Give the algorithm for -

    a. Heuristic ordering. b. Labeling algorithm.
16. Explain the working of gencode( ) function.
17. Give the algorithm for gencode( ).
18. What is the principle of dynamic programming?

19. Give an algorithm for code generation using dynamic programming.
20. Write a note on code generator.
21. Write tree rewriting rules for the following instructions :

    (1) { MOV #c, R_i }

    (2) { MOV a, R_i }

    (3) { MOV R_i, a }

    (4) { MOV R_j, *R_i }

    (5) { MOV c(R_j),R_i }

    (6) { ADD c(R_j), R_i }

    (7) { ADD R_j,R_i }

    (8) { INC R_i }

22. Write a note on code generation using tree rewriting rules.

◈◈◈

Model Question Papers for End-Semester Examination

PAPER I

Time : 3 Hours **Max. Marks : 60**

Instructions to the candidates :

(1) Each Question carries 12 Marks.

(2) Attempt any five questions to the following.

(3) Illustrate your answers with neat sketches, diagram etc., wherever necessary.

(4) If some part or parameter is noticed to be missing, you may appropriately assume it and should mention it clearly.

Attempt any Five Questions :

1. (a) Explain output of each phase of compiler for the following statement :

$a = b + c \times 60$ **[6]**

(b) Explain the Role of Lexical Analyzer in compiler construction Define Lexeme, Token and Pattern. Give suitable example. **[6]**

2. (a) Determine whether the following grammar is ambiguous? If yes, show resultant parses trees for one example string.

$S \rightarrow S + S \mid S \times S \mid a \mid b$ **[6]**

(b) List and explain different types of parser **[6]**

3. (a) Generate three address code for following program snippet **[6]**

```
do {
p=p+x[i]/y[i];
} while (i>100);
```

(b) Write syntax directed translation scheme for simple assignment statement. **[6]**

4. (a) Differentiate between top down parser and bottom up parser. **[6]**

(b) State and explain different sections in YACC specification file. **[6]**

5. (a) Generate quadruple, triple and indirect triple representation for following **[6]**

a = –u*v / w^ x+y*z

(b) What are different types of intermediate code representation. Give one example each **[6]**

6. (a) Define the term basic block. Explain any two transformations that can be performed on basic block. **[6]**

(b) Give an algorithm for DAG construction **[6]**

◈◈◈

PAPER II

Time : 3 Hours **Max. Marks : 60**

Instructions to the candidates :

(1) Each Question carries 12 Marks.

(2) Attempt any five questions to the following.

(3) Illustrate your answers with neat sketches, diagram etc., wherever necessary.

(4) If some part or parameter is noticed to be missing, you may appropriately assume it and should mention it clearly.

Attempt Any Five Questions :

1. (a) Explain in detail various phases of compilation, describe output of the following statement after each phase of compiler a = b+ c*60 **[6]**

(b) Explain following points with respect to compiler : **[6]**

(i) Grouping of phases.

(ii) No. of passes required.

(iii) Intermediate languages.

(iv) Tools needed.

2. (a) How lexical analysis detect errors? Explain with suitable example. **[6]**

(b) Define passes and phases of Compiler. Explain different phases of Compiler in detail. **[6]**

3. (a) Write the different rules for closure operation and then apply the same rules to compute the closure of the following grammar: **[6]**

$E' \rightarrow E$

$E \rightarrow E + T \mid T$

$T \rightarrow T - F \mid F$

$F \rightarrow (E) \mid id$

(b) What is the necessary and sufficient condition for a grammar to be LL(1)? With respect to parsing, explain the following terms: **[6]**

a. Ambiguous Grammar

b. Left Recursion

c. Shift-Reduce Conflict

d. Precedence Associativity

4. (a) Define the following terms with an example: **[6]**

(a) Synthesized attribute

(b) Inherited attribute

(c) S-attributed definition

(d) L-attributed definition

(b) Consider the following grammar: $E \rightarrow E + T \mid T$ **[6]**

$T \rightarrow num.num$

$T \rightarrow num$

(i) Write syntax-directed definition to determine the type of each sub-expression. The resulting type is an integer if two integers are added, otherwise it is real.

(ii) Construct an annotated parse tree for the input expression 10 + 20 + 15.2

5. (a) Write quadruples, triples, and indirect triples for the following expression: (x+y)*(y+z)+(x+y+z) [6]

(b) Translate the following program code into three-address code. [6]

```
int i
i = 1
while a < 10 do
    if x>y then a=x+y
    else a=x-y
```

6. (a) For the following code, construct the basic block, three-address code, flow graph and DAG. [6]

```
main ()
{
    int prod, i, a[20];
    prod = 0;
    i =1;
    do
    {
        prod = prod + a[i] & b[i]
        i = i + 1
    }
    while(i< 20)
}
```

(b) Consider the following code- [6]

```
void sort_array(int m, int n)
{
    int i, j;
int temp, s; if(n<=m) return i = m-1
j = n
temp = a[n]
while(1)
{
    do
    i = i +1
    while(a[i] < temp)
    do
    j = j+1
    while (a[j] > temp)
    if(i>=j) break s = a[i]
    a[i] = a[j]
    a[j] = s
```

```
}
s=a[i]
a[i] = a[n] a[n]
= s
sort_array(m,j)
sort_array(i+1,n)
}
```

For this code:

i. Generate the three-address code.

ii. Draw a flow graph.

iii. Apply the possible sources of optimization.

◈◈◈

www.ingramcontent.com/pod-product-compliance
Lightning Source LLC
LaVergne TN
LVHW062205171026
850499LV00044B/1864
* 9 7 8 9 3 8 9 6 8 6 6 2 3 *